Political Economy as Natural Theology

Since the early 20th century, economics has been the dominant discourse in English-speaking countries, displacing Christian theology from its previous position of authority. This path-breaking book is a major contribution to the interdisciplinary dialogue between economics and religion.

Oslington tells the story of natural theology shaping political economy in the late 18th and early 19th centuries, emphasising continuing significance of theological issues for the discipline of economics. Early political economists such as Adam Smith, Josiah Tucker, Edmund Burke, William Paley, TR Malthus, Richard Whately, JB Sumner, Thomas Chalmers and William Whewell, extended the British scientific natural theology tradition of Francis Bacon, Robert Boyle and Isaac Newton to the social world. This extension nourished and shaped political economy as a discipline, influencing its theoretical framework, but perhaps more importantly helping legitimate political economy in the British universities and public policy circles. Educating the public in the principles of political economy had a central place in this religiously driven program. Natural theology also created tensions (especially reconciling economic suffering with divine goodness and power) that eventually contributed to its demise and the separation of economics from theology in mid-19th-century Britain. This volume highlights aspects of the story that are neglected in standard histories of economics, histories of science and contemporary theology.

Political Economy as Natural Theology is essential reading for all concerned with the origins of economics, the meaning and purpose of economic activity and the role of religion in contemporary policy debates.

Paul Oslington is Professor of Economics and Dean of Business at Alphacrucis College in Sydney, Australia. He previously held a joint appointment as Professor in the Schools of Business and Theology at Australian Catholic University, and before that Associate Professor of Economics at the University of New South Wales, along with visiting positions at the University of Oxford, University of British Columbia, Regent College Vancouver and Princeton Theological Seminary and University. He is also an honorary Research Professor at the Australian Centre for Christianity and Culture in Canberra.

Routledge Frontiers of Political Economy

Political Economy as Natural Theology

Smith, Malthus and Their Followers

Paul Oslington

Routledge
Taylor & Francis Group

LONDON AND NEW YORK

First published 2018 by Routledge

2 Park Square, Milton Park, Abingdon, Oxfordshire OX14 4RN
52 Vanderbilt Avenue, New York, NY 10017

Routledge is an imprint of the Taylor & Francis Group, an informa business

First issued in paperback 2019

British Library Cataloguing-in-Publication Data
A catalogue record for this book is available from the British Library

Library of Congress Cataloging-in-Publication Data
Names: Oslington, Paul, author.
Title: Political economy as natural theology : Smith, Malthus and their
    followers / Paul Oslington.
Description: Abingdon, Oxon ; New York, NY : Routledge, 2017. | Includes
    bibliographical references and index.
Identifiers: LCCN 2017006189| ISBN 9780415454810 (hardback) |
    ISBN 9781315168463 (ebook)
Subjects: LCSH: Economics—Religious aspects—Christianity. |
    Economics—Religious aspects—History.
Classification: LCC BR115.E3 .O75 2017 | DDC 261.8/5—dc23
LC record available at https://lccn.loc.gov/2017006189

ISBN: 978-0-415-45481-0 (hbk)
ISBN: 978-0-367-86502-3 (pbk)

Typeset in Times New Roman
by Swales & Willis Ltd, Exeter, Devon, UK

Contents

Preface

Discussions over many years with many people have helped me think through issues in the relationship between economics and theology, without any claim that any of these agree with the arguments of this work. I thank Andrew McGowan, Anthony Waterman, Geoffrey Brennan, Ian Harper, Christopher White, Samuel Gregg, Peter Groenewegen, Geoff Harcourt, John Nevile, John Pullen, Greg Moore, Tony Aspromourgos, Stuart Piggin, Mark Hutchinson, Geoff Treloar, Robert Banks, Margaret Schabas, Ross B. Emmett, Brendan Long, Kim Hawtrey, Donald Hay, Gordon Menzies, Peter Docherty, Ian Smith, Andrew Hartropp, Peter Heslam, Robert Mochrie, John Hedley Brooke, Peter Harrison, Mark Brett, Wentzel Van Huyssteen, Deirdre McCloskey, Peter Boettke, John Milbank, Robert Nelson, Luigini Bruni, Neil Ormerod, Shane Clifton, Larry Iannaccone, Max Stackhouse, Paul Williams, David Richardson, Mary Hirschfeld, Albino Barrera and Andy Yuengert.

The work was begun at University of New South Wales, continued at Australian Catholic University, and completed at Alphacrucis College and University of Divinity. I am grateful for good colleagues and the supportive environment at Alphacrucis, where we are attempting to build a high-quality Pentecostal Christian university for Australia and beyond.

Most of all, thanks to my family, Gabrielle, Ruth, Timothy and Peter. The past few years have not been an easy time for our family, but your love and support has made this work possible.

1 Introduction

Economics matters because it has been the dominant discourse in English-speaking countries at least since the middle of the 20th century, arguably before that. Anthony Waterman (2004) suggests that economics has replaced Christian theology as the discourse which binds Western society together and carries authority. John Milbank's influential theological work begins from the marginalisation of Christian theology by contemporary social science, including economics, which he sees as deformed theology (Milbank 1990). The American economist Robert Nelson (1991, 2001, 2010) has attempted to read 20th-century economics as concealed theology, for instance identifying Samuelsonian public economics with liberal Protestantism, and the Chicago school with Calvinism.

There is a deep gulf between contemporary economic and religious discourse. Theologians tend to engage only superficially with mainstream economics, and economists on the whole ignore theology. There are exceptions of course to the generally superficial engagement of contemporary theologians with economics, for instance the works of Douglas Meeks (1990, 2014), Miroslav Volf (1991), Alan Storkey (1993), Kathryn Tanner (2004, 2005) and Mary Hirschfeld (2013). Biblical scholars find it difficult to avoid economics, though puzzlingly gravitate to varieties of Marxian or other types of non-mainstream economics (for instance, Boer 2003 as discussed in Oslington 2011c).

It is very rare for contemporary economists to engage deeply with theology. The economics of religion is a growing subfield of contemporary economics which seeks to explain religious behaviour and religious institutions using mainstream economic models (see the surveys of Iannaccone 1998, 2010; Oslington 2011e; Iyer 2016). However, modelling religious behaviour and institutions is something different to engaging deeply with theology.

A recent attempt by economists to reengage with theology has been in the sectarian "Christian economics" that arose in the 1970s in the US and Europe, especially in certain Calvinist and Roman Catholic circles. In my view this "Christian economics" movement is a theologically problematic response to the marginalisation of Christianity in Western culture in the preceding decades (discussed further in Oslington 2009, 2010 and briefly in Chapter 8, this volume). "Christian economics" runs parallel with the rise of a sectarian "Islamic economics" in response to the economic disappointments of the Muslim world through the 20th century and the association of economics with the heart of Western culture that is rejected by these Islamic groups (Kuran 2004).

Economics matters particularly in Australia with our heritage of utilitarianism and prosperity (Collins 1985; Gascoigne 2002). The church needs to engage more deeply with economic ways of thinking to connect with ordinary Australians and to have an influence for good on our public culture. A renewed theological engagement with economics also matters particularly in African and Asian societies, where Christianity is vibrant and economic change rapid. Something better is needed than the distorted prosperity theology that is widespread in churches.

This book contributes to the interdisciplinary dialogue between economics and theology by telling the story of the role of theology in the formation of political economy as a discipline in Britain in the 18th and 19th centuries, and the separation of ethics and theology from economics later in the 19th century.

It aims to:

- Deepen understanding of the formation of political economy as a discipline, writing the neglected theological elements back into the history of the discipline. It is a contribution to an alternative history of the formation of political economy emphasising theological context and influences, largely bypassing figures such as Ricardo and the Mills' who are overemphasised in existing histories.
- Provide a historical basis and theological resources for a renewal of dialogue between economists and theologians. There is no need to create artificial points of contact because strong historical connections already exist. History is neutral ground between the disciplines of economics and theology, and an excellent starting point for dialogue.
- Extend existing scholarship on natural theology to political economy, especially considering issues of theodicy raised by this extension.

The focus of the book is Britain, justified by this being the centre of political economic discussion in the period under study, and the country where the academic discipline of political economy initially took shape (Checkland 1951; Winch 1971, 1996, 2009). Some comments will be offered on America, mostly for comparison with Britain. It is acknowledged that important early contributions were made by the French Physiocrats (Meek 1963; Groenewegen 1977, 1989), the Italian civil economy school (Bruni and Zamagni 2007) and the German cameralists (Tribe 1997), but the scope of the book needs to be limited.

Discussion will be restricted to Christian theology, though interactions between economics and Islamic, Buddhist and other religious thought has become more important in recent years (for instance, Wilson 1997; Schumacher 1966; Kuran 2004; Elashker and Wilson 2006).

I am not dealing with the many important policy issues connected to the relationship between economics and theology. The greatest need is to clarify the relationship between economics and theology as a basis for future writing on policy issues that involve both economics and theology.

I am not taking up parallels between the relationship between theology and economics, and wider issues in theology and science (for instance Brooke 1991a; Harrison 1998, 2007), theology and psychology (Watts 2002), theology and sociology (Gill 2012), etc. The focus will be on the science of economics.

I will concentrate on the intellectual issues at stake, although it is acknowledged that not all the barriers to dialogue between economists and theologians are intellectual. The formation of economics as a discipline and the separation of economics from theology were for a mixture of intellectual reasons and reasons connected with the interests of those involved.

It must be emphasised that there are vast number of interesting and important questions at the boundary of economics and theology, and this book tackles only a small subset of them. It is not meant to be a comprehensive survey of the questions, let alone a definitive account of the relationships between economics and theology. There are other surveys of the growing interdisciplinary field of economics and theology (including Waterman 1987; Oslington 2003, 2009, 2014).

The book begins with a brief discussion of natural theology and the problem of theodicy that is intimately connected with natural theology. This chapter is essential reading for those less familiar with religious thought, and the historical chapters which follow draw on this discussion. Those needing more background in Christian theology may want to consult one of the standard introductions to the field, such as Alister McGrath's highly readable *Christian Theology* with its associated volume of excerpts from the classic works. As you read the historical chapters, bear in mind that I am offering a corrective to standard histories of economics, and so works such as Roger Backhouse's *Penguin History of Economics*, or Vaggi and Groenewegen's *Concise History of Economic Thought* may be useful to readers unfamiliar with economics. Do not bother with introductory economics textbooks which are typically dull and unenlightening about the intellectual framework of the subject. My final chapter offers some thoughts on the promise and difficulties of reviving the conversation between economists and theologians, and some ideas on possible intellectual frameworks for future engagement between the disciplines.

I hope this work stimulates further discussion of the issues among economists, theologians, historians and others. There is much work to be done in this field.

2 Natural theology
Philosophical and historical issues

Introduction

The purpose of this chapter is to briefly introduce and clarify one of the key categories in the book, that of natural theology, concentrating on the British tradition of scientific natural theology which the argument mostly draws upon. It will set the scene for subsequent chapters.

Natural theology and scripture

Francis Bacon at the beginning of the 17th century defined natural theology[1] as "divine philosophy derivable from God by the light of nature, and the contemplation of his creatures; so that with regard to its object, it is truly divine; but with regard to its acquirement, natural" (Bacon 1605: 142). For Bacon, it was a project of understanding the ways of God through examining the natural world, noting that this includes humanity. A common way of explaining natural theology in Bacon's time was that God had written two books for our benefit, the scriptures and the book of nature.[2]

Natural theology is often contrasted with revealed theology, but there is no rigid dividing line between the two. For Bacon and many other natural theologians, it is a distinction between types of revelation. Although the scriptures are held by most theologians to be of divine origin (whatever their particular view of inspiration), they were authored by created human beings and are an object in creation. They require interpretation by human beings under the guidance of the Holy Spirit.[3] [4]

A rigid split between scriptural and natural revelation is also undermined by scriptural encouragement for us to learn about God from creation.[5] In the Apostle Paul's Areopagus speech recorded in Acts 17:24–27:[6]

> The God who made the world and everything in it is the Lord of heaven and earth and does not live in temples built by human hands. And he is not served by human hands, as if he needed anything. Rather, he himself gives everyone life and breath and everything else. From one man he made all the nations, that they should inhabit the whole earth; and he marked out their appointed

times in history and the boundaries of their lands. God did this so that they would seek him and perhaps reach out for him and find him, though he is not far from any one of us.

In Romans 1:20 we read: "For since the creation of the world God's invisible qualities – his eternal power and divine nature – have been clearly seen, being understood from what has been made, so that people are without excuse". Many Psalms would seem to encourage natural theology; for instance, Psalm 19 begins:

> The heavens declare the glory of God; the skies proclaim the work of his hands. Day after day they pour forth speech; night after night they reveal knowledge. They have no speech, they use no words; no sound is heard from them. Yet their voice goes out into all the earth, their words to the ends of the world.

References such as Genesis 1:26–27 to humans being created in the image of God, and being endowed by God with senses and reasoning powers, also license natural theology.[7]

Varieties of natural theology

Natural theology has a long history and there are many varieties. It was important in pre-Christian Greek thought, especially among the Stoic philosophers. Christian versions of natural theology include Thomas Aquinas' Five Ways demonstrating the existence and attributes of God, Anselm's attempt to show God's attribute of perfection implies God's existence, John Calvin's arguments that the natural world shows God's power and goodness as well as our need of salvation, although it cannot disclose the means of salvation.[8]

In recent times, natural theology has fallen out of favour. For most scientists, it is no longer relevant. Among many philosophers, the objections in Hume's *Dialogues Concerning Natural Religion*, and Kant's *Critiques* and *On the Failure of All Attempted Philosophical Theodicies*, are regarded as devastating.[9] Among theologians, natural theology receives some attention from contemporary Roman Catholic philosophers and theologians, but little among Protestant theologians.

The bad repute of natural theology among contemporary Protestants is partly due to Karl Barth's famous utter rejection of it in a work with perhaps the shortest title in theological history *No!*[10] Barth was responding to a suggestion by Emil Brunner in *Nature and Grace* 1934 (in Barth and Brunner 1946) that "It is the task of our theological generation to find the way back to a true *theologia naturalis*" (1946: 59). Barth does not seem very interested in Brunner's definition of natural theology, instead defining it himself as any system which does not focus on revelation in Jesus Christ, and leaving readers in no doubt as to his views:

> If one occupies oneself with real theology one can pass by so-called natural theology only as one would pass by an abyss into which it is inadvisable to step if one does not want to fall. All one can do is to turn one's back upon

it as upon the great temptation and source of error, by having nothing to do with it and by making it clear to oneself and to others from time to time why one acts that way.

Barth adds the advice that one should not delay to stare at a serpent (Barth and Brunner 1946: 75–6).

Care is needed to identify exactly what Barth was objecting to, and his real target appears to have been the misuse of the Lutheran doctrine of the orders of creation to support the Nazis' repugnant policies. Despite Barth's reiteration of his rejection of natural theology when invited to deliver the Gifford Lectures on natural theology in 1938, we cannot take Barth as rejecting natural theology in all contexts.[11] Once the Nazi era had passed, Barth wrote more encouragingly of reintroducing natural theology through Christology. Stanley Hauerwas (2001) in his own Gifford Lectures provocatively reads Barth as a major natural theologian.

Another influence on contemporary Protestants has been the use of natural theology by some philosophers of religion (for instance, Plantinga 1980) as a point of departure for their rejection of foundationalist epistemology. Their target is demonstrative proof of God's existence, which they find in certain strains of natural theology, rather than natural theology itself. In fact, a natural theology which rests on the Christian doctrine of creation would seem exactly the kind of intellectual project these philosophers would support, and just the sort of program Alvin Plantinga sketches in his subsequent Gifford Lectures (Plantinga 2011).

The British tradition of scientific natural theology

A different style of natural theology to that of the Stoic writers or Thomas Aquinas' Five Ways is relevant to this book. This is the tradition of scientific natural theology which was one of the most important organising frameworks for intellectual life in Britain from the 17th to the mid-19th centuries. Young (1985) described it as the "common context" for the activity of scientists, philosophers and theologians over this period, and Gascoigne (1988), Brooke (1991a) and Harrison (2015) also emphasise its integrative role.[12] The key texts in this British tradition of natural theology include Francis Bacon *Advancement of Learning* 1605 and *Novum Organum* 1620, Robert Boyle *Disquisition about the Final Causes of Natural Things* 1688 (Boyle 1979), Isaac Newton *Philosophiae Naturalis Principia Mathematica* 1686, John Ray *Wisdom of God Manifested in the Works of Creation* 1691, Joseph Butler *The Analogy of Religion* 1736, Abraham Tucker *The Light of Nature Pursued* 1768, William Paley *Natural Theology* 1802, and the Bridgewater Treatises – a series of works commissioned in the 1830s "On the Power, Wisdom and Goodness of God, as Manifested in the Creation".[13]

It is important to recognise that the tradition of British scientific natural theology depended for its coherence on Christian doctrines of creation by a personal God and divine providence. This was not so for earlier Greek, and especially Stoic versions of natural theology. British scientific natural theology was not a project of autonomous reason demonstrating the existence of God, and so avoids the criticisms of Karl Barth and Alvin Plantinga. This is so even though works of natural theology sometimes took the form of proofs of the existence and goodness of God. And even despite statements that this was the purpose of such works. For instance, Isaac Newton wrote to Richard Bentley that the *Principia* was written "with an eye upon such Principles as might work with considering men for belief in a Deity, and nothing can rejoice me more than to find it useful for that purpose". There are reasons not to take statements like this at face value. Aside from Newton's private reasons to cast himself and his work as serving theological orthodoxy, atheists were pretty thin on the ground in Britain in this period, and there is little evidence that such atheists as existed were converted to Christian orthodoxy by reading works of natural theology. Something more than converting atheists is required to explain the huge amount of effort devoted to natural theology in Britain from the 17th to the 19th centuries. It cannot purely be speculative philosophical interest; for the main figures in the tradition were scientists.

Some non-demonstrative functions of natural theology are outlined by Brooke (1991a) and Brooke and Cantor (1998 ch. 5). Its integrative role is discussed by Harrison (2015: 150).

First, natural theology legitimated scientific endeavour – Robert Boyle in the 17th century described himself as a priest in the temple of nature, and William Whewell in the 19th century spoke of science as a perpetual song in the temple of nature. Both men as Christian clergymen used natural theology to justify their scientific work to themselves and others, by showing it had a religious purpose.

Second, operating within a fairly general natural theology framework allowed scientists to avoid scientifically pointless sectarian squabbles. This function became more important later in the period as Dissenters, Roman Catholics and others participated more actively in scientific institutions.

Third, natural theology provided a common language for various branches of scientific investigation, facilitating discussions across mathematics, biology, geology, chemistry, etc.

Fourth, natural theology suggested scientific theories. Boyle spoke of pregnant hints from a greater chemist than he, and Newton pored over the scriptures and religious history as he formulated his scientific theories. Whewell's commitment to teleology in science came from his theology.

Fifth, natural theology was a political resource that could be deployed by the establishment in support of the existing social order. Harmony and order in the natural world could be transferred to the social world, for instance to justify private property or inequality of rank. It does not seem to be an accident that these themes became more prominent at this time of political upheaval and threat to the established social order.[14]

Natural theology, creation and providence

Natural theology in its British scientific form depends for its coherence on the revealed doctrines of creation and providence.[15] A full discussion of the doctrine of creation is well beyond the scope of the book, but as will be clearer in later chapters, God's creation of everything that exists, including human beings and human economies, was the starting point for most 18th- and 19th-century natural theological political economists. Unless the object of study flowed from God's creative action, there would be no point in trying to better understand God through the study of economic arrangements and action. Most also recognised that the possibilities for understanding are limited by the fall, which impairs not just human moral capabilities but also our observational and reasoning capacities.[16]

The doctrine of providence is closely intertwined with natural theology. Providence is God's care for creation and involves both preservation of creation and God's governance of creation. It is a connecting doctrine, following on temporally and logically from the doctrine of creation, and looking towards the end of all things. Providence expresses God's love for human beings as well as the divine wisdom.

Later in the book, I will make use of the distinction between general and special providence; that is between God's regular lawlike activity and irregular activity. Special providence is not the same thing as miracles, which since the early modern period have often been seen as divine interventions into an otherwise autonomous natural order.[17] This idea of a miracle contrasts with the older conception where everything is in some sense caused by God, whether regular or irregular. Another distinction is between general and particular providence; that is between care of all things and God's particular care for the elect as part of the plan of salvation. Another way of seeing general and particular providence is as a distinction between God's wider care and care for individuals.[18]

One of the complications in discussing the Christian doctrine of providence is that it has been shaped by Stoic ideas of an autonomous, rational, lawlike universe with no need for a personal creator God. This complication is not of course unique to the doctrine of providence. Stoicism was popular in the 18th century, including with some of the authors discussed in this book, especially the young Adam Smith. Leaning too much towards Stoic conceptions of providence is a danger for our natural theologian political economists, but as will become clearer in the later chapters, most retained the idea that a personal and active God was caring for the universe. The rise of political economy in the early 19th century was in fact an example of divine providence for JB Sumner, one of the authors considered in later chapters. For others, political economy revealed something of the mechanisms of divine providence, increasing our appreciation of the divine wisdom and leading us to worship.

Like any Christian doctrine, providence can be twisted and used for dubious purposes. The "invisible hand" is a prime example, and its relationship to the doctrine of providence and some of its abuses will be discussed in Chapter 3. The use of the doctrine to justify imperial expansion and the mistreatment of indigenous peoples, and the alliance of "Christianity and commerce" in 19th-century Britain are other examples.[19]

My concern in this book is the use made of the doctrine of providence by those who shaped political economy as a discipline.

Natural theology and theodicy

The struggles of natural theological political economists to interpret economic suffering and evil, and reconcile them with the goodness and power of God, will be a major theme of the book. The best-known formulation of the philosophical problem is probably that of David Hume in his *Dialogues on Natural Religion*: "Is he willing to prevent evil, but not able? Then he is impotent. Is he able, but not willing? Then he is malevolent. Is he both able and willing? Whence then is evil?" (Hume 1993: 100).

A full account of theodicy is beyond the scope of the book, but a brief survey with an emphasis on the relevant early modern literature will help set the scene for subsequent chapters.[20] The dominant approach to evil in the Christian tradition, going back to Augustine, sees evil as a privation of the good.[21] Augustine struggled with the tension between denying evil and elevating evil powers to a role alongside God, which was the error of Manicheans. Eventually, he settled on a view that evil was real yet nothing. His struggle with Pelagians pushed him to a view that evil is not something we have a choice about, for the decisive choice had been made earlier by Adam, and before Adam a choice made by the angels. These views left Augustine to struggle towards the good, knowing that perfection was impossible, and the struggle hard because of original sin. The struggle was encouraged through his conviction that God had providentially ameliorated the effects of sin through institutions like government.

Before the early modern period, no particular need was seen to justify God – to answer the challenges like those in the quotation from Hume above. Suffering and evil were seen as a human problem, not a problem for God. If the question was asked, the answer was that God had a right to punish wrongdoing, and this was seen as a sufficient explanation for the suffering in the world. The biblical story of the fall is an explanation of evil, but there is no sense in which it is trying to defend God against something like Hume's challenge. The book of Job resists offering a theodicy, and Job's friends who attempt to explain his suffering are portrayed negatively. The closest readers get to an answer is God's appearance in greatness towards the end of the book. Job is a non-theodicy. The cross of Christ is another answer to evil that is not a theodicy.

It was in the 17th and early 18th centuries that the philosophical tradition of theodicy took shape.[22] God came to be seen as in some sense the cause of evil, and so the problem arose of justifying God's ways to humanity. As classically formulated by Leibniz in *Theodicy*, or by Hume in his *Dialogues*, it is the problem of logically holding together God's power, God's goodness and the reality of evil.

There is a continuing philosophical discussion and the main types of theodicies are:

- Greater good theodicies. Evil is necessary for God to achieve a greater good that cannot be achieved in any other way. For instance, developing the virtue of courage needs war or some other similar challenge, charity needs poverty and so on. Malthus' theodicy is considered in Chapter 4, where exertion is necessary to develop human capacities, is of this type.[23] The extreme case of this type of theodicy is Leibniz' argument that this is the best of all possible worlds that God could have created. This argument was mercilessly ridiculed by Voltaire's *Candide* in the wake of the Lisbon earthquake.

- Free will theodicies. These can be seen as a special case of greater good theodicies. Free will theodicies begin with the idea that humanity, with its moral dimension, would be meaningless without freedom to choose. Framed more theologically, our love of God would be empty unless we have a choice to do otherwise. The argument proceeds that evil is needed so that there is something else to choose as an alternative to the good, or God. A situation where bad choices do not have bad consequences would be very strange, perhaps impossible to sustain. So, if we are to have free choice we must have evil and suffering. This type of theodicy works best for moral evil, as opposed to natural evil, though it is possible to extend it by emphasising connections between humanity and the rest of creation.
- State of trial theodicies. These are a supplement to free will theodicies where this present world is a trial for the future life, and such a trial requires the existence of evil for a meaningful human choice between good and evil. This type of theodicy was important for Butler and Paley who will be considered in the next chapter.

As will be discussed in subsequent chapters, the emergence of political economy in the late 18th and early 19th centuries threw up new and complex versions of the problem of evil, which the early political economists responded to in various ways. The issue for this book is not whether theodicy is a coherent or fruitful enterprise.[24] Theodicy comes into the argument because the early political economists took it to be so, and my concern will be with the role of theology in shaping the new discipline of political economy.

Conclusion

The main point is that the British tradition of scientific natural theology was not about demonstrating God's existence; it was grounded in the revealed doctrine of creation and had quite different functions. This is fairly well travelled ground in the history and philosophy of science literature, but in the following chapters I will extend the linkage between natural theology and British science to the science of political economy, and draw out some issues raised by this extension.

Notes

1 General surveys of natural theology include Webb (1915), Swinburne (1991), Fergusson (2006), Brooke Re-Manning and Watts (2013).
2 The history of the two books' metaphor is discussed by Peter Hess (2003).
3 Everything requires interpretation, and the argument that interpretation is in fact the most basic philosophical problem is made by Gadamer (1960).

4 The ambiguity of the concept of nature complicates the issue. Natural is one of the most slippery concepts in the philosophical vocabulary. Lovejoy (1927) for instance identifies over twenty distinct meanings of the term. The distinction between natural and artificial is particularly problematic (Bensaude-Vincent and Newman 2007). The distinction between creation and nature (Welker 1999) also has to be borne in mind.

5 Barr (1993) and others discuss the scriptural passages.

6 Scriptural quotations are from the New International Version.

7 The precise meaning of humanity being in the image of God is debated. The dominant interpretation (according to Clines 1968) is that humanity shares something of the spirit of God, which distinguishes us from the animals. Other interpretations stress a sharing of dominion with God or the image of God as grounding our identity. Luther's view was that the image was sharing an original righteousness that was lost with the fall. Barth's view was that that is a sharing in God's relational character. For the purposes of this book, sorting out exactly what is shared is less important than there being something shared which gives a basis for a natural theology of humanity. If there is anything in Barth's (1932–70 III/1) proposal about sociality being an essential aspect of the bearing of the image of God, or Mouw's (2012) argument that all humanity together rather than a single individual bears the image, then the licence for a natural theology of humanity in their economic relationships is strengthened.

8 In addition to the above surveys, Thomas Aquinas' natural theology is discussed by Kretzmann (1999) and Calvin's approach to natural theology by Helm (2004).

9 Swinburne (1991, 2011) suggests that many philosophers misunderstand Hume and Kant's arguments against natural theology, and the arguments themselves are problematic. Hume's role in the decline of natural theology in the 19th century will be considered further in Chapter 7.

10 Barth and Brunner's debate, if it can be called that, is discussed by Barr (1993), McGrath (2008), Holder (2012) and others.

11 The Gifford lectures on natural theology are discussed by Witham (2005). Barth's 1938 lectures were entitled *The Knowledge of God and the Service of God According to the Teaching of the Reformation* and his view has not changed much since the 1934 exchange with Brunner. He opened his lectures "I certainly see with astonishment that such a science as Lord Gifford had in mind does exist, but I do not see how it is possible for it to exist. I am convinced that so far as it has existed and still exists, it owes its existence to a radical error" and "I am an avowed opponent of all natural theology" (Barth 1938: 5–6).

12 Fergusson (2014: 71) connects British natural theology with Deism, discussing the major 17th- and 18th-century figures and their doctrines. He observes that this often vaguely defined movement has had a very bad press, and accusing a writer of Deism essentially dismisses that writer. Gay (1968) assembles the most important Deist texts. Without entering into the arguments, merits or otherwise of Deism, I have followed Gascoigne and Brooke in emphasising the connections of natural theology to science.

13 The Bridgewater Treatises are discussed by Brooke (1991a) and Topham (1992, 1998).

14 Natural theology tends to support the existing social order because that is what theologians have before them to work with. This need not be so if awareness of sin, eschatology, or some other theological commitment, encourages the theologian to look for a non-observed natural or ideal state behind what is observed. This makes natural theologians in the Augustinian and Calvinist traditions, for instance, less disposed to use natural theology to buttress the existing order.

15 The doctrines of creation and providence are discussed by Fergusson (2010, 2013, 2014) and Elliott (2013). Walsham (1999) is illuminating on the history of the doctrine in the early modern period.

16 Harrison (2007) emphasises the role of the fall in relation to natural theology and the rise of modern science.

17 Charles Taylor (2007: 221ff) discusses changing conceptions of providence in the early modern period, on the anthropocentric shift and secularisation of the doctrine of providence. This shift from a doctrine of providence that focuses on God's activity to one that focuses on human apprehension of the natural order and ethics, is extremely important for political economy. Many of our natural theological political economists, whatever their position on innate moral sense, saw their discipline as helping human beings better discern the natural order that God had set up, and persuading human beings to live in harmony with it, for their happiness.

18 Swinburne (1998) discusses these distinctions between general and special providence.

19 These examples of the misuse of the doctrine of providence are discussed by Fergusson (2013). He concludes "One theological lesson emerging from all this is the need for a more modest account of providence that neither over determines our capacity for discerning purpose and progress in history nor too readily identifies divine intention with historical and social forces which may be very ambivalent when ethically assessed . . . At the same time, the language of providence needs to be retained rather than discarded" (Fergusson 2013: 670).

20 Theodicy is a vast topic and surveys include Murray (2009), Hick (1977), Swinburne (1998), Surin (1986). Crenshaw (2005) deals with the biblical material.

21 Gillian Evans (1982) discusses Augustine's extraordinarily influential account of evil, in the original context of his struggles with Manicheans and Pelagians.

22 Sam Newlands (2012) tells the story of the rise of theodicy in the 17th century.

23 John Hick characterises these as Irenaean theodicies in contrast to Augustinian theodicies. "There is to be found in Irenaeus the outline of an approach to the problem of evil which stands in important respects in contrast to the Augustinian type theodicy. Instead of the doctrine that man was created finitely perfect and then incomprehensibly destroyed his own perfection and plunged into sin and misery, Irenaeus suggests that man was created as an imperfect immature creature to undergo moral development and growth and finally be brought to the perfection intended for him by his Maker" (Hick 1977: 214). One may question whether Irenaeus or Augustine are offering theodicies in the modern sense, but if so, then Malthus' theodicy fits Hick's Irenaean type.

24 My own view (influenced by Surin 1986 and Clifton 2015) is that theodicy is a theologically problematic enterprise.

3 Early English theological roots of political economy[1]

According to David Hume's biographer EC Mossner, Butler's "Analogy *was to remain the one theological work of the century that he was to deem worthy of serious consideration and whose author was always to be highly respected by him" and "Hume was greatly interested in learning Dr Butler's opinion of his philosophy". For John Henry Newman Joseph Butler was "The greatest name in the Anglican Church".*

Josiah Tucker according to Dr Johnson was "one of the few excellent writers of the period. No person, however learned can read his writings without some improvement". Bishop Warburton suggested "Trade was his religion and religion his trade". For Karl Marx "Tucker was a parson and a Tory, but for the rest, an honourable man and a competent political economist".

Edmund Burke by contrast was disparaged by Karl Marx as "an out-and-out vulgar bourgeois".

William Paley "laid the foundation of the moral philosophy of many hundreds – probably thousands – of youth while under a course of training designed to qualify them for being afterwards the moral instructors of millions". According to JM Keynes, Paley's Principles of Moral and Political Philosophy *was "an immortal book" and Charles Darwin shared his admiration.*[2]

Introduction

This chapter is about the 18th-century English background to the rise of political economy, but much of the motivation comes from a Scot, Adam Smith, or at least the role that Smith plays in standard histories of economic thought. The tale that is often told is of Smith creating political economy ex-nihilo, and then passing it on to the English who tidied up some theoretical loose ends and professionalised it. Scholars in recent decades have corrected this tale, documenting the influence of many 18th-century predecessors, especially in relation to Smith's analytical apparatus (Meek 1963; Ross 1995; Skinner 1996; Rashid 1998). Even if influences on Smith are recognised, the story of political economy in Britain flowing from Smith usually remains.

Can we ask, what would have happened if the sickly Adam Smith had died in childhood? Would political economy have emerged in Britain in the early 19th century? I will argue that the key idea for subsequent economists of a coincidence of self-interest and the common good was clear in 18th-century English thought, and while it may have taken longer for political economy to achieve the same level of analytical sophistication without Smith and the influences transmitted through him from continental Europe, political economy would have taken a broadly similar course in 19th-century Britain without him.[3] Perhaps this 18th-century English background helps explain why political economy did not develop in Scotland after Smith's passing, despite Dugald Stewart's Edinburgh lectures on Smithian political economy after his death, which in fact seemed of most interest to English travellers.

Running this argument means allowing the English Enlightenment to be something more than a cause for a polite chuckle, and questioning the long running denigration of 18th-century English economic thought (following historians Roy Porter 2000, Gertrude Himmelfarb 2004, against Franco Venturi 1970). It also means recognising Adam Smith's English connections. Though he was a proud Scot, he was a strong supporter of the 1707 Union of Scotland with England and spent considerable amounts of time in London, including the crucial period leading up to the publication of the *Wealth of Nations* (Ross 1995).

Many scholars have suggested that 18th-century British moral philosophy is essentially an extended response to the challenge of Thomas Hobbes (for instance Raphael 1969; Hirschman 1977; Myers 1983; Milbank 1990, though Darwall 1999 resists this). Smith is often seen as the definitive response to Hobbes' view that a coercive state is the only way of maintaining order in a society of self-interested individuals – Smith's response being that self-interest in the context of the institutions of commercial society generates order and not chaos. Evidence of Smith having Hobbes in mind is slim, though it must be said that his patchy citation habits were even more so when notorious figures such as Hobbes or Mandeville were involved. Evidence of other key figures in the emergence of political economy seeing themselves as responding to Hobbes is even slimmer.

Theology is the crucial ingredient in this rewriting of the connections between 18th-century English economic thinking and the successful emergence of political economy in 19th-century Britain. This is especially so of the doctrine of providence, and debates about the relationship between self-interest and the good of society.[4]

Among the many 18th-century English philosophers who discussed economic questions, I will concentrate on Joseph Butler, Josiah Tucker, William Paley and Edmund Burke because the historical connections are clear with Hume and Smith, along with the direct connections with important 19th-century English political economists.[5] Butler and Paley exerted a particularly important influence on 19th-century English political economy independently of Smith.

Joseph Butler (1692–1752)

After a Presbyterian upbringing, Joseph Butler[6] was educated at a dissenting academy, Oriel College Oxford, before going on to distinguished Anglican appointments as Rector of Stanhope, Bishop of Bristol, Dean of St Pauls Cathedral and Bishop of Durham. He famously clashed with John Wesley over unlicensed Methodist preachers operating in his Diocese of Bristol. Butler's major works are his *Sermons Delivered in the Rolls Chapel* published in 1726, and his *Analogy of Religion* 1736.

Contemporary interest in Butler is mostly from philosophers – extracts from his *Sermons* often appear in anthologies among the "British Moralists" responding to Mandeville and Hobbes, but there is much less attention now to the *Analogy of Religion*. Very little has been written on Butler's influence on political economy since Jacob Viner's pioneering work on 18th-century Anglican social thought (some published in Viner 1960, 1972, but much remains unpublished). There are brief comments on Butler in Hirschman (1977: 46). Myers' (1983: 57–9) discussion of "self-interest and public welfare" downplays Butler's influence on political economy on the basis that Butler relied solely on an internal psychological balance to self-interest, in contrast to Smith who balanced self-interest against the self-interest of others in a market economy.[7]

We have no record of Butler's works in Adam Smith's library (Mizuta 2000), but there is other evidence Smith knew and respected Butler's work. Smith's good friend David Hume acknowledged Butler in the Introduction to his *Treatise of Human Nature*. Hume's correspondence records his respect for Butler's opinion of the work, and Butler seems to be the main model for Cleanthes in Hume's *Dialogues on Natural Religion*. Smith himself refers to Butler as that "late ingenious and subtle philosopher" (*TMS* I i 2.2: 14) when discussing topics like sympathy and conscience (for instance, *TMS* I iii 1.1: 11).[8]

Butler's fame in the 18th century rested on his *Analogy of Religion*, so it is here we must look for what Hume and Smith admired. Butler's outline of what religion teaches from the Introduction to this work is worth quoting in full because it sums up the Anglican theological framework which I am arguing was important for the development of political economy:

> Now the divine government of the world, implied in the notion of religion in general and of Christianity, contains in it – that mankind is appointed to live in a future state; that there everyone shall be rewarded or punished; rewarded or punished respectively for all that behaviour here, which we comprehend under the words virtuous or vicious, morally good or evil; that our present life is a probation, a state of trial and of discipline, for that future one; notwithstanding the objections, which men may fancy they have, from notions of Necessity, against there being any such moral plan as this at all: and whatever objections may appear to lie against the wisdom and goodness of it, as it stands so imperfectly made known to us at present; that this world being in

a state of apostasy and wickedness, and consequently of ruin, and the sense both of their condition and duty being greatly corrupted amongst men, this gave occasion for an additional dispensation of Providence of the utmost importance; proved by miracles; but containing in it many things appearing to us strange, and not to have been expected; a dispensation of Providence, which is a scheme or system of things; carried on by the mediation of a divine person, the Messiah, in order to the recovery of the world; yet not revealed to all men, nor proved with the strongest possible evidence to all those to whom it is revealed; but only to such a part of mankind, and with such particular evidence, as the wisdom of God thought fit.

(Butler 1736: xxxi–xxxii)

The most notable features of Butler's summary of Christian doctrine are his emphasis on rewards and punishments in the future life, and an imperfectly perceived divine providence operating in our present fallen life. These doctrines of the future hope, the moral and intellectual consequences of the fall, and divine providence I have argued are important components of the framework of Adam Smith's thought (Oslington 2011a, 2011b, 2012a). Together with the "objections that may appear to lie against the wisdom and goodness of it" and the associated enterprise of theodicy, they are also part of the animating framework of early 19th-century English political economy (Waterman 1991a, 2004).

As well as this shared theological framework, there are specific connections between Butler's ideas and those of Smith and 19th-century English political economy.

Beginning with mankind as he actually is

Butler begins his Rolls Chapel sermons by pointing out that he is not "enquiring into the abstract relations of things" but beginning his moral enquiry "from a matter of fact, namely what the particular nature of man is, its several parts, their economy or constitution; from whence it proceeds to determine what course of life it is" (Butler Preface to *Sermons* paragraph 12: 6).

Idea of nature (including human society) as a teleological system

Butler continues "Every work both of nature and of art is a system: and as every particular thing, both natural and artificial, is for some use or purpose out of or beyond itself" (Butler Preface to *Sermons* paragraph 14: 9–10). Butler then explains the purpose of this system "The interest or good of the whole must be the interest of the universal Being" (Butler Preface to *Sermons* paragraph 30: 18).

Affirmation of self-love, and showing that is not opposed to benevolence and virtue

Butler then moves to one of his main themes: "self-love and benevolence, virtue and interest are not to be opposed . . . self-love in its due degree is as just and morally good as any affection whatever" (Butler Preface to *Sermons* paragraph 39: 23–4). Further:

> Let it be allowed, though virtue or moral rectitude does indeed consist in affection to and pursuit of what is right and good, as such; yet, that when we sit down in a cool hour, we can neither justify to ourselves this or any other pursuit, till we are convinced that it will be for our happiness, or at least not contrary to it.
>
> (Butler *Sermons* Sermon XI "Upon the Love of our Neighbour" paragraph 20: 182 – this is the often anthologised "cool hour" passage)

Private and public good are providentially reconciled

Butler argues our affections "do in general contribute and lead us to public good as really as to private" (Butler *Sermons* Sermon I "Upon Human Nature" paragraph 7: 37).

Then he restates the point: "private affections, as tending to private good; this does not hinder them from being public affections too, or destroy the good influence of them upon society, and their tendency to public good" (Butler *Sermons* Sermon I "Upon Human Nature" paragraph 7: 37). Butler continues in language that could easily come from Smith, Whately, Jones, Whewell, or any number of early 19th-century political economists:

> [b]y acting merely from regard (suppose) to reputation, without any consideration of the good of others, men often contribute to public good. . . . they are plainly instruments in the hands of another, in the hands of Providence, to carry on the preservation of the individual and good of society, which they themselves have not in their view or intention.
>
> (Butler *Sermons* Sermon I "Upon Human Nature" paragraph 7: 38)

This is a clear statement by an influential figure of Adam Smith's key idea, fifty years before the publication of the *Wealth of Nations*.

The fall affects private and public good alike

Butler observes:

> [t]here is a manifest negligence in men of their real happiness or interest in the present world, when that interest is inconsistent with a present gratification; for the sake of which they negligently, nay, even knowingly, are the authors and instruments of their own misery and ruin. Thus they are as often unjust to themselves as to others, and for the most part are equally so to both by the same actions.
>
> (Butler *Sermons* Sermon I "Upon Human Nature" paragraph 15: 45)

Illusion

Just as for Smith, a wisely designed illusion is part of the divine system "however perfect things are, they must necessarily appear to us otherwise, less perfect than they are" (Butler *Sermons* Sermon XV "Upon the Ignorance of Man" paragraph 15: 239). Providence is used by Butler, just as by Smith, to explain motivation towards ends of the system that humans cannot see.

Leaving the good of the whole to God

Human ignorance for Butler, just as for Smith, means that humans should restrict their concerns to their own interests, which they are competent to judge, for "the happiness of the world is the concern of him who is the Lord and the Proprietor of it" (Butler *Dissertation on Virtue* 1726: 272). Further:

> Since the constitution of nature, and the methods and designs of Providence in the government of the world, are above our comprehension we should acquiesce, and rest satisfied with, our ignorance; turn our thoughts from that which is above and beyond us, and apply ourselves to that which is level to our capacities, and which is our real business and concern.
>
> (Butler *Sermons* Sermon XV "Upon the Ignorance
> of Man" paragraph 16: 240)

Contrary to Myers' suggestion that the harmony in Butler is just internal and psychological, Butler clearly suggests in the preface to *Sermons* and *Analogy* that the social system also operates to harmonise individual interests and the common good. A description of the mechanisms by which harmony is achieved is missing though in Butler. The same could be said of many early 19th-century English political economists.

Josiah Tucker (1713–99)

Tucker rose from humble Welsh circumstances through education at St Johns College Oxford to become Chaplain to Bishop Butler in Bristol, then Dean of Gloucester under Bishop Warburton.[9] Throughout his career, Tucker was a pugnacious participant in public debates over economic matters, including a famous exchange with David Hume over the tendencies of trade to equalise wealth between rich and poor countries,[10] and an exchange with Edmund Burke towards the end of his life over the economics of separation of the American colonies from Britain.

His major economic works were *Elements of Commerce and the Theory of Taxes* 1755 (privately circulated and only three copies exist), *Instructions for Travellers* 1757 and his *Treatise on Civil Government* 1781.

The literature on Tucker's economics is thin. It includes an adulatory biography by Clark (1903) and Schulyer's collection of texts (Tucker 1931) reviewed by Viner (1932), who agreed Tucker was "important for the history of ideas in the 18th century" but expressed skepticism about Tucker's contribution to economics. The more recent biography of Shelton (1981) distinguished Tucker from Smith in that Tucker required government as well as the market to reconcile private and public interest. By contrast, Rashid (1982, 1998) elevates Tucker in disparaging Adam Smith's contribution to political economy.

The biographical connections between Tucker, Hume and Smith are close. Eleven of Tucker's books are in Smith's library (Mizuta 2000). As noted earlier, there was an extended exchange between Hume and Tucker over trade between rich and poor countries which shaped the views on trade of Hume's close friend, Adam Smith. Tucker's point that the expansion of the market facilitates mutually beneficial trade is prominent in Smith's discussion of free trade.

Ideas and even specific language from Tucker appear in Smith and early 19th-century political economy.[11]

Providential underpinnings of the economic system

One of Tucker's earliest economic works begins "Providence intended that there should be mutual dependence and connection" between people (Tucker *Essay on Trade* 1749: ii) and then goes on to apply this principle to trade between people in different nations. Like most 18th-century writers, Tucker recognised the doctrine of providence as the background for discussion of the economic system. Right action by individuals in markets or by government is that which aligns to God's providential designs. As Tucker wrote:

> The powers with which it has pleased the munificent Creator to form mankind, are suited to such important ends, that a wrong application of them cannot but be productive of great infelicity; as a right use of such endowments is the source of all enjoyments for which human nature was created.
>
> (Tucker *Elements* 1755: 55)

Self-love is powerful but in need of direction

Tucker calls "Self-love, the great mover of created beings" (Tucker *Elements* 1755: 58). For Tucker, like Smith, the weakness of benevolence means that "the main point to be aimed at, is neither to extinguish nor enfeeble self-love, but to give it such a direction, that it may promote the public interest by pursuing its own" (Tucker *Elements* 1755: 59).

Commerce, government and religion reconcile self-love and public interest

> Let us therefore enter upon the ensuing work with the following maxim strongly upon our minds, that universal commerce, good government, and true religion, are nearly, are inseparably connected. For the directions and regulations of each of these, are no other than to make private coincide with public, present with future happiness.
>
> (Tucker *Elements* 1755: 60)

Tucker's argument that the divergence of interests between merchants and the country as a whole means the role of government is to "frame Laws and Regulations relating to trade in such a manner, as may cause the private interest of the merchant to fall in with the general good of his country" (Tucker *Essay on Trade* 1749: viii).

For Tucker, things should be arranged so that "every individual (whether he intends it or not) will be promoting the good of his country, and of mankind in general, while he is pursuing his own private interest" (Tucker *Elements* 1755: 61). Later he wrote:

> The rules of religion, and the rules of social industry do perfectly harmonize; and that all things hurtful to the latter, are indeed a violation of [the] former. In short, the same Being who formed the religious system, formed also the commercial; and the end of both, as designed by Providence, is no other than this, that private interest should coincide with public, self with social, and the present with future happiness. Those men therefore, who would represent the principles of religion, and the principles of commerce as at variance with each other, are in reality friends to neither, and quite ignorant of both.
>
> (Tucker *Travellers* 1757: 266)

In another work: "I am thoroughly convinced that the Laws of Commerce, when rightly understood, do perfectly coincide with the Laws of Morality, both originating from the same good Being, whose mercies are over all his works". This is used by Tucker as an argument against slavery when combined with the observation that slavery is an inefficient method of production in the colonies (Tucker *Letter to Burke* 1775: 383).

In Tucker we have a clear and powerful statement of the harmony between self-love and the common good, though Tucker is not a proponent of laissez-faire, as government has an important role in directing self-love to its proper end. This is contrary to the conclusion of Shelton, who in my view neglects the common naturalness of both government and self-interest, perhaps because of his neglect of the theological framework of Tucker's thought. For Tucker, both the government and the market are providential institutions, as they are for Adam Smith.

William Paley (1743–1805)

Paley was a Cambridge student with a particular talent for mathematics, senior wrangler and then Fellow at Christ's College Cambridge before marrying and moving to the posts of Archdeacon of Carlisle then Archdeacon of Wearmouth.[12] His major works were *Principles of Moral and Political Philosophy* 1785 (based on his 1776 Cambridge lectures), *Horae Paulinae, or the Truth of the Scripture History of St Paul* 1790, *Evidences of Christianity* 1784, *Natural Theology* 1802 and some posthumously published *Sermons* 1806.[13]

Today, Paley is not much read and is generally regarded as exploded by Darwin's *Origin of Species* 1859, if not earlier by Hume's *Dialogues on Natural Religion*. This contemporary view overlooks the continued popularity of Paley's works deep into the 19th century – Keynes, for instance, called his *Principles of Moral and Political Philosophy* "an immortal book" and Darwin greatly admired the book. Rather than Paley's arguments being exploded by Hume and Darwin, the late 19th-century decline in his popularity was due to the collapse of the natural theological framework for British scientific and religious discussion. The popular reception of Darwin's *Origin of Species* had something to do with the collapse of natural theology, but struggles over theodicy, increasing professionalisation of science, and church politics were arguably more important (Brooke 1991a).

As well as a natural theological framework, Paley took a cumulative probabilistic method of argument from Butler's *Analogy*. However, Paley's theological utilitarian ethics left no role for Butler's conscience. Paley denied that moral sense or conscience was a useful guide for morality:

> Upon the whole, it seems to me, either that there exist no such instincts as compose what is called the moral sense, or that they are not now to be distinguished from prejudices and habits; on which account they cannot be depended upon in moral reasoning.
>
> (Paley *PMPP*: 11)

Purpose of scripture is limited, we reason from creation

As a natural theologian, Paley reasoned from what God has given us in the created order, including human nature; this was what would deliver moral and political guidance. In his Introduction to *PMPP*, Paley suggested to his readers "Whoever expects to find in the Scriptures a specific direction for every moral doubt that arises, looks for more than he will meet with" (Paley *PMPP*: 3) and "Morality is taught in Scripture . . . general rules are laid down . . . these rules are occasionally illustrated" (Paley *PMPP*: 4), and further that, "The Scriptures commonly presuppose in the persons to whom they speak, a knowledge of the principles of natural justice; and are employed not so much to teach *new* rules of morality, as to enforce the practice of it by new sanctions, and by a greater certainty" (Paley *PMPP*: 5). In case the reader is still in any doubt, "The Scriptures do not supersede the use of the science of which we profess to treat, and at the same time acquit them of any charge of imperfection or insufficiency on that account" (Paley *PMPP*: 6).

The world as a system for happiness

Paley begins his substantive moral argument with an observation about the purpose of the created order "God hath called forth his consummate wisdom to contrive and provide for our happiness, and the world appears to have been constituted with this design" (Paley *PMPP*: 41).[14]

Our limited understanding

He then picks up Butler's theme of human beings' limited understanding of God's government of the world, arguing we should focus on our individual role and use utility as our best (though imperfect) guide to action. Paley combines this theme with the previous observation about the purpose of the system:

> God wills and wishes the happiness of his creatures. And this conclusion being once established, we are at liberty to go on with the rule built upon it, namely, that the method of coming at the will of God, concerning any action, by the light of nature, is to inquire into the tendency of that action to promote or diminish general happiness.
>
> (Paley *PMPP*: 42)

This means "actions are to be estimated by their tendency to promote happiness. Whatever is expedient, is right. It is the utility of any moral rule alone, which constitutes the obligation of it" (Paley *PMPP*: 42). So, in contrast to his much less influential fellow utilitarian contemporary Jeremy Bentham, utility is not a principle that has moral force in itself, but rather is a way of approximating the will of God which has the moral force of the creator. Paley's argument is similar to Butler's except that utilitarian reasoning rather than conscience is the guide to action in an imperfect world.

Self-interest and the public good

Paley's *Principles of Moral and Political Philosophy* paints a picture of the harmony of self-interest and the common good, within the English institutional setting. By ruling out moral sense, it is only the properties of the larger social system that are left to reconcile self-interest and the common good. Some mechanisms of reconciliation are discussed in the long economic chapter of the *Principles* "Of Population and Provision" (Paley *PMPP* Book VI ch11). Population and provision are kept in equilibrium by mechanisms operating through changes in the accustomed mode of living of the people, changes in the quantity of provisions and changes in the distribution of provisions (Paley *PMPP*: 424–32). The public benefit of trade is discussed (for instance Paley *PMPP*: 437). Self-interest in Paley's economic chapter is the practical outworking of attending to our role in an imperfectly understood scheme of divine government, and he reminds his readers that "In the magnitude and complexity of the machine, the principle of motion is sometimes lost or unobserved" (Paley *PMPP*: 436). Prices seem to play no part in Paley's mechanisms, so while it is a less sophisticated model than offered by Adam Smith it has the same overall character of reconciling self-interest and beneficial outcomes for society. There is not the same emphasis as in Smith on the outcomes being unintended, although Paley does give examples of this, such as his discussion of the desire for luxuries having the unintended consequence of maintaining employment of the population (Paley *PMPP*: 436).

Problem of evil

The theological problem of economic suffering was raised famously by Malthus in his *Essay on the Principle of Population* 1798, and Malthus offered a controversial theodicy in an attempt to deal with the problem (Waterman 1991a; Oslington 2015a). The problem is less pressing for Paley than Malthus as he models an easier equilibrium between population and provision, but the problem still exists. Paley's mature view in *Natural Theology* follows Butler; that this life is a trial for the future life, though with traces of an alternative view that suffering provokes qualities which endure into the future life.

> Now we assert the most probable supposition to be, that it is a state of moral probation; and that many things in it suit with this hypothesis, which suit with no other. It is not a state of unmixed happiness, or of happiness simply: it is not a state of designed misery, or of misery simply: it is not a state of retribution: it is not a state of punishment. It suits with none of these suppositions. It accords much better with the idea of its being a condition calculated for the production, exercise, and improvement of moral qualities, with a view to a future state, in which these qualities, after being so produced, exercised, and improved, may by a new and more favouring constitution of things, receive their reward, or become their own.
>
> (Paley 1802 ch. XXVI: 271)[15]

Extension of natural theology to human society and economics

Adam Smith extended natural theology beyond the physical world (Oslington 2011a), and Paley seemingly independently does this in his last book *Natural Theology*. The point is not whether Paley's arguments about divine design in the social and economic realms are ultimately persuasive, but rather that Paley (like Smith) made the attempt, and that this attempt shaped the subsequent development of political economy in England. Paley's influence is clear in Malthus' *Essay on the Principle of Population* (1798: 201) where Malthus states that "it seems absolutely necessary that we reason from nature up to nature's God and not presume to reason from God to nature", and goes on to speak of "the book of nature where alone we can read God as he is". In correspondence Malthus commented that "The proofs of design are indeed everywhere so apparent that it is hardly possible to add much to the force of the argument as stated and illustrated by Paley" (Malthus to Whewell 1833, as quoted in Hilton 1988: 51). Many more examples could be quoted from early 19th-century political economists.

Edmund Burke (1729–97)

In the argument of this chapter, Burke occupies a somewhat different place to Butler, Tucker and Paley. Rather than being a source of a theological framework and the key idea of harmony of interest, Burke is an alternative conduit to

Adam Smith for these ideas into the 19th century, especially into 19th-century English policy and popular discussion.[16]

There is a vast literature on Burke, the Anglo-Irish writer, politician and self-described student of political economy "from his early youth to near the end of my service in parliament" (Burke 1796, quoted in Winch 1996: 125). His most important writings on political economy were his *Observations on The Present State of the Nation* 1769, Parliamentary *Speech on Economical Reform* 1780 where he attacked the Royal household's "prodigality and corrupt influence" (p. 161) and outlined principles of reform, *Reflections on the Revolution in France* 1790, *Thoughts and Details on Scarcity* originally written in 1795 for William Pitt in response to severe food shortages in that year and which was later edited for posthumous publication, and Burke's *Letter to a Noble Lord* 1796 where he discussed political economy as part of his response to the Duke of Bedford's criticism of him drawing a parliamentary pension.

The secondary literature on Burke's economics has been dominated by CB MacPherson (1962, 1980, 1987) for whom the key question was how to reconcile his conservatism and his economic liberalism; how Burke could be both the "champion of tradition, hierarchy, privilege and prejudice" and yet have an "unqualified embrace of the capitalist market economy" (1987: 299). MacPherson's best answer was that Burke believed the prosperity delivered by economic liberalism maintained something of the old order. This however was an unstable reconciliation because prosperity may undermine character, as in Burke's famous remark that "the age of chivalry is gone. That of sophisters, economists, and calculators has succeeded; and the glory of Europe is extinguished forever" (Burke 1790: 446). MacPherson also suggested that Burke saw "the operation of the capitalist market economy required that the hard core of hierarchical order should be maintained" (1987: 300). It is difficult now to follow MacPherson's reading of Burke after Jacob Viner's (1963) devastating review of his work. Viner, after detailing a long list of anachronistic and forced interpretations, concluded that "MacPherson tries to fit the 17th-century theorizing into a model built around the concepts of a possessive market society" (1963: 550) and judged MacPherson's work a "greater loss to learning" than gain to "social salvation" (1963: 559). Winch (1996) is similarly critical of MacPherson.

Burke's connections with Smith are interesting (explored by Jacob Viner in his *Guide to John Rae's Life of Adam Smith* 1965: 23–33 and by Donald Winch *Riches and Poverty* 1996: 127–200). Smith was reported to have said of Burke that "he was the only man who, without communication, thought on these topics [political economy] exactly as he did" (Bisset's 1800 anecdote, quoted in Winch 1996: 125). There are several letters, beginning with Burke to Smith 10 September 1759 after Burke received a copy via David Hume of Smith's *TMS*. Burke and Smith did not meet until 1777, the year after the publication of *WN*, when Burke was forty-eight. Smith's library included many of Burke's books, speeches and pamphlets (Mizuta 2000). It seems that Smith made some alterations to later editions of the *WN* in response to Burke (Winch 1996: 209). Smith was no doubt among the great and learned men Burke was alluding to when he claimed that he had studied political economy "since his early youth" and that "great and learned men thought my studies were not wholly thrown away, and deigned to communicate with me now and then on some particulars of their immortal works" (Burke 1796 quoted in Winch 1996: 125).[17]

If the biographical evidence points to Burke's economic attitudes being formed independently of Smith and before he read Smith's *WN*, and influences subsequently ran in both directions between Burke and Smith, then what were the other influences on Burke's economics? The best candidate is Josiah Tucker, with whom Burke had well-documented connections (Pocock 1985a; Winch 1996), but Tucker is only the most obvious of the group of Anglicans who saw a theologically grounded harmony in the emerging market order.

Discussion of Burke's economics tends to focus on *Thoughts and Details on Scarcity* where there are some passages that would not seem out of place in a 1980's speech of Margaret Thatcher or Ronald Reagan. However, such passages must be read in the context of Burke's desire in 1795 to stop what he saw as hasty and damaging government intervention in food markets, at a time when Britain was at war. Burke pleaded with William Pitt to:

> [r]esist the idea, speculative or practical, that it is within the competence of government, taken as government, or even of the rich, as rich, to supply to the poor, those necessaries which it has pleased the Divine Providence for a while to withhold from them. We, the people, ought to be made sensible, that it is not in breaking the laws of commerce, which are the laws of nature, and consequently the laws of God, that we are to place our hope of softening the Divine displeasure to remove any calamity under which we suffer, or which hangs over us.
>
> (Burke *Thoughts and Details on Scarcity* 1795: 210)

Burke emphasised the harmony of interests, against those who wanted to blame farmers and speculators for the food crisis:

> It is therefore the first and fundamental interest of the labourer, that the farmer should have a full incoming profit on the product of his labour. The proposition is self-evident, and nothing but the malignity, perverseness, and ill-governed passions of mankind, and particularly the envy they bear to each other's prosperity, could prevent their seeing and acknowledging it, with thankfulness to the benign and wise disposer of all things, who obliges men, whether they will it or not, in pursuing their own selfish interests, to connect the general good with their own individual success.
>
> (Burke *Thoughts and Details on Scarcity* 1795: 199–200)

These passages in *Thoughts and Details on Scarcity* must be balanced by other discussions of economic matters in Burke's previous and later writings.[18] Government is regarded as a natural complement to the market and discussed favourably in *Observations on The Present State of the Nation* 1769, *Economical Reform*

1780 and *Reflections* 1790. Among Burke's criticisms during the impeachment of Warren Hastings was his failure to act to prevent famine in India.

The other important point to make about Burke's economics is that the functioning of a commercial society depends on manners, which in turn, like much else in the social order, depends on religion. The causality in Burke runs from religion to manners to economics, and there is little trace in Burke of Adam Smith's concern about a commercial order undermining manners and religion upon which the market order depends (for instance, Smith's discussion in *WN* (1776) of the deleterious effects on workers of the division of labour, for which education is suggested to ameliorate).

Burke's much quoted statement that "the age of chivalry is gone. That of sophisters, economists, and calculators has succeeded; and the glory of Europe is extinguished forever" (Burke 1790: 446) immediately follows his description of the invasion of Marie Antoinette's bedchamber by the revolutionaries, and would seem to be referring to that and related events. Given that context, the "economists" denigrated are most likely to be the French economists associated with the revolutionaries and fond of rationalistic speculation, rather than British writers on economic matters. Burke is consistent elsewhere in his criticism of rationalism in political and economic matters. So, read in proper context, this often quoted statement identifies Burke more closely with the 18th-century Anglican writers on political economy (as well as with Smith) rather than distancing Burke from them.

If Burke was an important conduit of these ideas into early 19th-century policy and popular discussion, then Burke's version of them is extreme and over-theologised compared to Adam Smith. Perhaps some of the less wise market advocacy in 19th-century England comes from reading Burke more than from reading Adam Smith. Our discussion of Burke (as well as Tucker) warns against driving a wedge between the twin providential institutions of market and government. Government overreach is criticised by Burke rather than government itself.

Conclusion

This chapter has been about the influence of 18thcentury English thought on Adam Smith, and on 19th-century political economy through Smith, and apart from Smith. Butler, Tucker, Paley, Burke and Smith shared a natural theological framework, and the idea of harmony of self-interest and the general good. Our 18th-century Anglicans placed less emphasis on sin and the effects of the fall than Smith, and also less emphasis on the hiddenness or illusory quality of the reconciliation of self-interest with the common good. They also seem less aware than Smith of the potential of commercial society to erode the culture which supports it, and the potential instability this erosion brings to the system. These differences in my view reflect the greater role of Calvinist theology in Smith's intellectual framework compared to the English writers.

I suggest that Butler, Tucker and Paley made Adam Smith possible in the sense that the English intellectual elite were well prepared for the idea at the core of the *Wealth of Nations* that there is a providential harmony of interests in commercial society.

So, would political economy have emerged in Britain in the 19th century if Smith had died in childhood? We can only speculate, but my own view is that it would have taken a similar shape, though theoretical development would have been slower without his bringing together economic ideas and evidence from many sources, especially the latest theoretical developments from continental Europe. Without Smith, perhaps, we would have had to wait for JS Mill in the mid-19th century for a grand theoretical synthesis of political economy.

How does this work enrich our understanding of the history of political economy as a discipline? First, it suggests softening the division between English and Scottish economic thinking. They share a broadly similar framework and the key idea of a harmonious economic order underpinned by divine providence. Second, the importance of theology for understanding the formation of political economy is reinforced. English theological sources as well as the moderate Calvinism of the Scottish enlightenment need more attention. All this is perfectly consistent with a central role for natural theology in the story of political economy. Natural theology of the type we have been discussing after all came to Smith through his admiration of Isaac Newton.

Notes

1 This chapter draws on a paper presented at "The History of Economic Thought Society of Australia" conference in July 2013, and I thank University of Divinity for a travel grant which enabled me to present the paper. It was subsequently presented at the David Nichol Smith Workshop on 18th-century studies at the University of Sydney in 2014.

2 The quotation from EC Mossner's (1980) *Life of David Hume* comes from p. 11. Newman's opinion of Butler is from his *Apologia* (1864) p. 277 and similar remarks in his correspondence. Marx' view of Burke is recorded in volume I of *Capital*. Paley is praised by Whately in the introduction to his 1859 edition of Paley's works. Keynes comment is from *Essays in Biography* 1933.

3 This does not deny that the key idea could also have come into British political economy from earlier continental Jansenist thought of Nicole and Domat, through Boisguilbert, Cantillon, Mandeville, Hume and Smith (Waterman 2008a, drawing on Faccarello 1999).

4 This chapter also pushes the beginnings of the English School of Political Economy identified by Waterman (2008b) further back into the 18th century, and suggests it had English native roots.

5 Notable omissions among the English include George Berkeley and Abraham Tucker. Scottish predecessors of Smith such as Gershom Carmichael, Francis Hutcheson, Lord Kames and David Hume will not be considered here.

6 Further information about Butler's life is available in Cunliffe (2004), which is a much more balanced account than Leslie Stephen's (1899a) earlier treatment of Butler (and his treatments of Josiah Tucker (1899b) and Paley (1899c)). The clash between Wesley and Butler is described in F. Baker (1980) "John Wesley and Bishop Joseph Butler: A Fragment of Wesley's Manuscript Journal August 1739" *Proceedings of the Wesley Historical Society* 42 (May): 93–100.

7 A reassessment of Butler's role in the history of economics implicitly repositions Hobbes, since Hirschman (1977) and Myers (1983) saw Smith as responding to

Hobbes' argument that the state of nature was chaotic and nasty, and that state power was the solution to this problem. Smith on their account was arguing, against Hobbes, that state power is not needed to achieve economic order. Smith could not afford to acknowledge debts to notorious atheists Hobbes and Mandeville, though Smith at one point in *TMS* sets his own moral theory against Hobbes, criticising Hobbes for supposing there is no natural distinction between right and wrong, making these a matter for the arbitrary will of the civil magistrate. Hobbes appears only incidentally in the *WN*. If Butler was responding to Hobbes, and Butler influenced Hume and Smith, then Hobbes has more historical influence on political economy than is commonly recognised. Hont (2005) gives a quite different account of the connection between Hobbes, Hume and Smith, where the Scots add an economic dimension to Hobbes' purely political natural law theory.

8 Mossner (1936) and Penelhum (1988) discuss the relationship between Butler and Hume. Further biographical evidence that Butler was respected by Hume and Smith is provided by Ross (2010). Raphael and Macfie's introduction to their edition of Smith's *TMS*: 11 suggests that the connection between Butler and Smith was mediated through Hutcheson, though the evidence for this suggestion is unclear.

9 Further information about Tucker's life and works may be found in Shelton (1981, 1987) and Cornish (2004).

10 The exchange between Tucker and Hume was noted by Rotwein (1955) and discussed by Semmel (1965) and in much greater depth by Hont (1983, 2005). Hume suggested in his *Political Essays* (1752) that trade between rich and poor countries cannot generate limitless wealth for the rich country, because lower wages in the poor country will eventually give the poor country a trade advantage, and narrow the wealth gap between them. Hume read in 1758 via Kames an essay by Tucker (1758) in which Tucker suggested that the expansion of the market would counteract the effect of lower wages so that trade could continue to enrich both countries. Hume revised his view in a new essay "On the Jealousy of Trade" added in 1758 to his *Political Essays*. As Hont (2005) points out, both Hume and Tucker's arguments contained the idea of mutually beneficial trade and international specialisation. Tucker claimed victory in the exchange, but Hume viewed "On the Jealousy of Trade" as merely clarifying his original argument.

11 A striking but theoretically inconsequential example is Tucker's remark that England is a nation of shopkeepers. This appears in Adam Smith, is quoted by Napoleon, and many others down to Mrs Thatcher in the 1980s.

12 Paley's clerical career was rumoured to have been curtailed by the discomfort caused to Anglican authorities by the so-called pigeon passage in his *PMPP*: "If you should see a flock of pigeons in a field of corn; and if instead of each picking where and what it liked, taking just as much as it wanted, and no more you should see ninety-nine of them gathering all they got, into a heap; reserving nothing for themselves, but the chaff and the refuse; keeping this heap for one, and that the weakest, perhaps worst, pigeon of the flock; sitting round, and looking on, all the winter, whilst this one was devouring, throwing about, and wasting it; and if a pigeon more hardy or hungry than the rest, touched a grain of the hoard, all the others instantly flying upon it, and tearing it to pieces; if you should see this, you would see nothing more than what is every day practised and established among men" (Paley *PMPP*: 63).

13 Further biographical information about Paley may be found in Le Mahieu (1976) and Cole (1988, 1991). Waterman (1996, 2008c) discusses Paley's relationship to Adam Smith and Paley's sophisticated model of population and growth in *PMPP* that led Keynes to call him "the first of the Cambridge economists". Paley may have seen Smith's *WN* 1776 before finalising his *PMPP* in 1785, but traces of dependence are absent from *PMPP*. We cannot rule out reports of Smith's 1750s' Glasgow lectures influencing Paley. Neither can we rule out reports of Paley's Cambridge lectures influencing Smith, though this is much less likely. Paley's enormous influence on English social and economic thinking is discussed by Norman (1976: 9).

14 Paley's providential "finger of God" (*PMPP*: 41) has received much less attention in the literature than Adam Smith's "invisible hand".

15 Paley was dying of painful cancer while writing his natural theology. There is no mention of this in the text, though perhaps his comment about bodily pain reflects this experience (*Natural Theology*: 255ff.). Paley is no Dr Pangloss, and unlike Voltaire's famous character from *Candide* recognises that imperfection and evil are realities of a created order.

16 Seeing Burke and Smith as parallel, though linked, sources of 19th-century economic thinking was suggested by Winch (1996). I am emphasising the Butler-Paley-Malthus line as an influence on economic theory and Burke as an influence on policy and popular discussion. Winch (1996: 373) also elevated Malthus as a "joint founder" with Smith of the discipline of political economy.

17 Since Smith died in 1790, this claim must refer to Burke's early work, ruling out from consideration Burke's *Reflections on the Revolution in France*, as well as his *Thoughts and Details on Scarcity*. The claim could refer to student essays published in the Trinity College Dublin *Reformer* where Burke discussed political economy, or more likely his *Observations on The Present State of the Nation* 1769, which contains detailed arguments about the benefits of trade with the colonies, supported by statistical evidence.

18 Balanced perspectives on Burke's economics are provided by JGA Pocock's (1985b) reading of the *Reflections on the Revolution in France*, and Renee Prendergast's (2000) survey of the economic content in Burke's other writings.

4   Adam Smith as natural theologian[1]

Modern professors of economics and ethics operate in disciplines which have been secularized to the point where the religious elements and implications which were once an integral part of them have been painstakingly eliminated . . . [scholars] either put on mental blinders which hide from their sight these aberrations of Smith's thought, or they treat them as merely traditional and in Smith's day fashionable ornaments to what is essentially naturalistic and rational analysis . . . I am obliged to insist that Adam Smith's system of thought, including his economics, is not intelligible if one disregards the role he assigns in it to the teleological elements, to the "invisible hand".[2]

Introduction

Notwithstanding the arguments of the previous chapter, Smith is the central figure in the rise of political economy as a discipline. Smith is almost alone among dead economists in continuing to attract the interest of contemporary mainstream economists. Finding some idea in Smith (or more commonly attaching an idea to Smith, regardless of the textual and contextual basis) still carries weight in the economics profession. For these reasons, Smith is an important figure in any account of connections between theology and economics.

I will begin by establishing the plausibility of a theological reading of Smith using biographical and contextual evidence, and examination of his works. I will then consider several test cases of the fruitfulness of a theological reading of Smith: Smith's invisible hand, the role of theodicy and the future hope in Smith's system.

Adam Smith's religious background

Biography is helpful to identify possible religious influences on Smith's intellectual development.[3] As pointed out by his biographer (Ross 1995), it would be very strange if the religious ideas were unimportant in forming any scholar in the religiously saturated environment of 18th-century Scotland. Adam Smith was brought up by his devout Calvinist mother after the early death of his father, and like most of his Scottish contemporaries attended church regularly throughout his life, associating with the moderate party in the Presbyterian Church (described by Sher 1985). The Snell Scholarship that he won to enable him to study at Balliol College Oxford from 1740 entailed a commitment to take Holy Orders. On his appointment to the Chair in Logic and then Moral Philosophy at the University of Glasgow in 1751, Smith signed the Calvinist Westminster Confession before the Glasgow Presbytery and took the required Oath of Faith.

Smith was reticent about religious matters in public as he was about other matters likely to arouse needless controversy, and we have no evidence from correspondence or contemporary reports of insincerity of his public professions of faith.

The removal of a passage about the atonement from the 1790 6th edition of the *Theory of Moral Sentiments* has attracted a great deal of attention.[4] However, there are other explanations for the changes to the passage besides Smith abandoning an earlier commitment to an orthodox doctrine of the atonement. Smith was above all keen to avoid controversy about religious matters, and the nature and scope of the atonement was a subject of acrimonious dispute in the Kirk during the period in which Smith wrote. While doctrines such as providence are integral to Smith's system, nothing hinged on the atonement, so discussing this disputed Christian doctrine had risks and no particular benefit for Smith. We just do not have enough information to settle the question of why Smith changed the passage.

Some writers on Smith's religious views have pointed to his various criticisms of the church. However, these must be interpreted in their 18th-century Scottish context where Roman Catholicism and Popery were popular targets. When Smith criticised "superstition", readers would recognise these as the targets, not the Presbyterian Church. Similarly, Methodism and associated tendencies are the target when Smith refers to "enthusiasm". Even filtering out the sectarianism, there remain many critical comments on religious practice, especially criticisms of various perversions of what Smith sees as true religion. Any interpreter who takes criticism of religious practice as evidence of a lack of faith or commitment has little experience of churches. Usually the opposite is true.[5]

Smith was an intimate friend of David Hume, but we cannot jump to the conclusion that the religious views of friends are identical or even similar. On many matters, Smith took sharply different positions to his friend Hume, and Smith did not wish to be associated with the publication of Hume's *Dialogues on Natural Religion*. Smith's praise of his dying friend's character and remark that Hume approached death with "more real resignation to the necessary course of things than any whining Christian ever dyed with pretended resignation to the will of God" (Smith to Wedderburn 14 August 1776, in Smith 1986) seems to have been provoked by Boswell's insensitive visit seeking Hume's deathbed conversion, and it is a mistake to read too much into this remark. The most in my view we can conclude is that many of the religious issues dealt with by Hume in his published works were discussed by the two men.

If we move on from Smith's life to Smith's texts then we find an abundance of religious language. He regularly refers to "the Deity", "the author of nature", "the great Director of nature", "lawful superior", etc. There are repeated references to divine design and providence. For instance:

> Every part of nature, when attentively surveyed, equally demonstrates the providential care of its Author, and we admire the wisdom and goodness of God even in the weakness and folly of man.
>
> (*TMS* II iii 3 2: 106)[6]

> The happiness of mankind, as well as all other rational creatures, seems to have been the original purpose intended by the author of nature, when he brought them into existence . . . By acting according to the dictates of our moral faculties, we necessarily pursue the most effectual means for promoting the happiness of mankind, and may therefore be said, in some sense, to co-operate with the Deity, and to advance as far as in our power the plan of Providence.
>
> (*TMS* III 5 7: 166)

> The idea of that divine Being, whose benevolence and wisdom have, from all eternity, contrived and conducted the immense machine of the universe, so as at all times to produce the greatest possible quantity of happiness, is certainly of all the objects of human contemplation by far the most sublime.
>
> (*TMS* VI ii 3 5: 236)

In relation to morality, Adam Smith wrote: "the governing principles of human nature, the rules which they prescribe are to be regarded as the commands and laws of the Deity" (*TMS* III 5 3: 163).

What religious ideas then may have influenced his economics? Smith scholarship in recent decades has shown how the economic analysis of the *Wealth of Nations* is part of a carefully constructed system, encompassing moral philosophy, jurisprudence and philosophy of science (for instance, Ross 1995; Skinner 1996; Winch 1996; Fleischacker 2004).

I will now discuss several philosophical and religious traditions which have been suggested as important for Smith.

Stoicism

Many commentators have pointed to Stoicism as the source of the religious language in Smith's works, and many Enlightenment Scots including the young Smith were interested in Stoic ideas.

For example, Raphael and Macfie's introduction to the standard edition of the *Theory of Moral Sentiments* states: "Stoic philosophy is the primary influence on Smith's ethical thought. It also fundamentally affects his economic theory" (Introduction to *TMS*: 5) and "Adam Smith's ethics and natural theology are predominantly Stoic" (Introduction to *TMS*: 10). Others emphasising the Stoic influence include Waszek (1984) and Hill (2001).

As evidence, they point to the importance of self-preservation in Smith, the importance of self-command as a virtue, Smith's commitment to a harmonious natural order, and his universalism. While there is no denying Stoic influences on Smith, contemporary writers in my view have been too ready to assume this deals fully with Smith's religious language, disposing of Christian theology as an influence.

One reason why this is unsatisfactory is that it treats Christianity and Stoicism as mutually exclusive, when in fact they are historically intertwined, especially for Enlightenment Scots (Bouwsma 1975). It is also difficult to reconcile an exclusively Stoic Smith with his own words "The plan and system which Nature has sketched out for our conduct, seems to be altogether different from that of the Stoical philosophy" (*TMS* VII ii I 43: 292), or with Smith's conspicuous failure to adopt Stoic resignation towards economic deprivation in 18th-century Scotland.

Aristotelianism

Smith wrote many rude things about the scholastic Aristotelians of his day, flowing partly from his unrewarding studies at Oxford. However, his contempt for scholastic Aristotelians does not extend to Aristotle himself; there is no direct criticism of Aristotle in the discussion of systems of moral philosophy in the *Theory of Moral Sentiments*. Scholars in recent years have pointed out an Aristotelian teleological substructure to his thought (Vivenza 2001, 2009; Hanley 2009) which should not be surprising as Aristotle provided the basic structure of the educational system with which Smith grew up, onto which then-fashionable Stoic and Newtonian ideas were grafted (Stewart 1991).

Protestant natural law

The natural law tradition has long been recognised as part of Adam Smith's background, especially the continental Protestant natural law philosophy of Hugo Grotius and Samuel Pufendorf. Gershom Carmichael, the first holder of Smith's Glasgow chair in moral philosophy was an important mediator of the tradition, producing an edition of Pufendorf for use in the university. Haakonssen (1981, 1998) and Moore (2006) discuss the continental natural law tradition and its importance for Smith and other Enlightenment Scots. More information about the Scottish universities in the late 17th and 18th centuries, together with translations of the works of Smith's predecessors Carmichael and Hutcheson, have given us a better understanding of the place of this strand of natural law theory in the Scottish Enlightenment.

At a minimum, natural law theory was important in structuring the moral philosophy curriculum Smith taught at Glasgow, and was the disciplinary matrix out of which political economy grew. The extent to which Smith's ethics remains within the natural law universe is debatable.

Scottish Enlightenment Calvinism

A more important influence in my view was the Calvinist theological tradition that provided the intellectual framework for the Presbyterian Church which dominated Scottish life in the 18th century. We have already observed that Smith signed the Calvinist Westminster Confession of Faith and associated with the moderate party of the Scottish Presbyterian Church.

David Fergusson (2007: 5) nicely sketches their theological outlook: "The dominant theology of moderate intellectuals in the era of the Scottish Enlightenment" as the following:

> The role of God as creator and sustainer of the world is emphasised. The signs of the divine presence are evident in the natural world; in this respect, the design argument is widely assumed to be valid. The beneficial role of religion in civil society is stressed. Religion contributes to social order and harmony. When purged of irrational fanaticism and intolerance, faith exercises a cohesive function through the moral direction and focus it offers human life. As benevolent and wise, God has ordered the world so that its moral and scientific laws contribute to human welfare. The prospect of an eschatological state in which virtue and felicity coincide, moreover, provides further moral motivation.

Smith fits this moderate Calvinist picture perfectly.

As well as the areas of agreement, it is important to understand the main theological issues at stake in Smith's Scotland. Fergusson (2007: 5) gives these as:

(a) the role of reason in establishing the existence and nature of God;
(b) the relationship of faith and reason;
(c) the dependence of ethics on religion;
(d) the rational status of Scriptural claims.

Smith's approach was to deploy theology when relevant, yet tread carefully around areas of controversy not essential to his argument. In relation to (a), it would be very nice to have a full set of student notes on Smith's Glasgow lectures on natural theology. However, the likelihood of them now turning up in a Scottish attic is slim. In his published works, no space is devoted to proofs of God's existence, and Smith takes the existence of God, God's creative and providential activity, and the goodness of God as given. My sense is that Smith had no taste for the rationalistic proofs of some of his contemporaries, both because of a scepticism about founding religion on reason and because such proofs were labouring the obvious. In relation to (b), faith for Smith is not in conflict with reason, and he shares with his friend Hume an interest in the rational explanation of religion and religious institutions, for instance in Book V of the *Wealth of Nations*. There is no suggestion by Smith that such explanation undermines religion. Smith's position on (c) is subtle. His account of the role of sentiments in the moral life develops with little reference to theology, apart from pointing out that these sentiments are implanted in human beings by God. However, the moral principles which emerge from his account of the moral life are divinely sanctioned, as one would expect if human nature which Smith is analysing is the product of divine creation and providence. Even the flaws in human nature are part of the divine plan. The status of scripture (d), perhaps the most controversial theological issue, is wisely bypassed by Smith.

An appreciation of the Calvinist theological elements in Smith is not helped by stereotypes and misconceptions of Calvinism which abound in the literature. Neither Calvin nor the main strands of subsequent Calvinist theology were opposed to scientific investigation. The normative statement for Scottish Presbyterianism was the Westminster Confession of Faith, which Smith signed to take up his Glasgow Chair. The opening sentence states that "the light of nature, and the works of creation and providence do so far manifest the goodness, wisdom, and power of God, as to leave men inexcusable", quoting scripture (Romans and Psalms) in support. There is the important caveat "that knowledge of God, and of His will, which is necessary unto salvation" cannot come from nature. For Calvinists, our sensory and moral capacities are limited and twisted by the fall.

Smith accepts the Calvinist view, writing of the "irregularity in the human breast" (*TMS* II iii 3 2: 105), "the great disorder in our moral sentiments" which has a utility in which we can "admire the wisdom of God even in the weakness and folly of man" (*TMS* VI iii 31: 253), of vices and follies of mankind which are a necessary part of the plan of the universe (*TMS* I ii 3 4: 36). Ignorance of "all the connexions and dependencies of things" (*TMS* VI ii 3: 236) conditions our action, though we are comforted by the thought that God the "benevolent and all-wise Being can admit into the system of his government, no partial evil which is not necessary for the universal good" (*TMS* VI ii 3: 236). Our limited and distorted human capacities are part of Anthony Waterman's (2002) argument that there is an Augustinian theodicy of markets in Smith.

Another misconception is that commitment to the doctrine of divine providence rules out investigation of causal mechanisms. In an Aristotelian framework there is a distinction between efficient and final causes, which Smith deploys in a few places to explain the relationship of the mechanisms he is describing to divine providence (for instance *TMS* II ii 3 6: 87). For 18th-century Scots, especially historians, commitment to the doctrine of providence and interest in the causal mechanisms reinforced each other. God had turned the evil (at least in the eyes of Smith and his moderate Presbyterian contemporaries) of the Jacobite revolt into good for Scotland, just as in biblical times the evil deed of Joseph's brothers led to the salvation of the nation of Israel when they were fed by him in Egypt.

The Calvinist context has received much less attention than it should in recent Smith scholarship, and chapters in my earlier edited volume (Oslington 2011a) attempted to remedy this.

British tradition of scientific natural theology

Natural theology and his moderate Scottish Enlightenment Calvinism were the two most important traditions for Smith. They are not in tension – one need only consider the opening sentences of the Westminster Confession quoted earlier.

Jacob Viner (1927, 1972, 1978) long ago suggested the importance of this tradition for Smith, but it has received less attention than it should, somewhat surprisingly given the large amount of attention to natural theology in the contemporary history and philosophy of science literature.

We know Smith and other Enlightenment Scots admired Isaac Newton, that he had a thorough knowledge of Newton's works, and he held up Newton's scientific methods in his History of Astronomy as a model for the future science advances. This essay culminates with a description of Newton's contributions and the judgment that "the superior genius and sagacity of Sir Isaac Newton, therefore, made the most happy, and, we may now say, the greatest and most admirable improvement that was ever made in philosophy" (Smith 1980: 98). Furthermore, early readers of the *Wealth of Nations*, such as Governor Pownall of Massachusetts, commented on its Newtonianism. The role of self-interest in Smith's system was also compared to the role of gravity in Newton's system.

Smith's lectures on moral philosophy in the early 1750s began with natural theology. A student John Millar reported that "His course of lectures . . . was delivered in four parts. The first contained Natural Theology; in which he considered the proofs of the being and attributes of God, and those principles of the mind on which religion is founded" (reproduced in Dugald Stewart's *Account of the Life and Writings of Adam Smith*, originally published in 1790, now Smith 1980: 274). These early lectures became the foundation of Smith's system, with the second part on moral philosophy becoming the *Theory of Moral Sentiments* published in 1759, and the final part being developed into the *Wealth of Nations* published in 1776.

A key part of the argument for reading Smith as a natural theologian is that his works are full of the distinctive language and thought forms of British scientific natural theology. A couple of passages from the many that could be cited:

> All the inhabitants of the universe, the meanest as well as the greatest, are under the immediate care and protection of that great, benevolent and all-wise Being, who directs all the movements of nature; and who is determined, by his own unalterable perfections to maintain in it at all times, the greatest quantity of happiness.
>
> (*TMS* VI ii 3 1–2: 235)

> In every part of the universe we observe means adjusted with the nicest artifice to the ends which they are intended to produce, and admire how everything is contrived for advancing the two great purposes of nature, the support of the individual and the propagation of the species . . . [and studying this leads us to admire] the wisdom of man, which in reality is the wisdom of God.
>
> (*TMS* II ii 3 6: 87)

Now consider some of the test cases of the fruitfulness of a theological reading of Smith.

Adam Smith's invisible hand

Importance

The invisible hand image is at the centre of contemporary debates about the capacities of markets, and is one of the reasons in Stephen Darwall's words "why we should take more than a scholarly interest in Smith" (1999: 140). For the Nobel Prize-winning economist George Stigler (1976: 1201), the invisible hand idea was the "crown jewel" of the *Wealth of Nations*, expressing Adam Smith's "one overwhelmingly important triumph: he put into the centre of economics the systematic analysis of the behaviour of individuals pursuing their self-interest under conditions of competition". For Deirdre McCloskey (2006: 456–8), the hand reconciles private self-interested action with the common good. Mark Blaug (2008) in a recent survey concluded that for economists the invisible hand expresses three interconnected ideas: "the private actions of individuals can have unforeseen and unintended social consequences", that these are "harmonious in mutually promoting the interests of all members of society" and they generate "order". Even critics of mainstream economics such as Duncan Foley (2006) interpret the invisible hand in a similar way, though regarding it as summarising the errors of the case for the market economy; as did Adam Smith's mistake which has cursed subsequent economic analysis. Another Nobel Prize winner Joseph Stiglitz (2002) has suggested the hand as understood by most economists is invisible because it is not there.

All these contemporary writers refer back to Adam Smith's use of the image in *Theory of Moral Sentiments* and *Wealth of Nations*, so it is important to understand its meaning in the original writings. This is so even if economists perfectly legitimately wish to go beyond Smith's usage in contemporary debates about the capacities of markets.

Despite the invisible hand being increasingly invoked by economists, its place and meaning in Adam Smith's work remains obscure. The religious associations of the image are particularly obscure. Early readers, though they did not emphasise the hand within Smith's system as much as contemporary writers, regarded its religious associations as obvious.[7] For Smith's early readers it was a divine hand. Among contemporary intellectual historians the religious associations remain important, though there is no consensus about their exact nature. Jacob Viner's view was quoted at the beginning of the chapter. Alec Macfie, one of the editors of the standard edition of Smith's works, wrote that "the Invisible Hand is only one of many names given in the *Moral Sentiments* to the Deity" (Macfie 1970: 111). One of the most careful contemporary Smith scholars Gloria Vivenza concluded her survey of contextual and rhetorical analysis of Smith's invisible hand: "it is almost unavoidable to give it a teleological, if not theological, sense" (Vivenza 2005: 52). Patricia Werhane's view (1991: 102) is that the invisible hand as God's hand is "probably an incorrect reading" because of immediate context, though she accepts that such a view is consistent with Smith's other "metaphysical speculation".

Establishing its meaning in Smith's writings is not the hopeless task as some commentators suggest (for instance, Samuels 2009). What is required is close attention to the texts in their original context, including the religious context. Recent contributions along these lines include Macfie (1970, 1971), Rothschild (1994), Winch (1996, 1997), Grampp (2000), Waterman (2004), Kennedy (2008), Brewer (2009) and Harrison (2011a, 2011b). This new work on Smith's religious background picks up questions raised in Jacob Viner's (1927) classic paper, and largely neglected in the decades which followed.[8]

This section of the chapter examines Adam Smith's invisible hand in the context of 17th- and 18th-century theology, especially Smith's scientific exemplar Isaac Newton's theories of divine action and providence. The aims are first, to get the history right, so as to properly appreciate the place and meaning of the invisible hand image in Smith's writings. Smith did not invent the invisible hand.[9] What was novel and interesting is the use he made of the image as he grappled with the developing market economy of 18th-century Scotland.

Second, to clarify the nature of the invisible hand image as an aid to those deploying it in contemporary discussions about the capacities of markets. Vague references to the invisible hand detract from many otherwise sound discussions of the capacities of markets.

Third, to augment our stock of ideas for dealing with relationships between religion and free markets through a recovery of Smith's views expressed through the invisible hand image. It models a more modest and historically grounded approach to the relationship between religion and economics.

Isaac Newton on divine action and providence

Within the British tradition of scientific natural theology, Isaac Newton's theories of divine action and providence are the specific background to the interpretation I am offering of Smith's invisible hand.

Newton affirms a strong version of the doctrine of providence. In his universe, everything that happens is in some sense an act of God. For scientific work to be fruitful, God's activity must be reasonably regular or law like, and Newton believed his success in explaining the universe in terms of regular laws made divine involvement more rather than less plausible. A clockwork universe demonstrated the wisdom and power of God.

Newton followed the British scientific natural theological tradition in distinguishing between general providence – God's care expressed in the regularity of the universe – and special providence – God's irregular acts. He sums this up nicely in correspondence: "[God is] constantly cooperating with all things in accordance with accurate laws, as being the foundation and cause of the whole of nature, except where it is good to act otherwise" (MS245 folio 14a, Library of the Royal Society London, quoted in Force 1990: 87). There is no sense in which any irregular actions of God undermine God's regular action. General and special providence are both part of the divine economy of nature.

For Newton it is not just that special providential action is allowable, but that God has willed a universe where such action is required (Brooke 1991a: 147). In the *Principia*, Newton writes of the orbits of planets needing periodic adjustment, and of comets tails restoring matter lost by the Sun and planets (discussed by Brooke 1991a: 148, and also commented on by Smith in his *History of Astronomy*). Newton was also fond of the analogy that God could move the universe as we move our bodies, although he rejected pantheism that made God the soul of the universe (Brooke 1988: 169). In Query 31 of the *Optiks*, Newton describes God as a:

> [p]owerful ever-living Agent, who being in all places is more able by his will to move the bodies within his boundless and uniform sensorium, and thereby to reform the parts of the universe, than we are by our will to move the parts of our own bodies.
>
> (Newton 2004: 138)

Another example of body imagery is a 1692 letter to Bentley where Newton describes a "divine arm" placing planets (Newton 2004: 100).

So a divine hand acting irregularly to maintain order seems perfectly legitimate within the Newtonian view of divine action, and the arm-hand imagery has precedents in Newton's own discussion of the planetary system.

The invisible hand passages in Smith's writings

Now turn to the passages. The interpretation I am offering of Smith's invisible hand is that it expresses the doctrine of providence. Others have pointed out the connections between the doctrine of providence and Smith's ideas about self-interested behaviour mediated through market institutions working for the general good (notably Viner 1927, and more recently Waterman 2004). The crucial nuance I am adding to make sense of the invisible hand is the distinction between general and special providence. The invisible hand metaphor is Smith's acknowledgement of the possibility of special providential divine action in the economic system to guarantee its stability. In Smith's understanding of the divine economy, the special providential invisible hand balances the general providential activity of God in markets.

The History of Astronomy

The first of the three appearances of the invisible hand in Adam Smith's work is in his early essay *The History of Astronomy*, section III "Of the Origin of Philosophy" (in the standard edition of *Essays on Philosophical Subjects*, Smith 1980: 48–50).

The passage is part of an argument about how philosophy (which for Smith and other 18th-century authors includes what we would now call science) originates in wonder and curiosity about the irregularities of nature. Smith begins the section describing how savages view events in nature which attract their attention as products of an "invisible and designing power . . . whose operations are not perfectly regular" (Smith 1980: 49). It is the irregular events, Smith emphasises, which attracted the attention of the savages and ancient polytheists, and were ascribed to gods. Smith's words are:

> For it may be observed, that in all Polytheistic religions, among savages, as well as in the early ages of Heathen antiquity, it is the irregular events of nature only that are ascribed to the agency and power of their gods.
>
> (Smith 1980: 49)

He then introduces the invisible hand to explain that the gods are not perceived by savages or ancient polytheists in the regular events of nature. His words are:

> Fire burns, and water refreshes; heavy bodies descend, and lighter substances fly upwards, by the necessity of their own nature; nor was the invisible hand of Jupiter ever apprehended to be employed in those matters. But thunder and lightning, storms and sunshine, those more irregular events, were ascribed to his favour, or his anger.
>
> (Smith 1980: 49–50)

To reinforce the point, Smith adds:

> [i]ntelligent beings, whom they imagined, but knew not . . . did not employ themselves in supporting the ordinary course of things, which went on of its own accord, but to stop, to thwart, and to disturb it. And thus, in the first ages of the world, the lowest and most pusillanimous superstition supplied the place of philosophy.
>
> (Smith 1980: 50)

Then Smith goes on to suggest that as law and order take hold and wealth grows, philosophy develops and the regular events also come to be ascribed to this divine power. The text is:

> But when law has established order and security, and subsistence ceases to be precarious, the curiosity of mankind is increased, and their fears are diminished. The leisure which they then enjoy renders them more attentive to the appearances of nature, more observant of her smallest irregularities, and more desirous to know the chain which links them altogether . . . Wonder, therefore, and not any expectation of advantage from its discoveries, is the first principle which prompts mankind to the study of Philosophy, of that science which pretends to lay open the concealed connections that unite the various appearances of nature.
>
> (Smith 1980: 50–51)

Smith is suggesting in the passage that after the rise of philosophy the irregular events as well as the regular events (not instead of the regular events) are ascribed to the gods. This is indicated by the structure of the passage, Smith's statement that for the ancients "only" the irregular events (Smith 1980: 49) are attributed to the gods, and his gentle depreciation of the ancients' inability to perceive divine activity in regular events of nature.[10] In my view, Smith in this early work is playing with the invisible hand image, and the issue of regular versus irregular divine action that he will develop further in his mature works.

Theory of Moral Sentiments

The second invisible hand passage is in the *Theory of Moral Sentiments* Part IV section I (Smith 1759: 185). It is a discussion of how the rich man endowed with insatiable desires has a stomach of limited capacity, so that in the end the rich man consumes only as much as a poor man. Smith observes that in this way the rich "in spite of their natural selfishness and rapacity" are:

> [l]ed by an invisible hand to make nearly the same division of the necessaries of life, which would have been made, had the earth been divided into equal portions among its inhabitants, and thus without intending it, without knowing it, advance the interest of the society.

Elsewhere in the *Theory of Moral Sentiments*, self-interest, including that of the rich, has a providential role in a market economy. This passage does not express that idea; instead, the divine hand is working against the greed of the rich, levelling out consumption and maintaining the stability of the market system. Smith understands that stability depends on adherence to the rules of justice and a not too obscenely unequal distribution of consumption. This is why the divine hand restraining the consumption of the rich serves to maintain the stability of the market system.

The hand appears, I speculate, because Smith, observing the beginnings of a modern market economy in 18th-century Scotland, saw the importance of the question of the long-term stability of such a system. Perhaps, like Newton's planetary system, a market economy cannot generate within itself the conditions for its own stability. The hand stands for something outside the system, like God, able to ensure its stability.

To summarise, I am drawing on the biographical and contextual evidence about Smith's religious background and previous interpretations of the hand of the *Theory of Moral Sentiments* as divine.[11] My interpretation adds the twist that the hand is special providence, balancing the general providential force of self-interest in markets.

Wealth of Nations

The third and most quoted invisible hand passage is from the *Wealth of Nations* IV ii (Smith 1776: 456). It is part of a chapter on restraints on foreign trade where

Smith discusses merchants seeking the greatest return on their capital, against the general background of self-interested behaviour in a market economy.

In the passage, the Scottish merchant weighs the greater security of investing in domestic industry against the possibility of greater profits abroad, and is led by an invisible hand to invest domestically. The text is:

> By preferring the support of domestic to that of foreign industry he intends only his own security; and by directing that industry in such a manner as its produce may be of greatest value, he intends only his own gain, and he is in this, as in many other cases, led by an invisible hand to promote an end which was no part of his intention.
>
> (*WN*: 456)

Smith comments "by pursuing his own interest he frequently promotes that of the society more effectually than when he really intends to promote it. I have never known much good to be done by those who affected to trade for the public good" (*WN*: 456) before returning to the theme of domestic vs foreign industry. The usual view of this passage is that it expresses Smith's theory of the market transforming self-interest into unintended benefits for all (perhaps even maximising national income) has been challenged by a number of recent authors.

Bishop (1995) focuses on the inconsistency between Smith's strong criticism of merchants and manufacturers and the dominant interpretation that the invisible hand validates the pursuit of self-interest. He quotes some of Smith's denunciations, including the following:

> The interest of the dealers, however, in any particular branch of trade or manufactures, is always in some respects different from, and even opposite to, that of the publick . . . The proposal of any new law or regulation of commerce which comes from this order, ought always to be listened to with great precaution, and ought never to be adopted till after having been long and carefully examined, not only with the most scrupulous, but with the most suspicious attention. It comes from an order of men, whose interest is never exactly the same with that of the publick, who have generally an interest to deceive and even to oppress the publick, and who accordingly have, upon many occasions, both deceived and oppressed it.
>
> (*WN*: 267)

Bishop then resolves the contradiction by restricting the applicability of the invisible hand to the investment of capital: "merchants and manufacturers benefit society when they invest their capital for maximum profit; they harm society when they combine to form monopolies, or when they deceive legislators into granting monopolies to them". This argument has merit, but in my view a more fundamental reassessment of the dominant interpretation is required.

William Grampp (2000) in a major article on the invisible hand in the *Wealth of Nations* raises different objections:

1   Nothing is said in the passage about the price mechanism or competition or any of the other things the hand supposedly stands for.
2   There is no mention of the hand in the earlier sections of the *Wealth of Nations* that discuss markets, competition and the price mechanism. If the hand is part of his argument about markets why does he only use it once, and why does he wait several hundred pages and bury it in a passage about foreign trade?
3   Too much weight has been put on this phrase, "in this, as in many other cases" in making the hand into a general law. Smith simply suggests there are other cases, not that the operation of the hand can be relied on in every case.
4   Too much weight has also been put on the "as if" qualification of the invisible hand that is not in the passage.[12] Smith suggests the action is actually by some hand, not a diffuse process.

On the basis of these objections to the dominant view, Grampp (2000) seeks another interpretation that is truer to the actual context and wording of the passage. For him, the invisible hand in the *Wealth of Nations* is "simply the inducement a merchant has to keep his capital at home, thereby increasing the domestic capital stock and enhancing military power" (Grampp 2000: 441). The end which is no part of the merchant's intention is maintaining the Scottish capital stock.

I agree with Grampp's objections to the dominant view and his reading of the passage that the invisible hand operates to restrain capital flight from Scotland. However, his close reading of the text ignores the religious background of the invisible hand which Smith and his readers would have had in their minds.

Both these authors open the way for the reinterpretation I am offering of the invisible hand as the special providential hand of God.

Smith sees God providentially watching over Scottish society, and if too much Scottish capital went abroad seeking higher returns, then Scottish economic development would be compromised. The providential hand operating through the mechanisms of the merchants' fear of the risk of overseas investment, which may or may not be illusory, works to keep Scottish capital at home.

A plausible interpretation of Smith's invisible hand?

How plausible is it to interpret the invisible hand as the special providential hand of God, which works to maintain the stability of the system; a hand operating to balance the general providential hand of God operating through the market mechanism? This interpretation has a number of attractions.

First, it gives due weight to providential aspects of Smith's work identified by many scholars, adding a nuance in the distinction between special and general providence. Such a distinction is well grounded in Smith's philosophical and theological context.

Second, it offers a plausible account of where Smith's hand language comes from – the providential associations of the invisible hand language in Smith's Scotland, and perhaps specifically Newton's discussion of God moving parts of the universe as parts of a body. It is plausible because of the strong link between

Smith and Newton, and Smith's first use of the hand image being in a work which discusses Newton's scientific approach. Of course, it is always difficult to identify sources with certainty, and I would not want to be dogmatic about this.

Third, the interpretation fits each of the three invisible hand passages. Some of the other proposals, such as Grampp's, fit only one of the passages and create considerable interpretative problems for the other passages. These interpretive problems can only be avoided by the implausible suggestion that Smith's three references to the invisible hand are unrelated.

Fourth, it gives a plausible account of the development of the idea over time in Smith. In each of the three passages, the divine hand acts against general providential market forces to maintain the stability of the system. As we move through the three passages, the description of the action of the hand becomes clearer, though it must be conceded that even in the *Wealth of Nations'* discussion of merchants balancing security and profits there is nothing as detailed as the Newtonian description of the mechanism of comets shifting matter around the universe.

Fifth, this interpretation makes sense of the lack of prominence of the invisible hand in Smith's writings. If the hand represents irregular special providential action, then we would not expect it to be popping up everywhere in Smith's works.

Sixth, it deals with the ironic, almost joking tone which Rothschild (1994) sees in the passages. This tone expresses Smith's ambivalence about special providence; divine intervention to maintain the stability of the system is for Smith a wistfully expressed hope, rather than a certainty. Such a tone is appropriate, as special providential action is by definition rare and unpredictable.

Conclusions on Smith's invisible hand

This discussion of the invisible hand makes three contributions to the literature. First, in relation to resolving the meaning of the invisible hand in Smith's work, the case for the interpretation offered here comprises the argument for the Calvinist and natural theological background to Smith's work, the reading of the passages against this background, and the reasons given in the previous section for its superiority to previous interpretations. The meaning of the invisible hand is an intellectual puzzle worth resolving, and I hope that the interpretation offered here will be seriously considered, and even if found to be in need of modification, I hope it will stimulate deeper study of the theological background of Smith's work, including Smith's theodicy, the role of human ignorance and folly, and the role of the future life in his system.

Second, unlike some other intellectual puzzles, the meaning of the invisible hand matters greatly for arguments about free markets and ethical behaviour in business. It must be one of the most used yet least understood phrases in contemporary ethical discourse. Often, invoking the invisible hand is a lazy substitute for an argument for markets and selfishness, which undermines rather than assists the argument. The interpretation offered here detaches the invisible hand from the general case for markets – Smith's invisible hand expresses something different, but is ultimately consistent with his general case for markets. Public policy and business ethics' discussions would be greatly improved by carefully making the theoretical and empirical arguments for markets in particular circumstances without the discussion being clouded by references to the invisible hand.

Third, this section of the chapter contributes to a more reasonable discussion about the relationship between economics, ethics and religion. Economists and theologians get on notoriously badly; mutual misunderstanding and acrimony unfortunately have been the norm. Grounding the discussion in history provides neutral territory for economists, philosophers and theologians to meet, as well as some common reference points.

Finally, all involved in the discussion could learn from Smith's reticence in pronouncing on these matters, for both the workings of the economy and the workings of divine providence are complex. Smith's invisible hand reference respects both the doctrine of providence, including the possibility of special providential action, and the scientific task of explaining the regular workings of the economic system.

I would suggest that the test case of reading Smith's invisible hand theologically has proved fruitful, reinforcing the argument that theology shaped Smith's work. The next test case is the problem of suffering and evil.

Adam Smith's theodicy

The problem of suffering and evil

Philosophers and theologians have written a great deal on the problem of suffering, or the problem of evil as it becomes when suffering flows from human moral choices. When a God who is supposed to be both powerful and good is involved, we have the problem of theodicy, or the problem of justifying the ways of God to human beings.

As discussed in Chapter 2, David Hume's challenge in the *Dialogues on Natural Religion* (written in the 1750s, published 1779) was "Is he willing to prevent evil, but not able? Then he is impotent. Is he able, but not willing? Then he is malevolent. Is he both able and willing? Whence then is evil?". Answering Hume (along with many sensitive religious and non-religious persons who have asked similar questions) is the task of theodicy. Some philosophers and theologians have refused the question because they regard any answer as morally offensive, even blasphemous; some refuse because of a concern that theodicies undermine the struggle to improve the world, or sometimes because the task of constructing a theodicy is considered futile.

One response to Hume's question discussed in Chapter 2 is to point out some greater good that is made possible by the existence of suffering. This argument assumes that the suffering and good are inseparable and rely on a method of weighing them. A greater good could be free will – and the argument would be that a world where humans make bad choices is better than a world with no choice. A variation is the argument that earthly life is a trial for the future life, with suffering as a necessary aspect of trial, justified by the overwhelming good of the future life. The most famous is Leibniz' *Theodicy* (1710), where he argued that our world with all the suffering and evil it contains is indeed the best of possible worlds. A similar argument was made by the Englishman William King (1702). Such theodicies arose in the 17th and 18th centuries in response to the criticisms of the older tradition flowing from Augustine that held evil to be the lack of a good that should be found, a tradition which denies evil an existence independent of the good it is parasitic on. Augustine theodicies minimise the power of evil in the face of God's purposes, even sometimes its existence.

Economic theodicies

We lack specifically economic theodicies. Philosophical and theological reflection on economic suffering and evil is not as well developed as in other types of suffering and evil. One of the difficulties in a complex global market economy is connecting suffering to human choices, connections which are essential to certain types of theodicies. The suffering of an African family unable to afford sufficient food for sustenance flows from market prices for food and for their labour. Market prices are determined by the actions of millions of others across the world with a complexity that destroys the connections of foreseeability and intention to the results for the African family. The institutions of market economy tend to ethically insulate human choices from their results, despite the undeniable dependence of results on aggregate choices.

Adam Smith's theodicy

Although 18th-century Scotland had no shortage of suffering, Smith's economic outlook was optimistic, certainly more so than Malthus who composed the best known economic theodicy (to be considered in Chapter 5) in the 1798 first edition of his *Essay on the Principle of Population* during a period of war and food shortages.

As argued earlier in this chapter, Adam Smith's thought was shaped by his theological background – especially his moderate Scottish Enlightenment Calvinism and the British tradition of scientific natural theology. Theodicies usually went with this type of natural theology so it would be reasonable to expect one from Smith.

There are intriguing connections between Smith and David Hume, the philosopher who put the problem of theodicy most sharply. They were close friends, to the extent that Smith was entrusted with the publication of Hume's *Dialogues on Natural Religion*, though eventually Smith withdrew from this commitment and others oversaw their posthumous publication. Reasons for Smith's withdrawal are debated, but a fear of public association with Hume can be ruled out for he wrote an appreciative postscript to Hume's *My Own Life* which he says brought upon him "ten times more abuse than the very violent attack on the whole commercial system of Great Britain" (Adam Smith to William Strahan, 9 November 1776 in Smith 1986). Smith, through his extensive reading, European travels and discussions with Hume, was probably aware of the contemporary discussions of theodicy, including Leibniz' work. Smith also admired and had contact with Voltaire, so may have been aware of the lines of attack on "best of possible worlds" theodicies to be made in Voltaire's *Candide* 1759, following the disastrous Lisbon earthquake of 1755. It cannot be a coincidence that an earthquake is the example of a natural catastrophe Smith uses when discussing human response to suffering.

Smith certainly affirms the doctrines of creation and providence, and the power and goodness of God which are essential components of the problem of evil as formulated by Hume. Two examples from his *Theory of Moral Sentiments* 1759:

> [t]he idea of that divine Being, whose benevolence and wisdom have from all eternity, contrived and constructed the immense machine of the universe, so at all times to produce the greatest quantity of happiness, is certainly of all the objects of human contemplation by far the most sublime.
>
> (*TMS* VI ii 3 5: 236)

Also:

> [t]he happiness of mankind, as well as all other rational creatures, seems to have been the original purpose intended by the author of nature, when he brought them into existence . . . By acting according to the dictates of our moral faculties, we necessarily pursue the most effectual means for promoting the happiness of mankind, and may therefore be said, in some sense, to co-operate with the Deity, and to advance as far as in our power the plan of Providence.
>
> (*TMS* III 5 7: 166)

Smith seeks to place evil in the context of God's government of the universe for our good:

> [e]very part of nature, when attentively surveyed, equally demonstrates the providential care of its Author, and we may admire the wisdom and goodness of God even in the weakness and folly of man.
>
> (*TMS* II iii 3 2: 105–6)

Also:

> [t]his benevolent and all-wise Being can admit into the system of his government, no partial evil which is not necessary for the universal good.
>
> (*TMS* VI ii 3 3: 236)

There is nothing in Smith's works like the explicit theodicy we get in the first edition of Malthus' *Essay*, but nevertheless is a reasonably full and consistent treatment of suffering and evil. Smith's work abounds with discussion of human imperfections, especially those of merchants and rulers, and, of course, the shortcomings of Roman Catholic clergy – discussion which was guaranteed to be well received in 18th-century Presbyterian Scotland. Not that Smith sees these groups as any worse morally than others. All share a fallen human nature, but these groups are exposed to greater temptation and have less effective restraints on their behaviour.

It is not always easy to place an author on the grid of philosophical theodicies, but I would resist placing Smith among the upholders of a naïve "best of all possible worlds" theodicies as has been the tendency in existing commentary on his approach to suffering (for instance, Jacob Viner). There is certainly ample evidence that Smith believes the universe to be a system directed towards human good, but no trace whatsoever of comparisons with other possible worlds. It is also hard to imagine a friend of Hume and Voltaire holding such a position.

If Smith is to be placed anywhere, perhaps it should be with the older privation theorists of evil. The strength of this Augustinian tradition in Smith's Calvinist Scotland and the attachment of his friend Hume to similar ideas, make such a placement of Smith historically plausible.

In Smith's work, including the quotations above, evil is not prominent, never an independent force, and never strong enough to threaten God's purposes. It is often qualified as a "partial evil". There are numerous examples of how human failings contribute to the achievement of God's purposes or the "prosperity of the universe" in the above quotation. For instance, our vain desire to possess "trinkets and baubles" promotes industry even though such things are ultimately unsatisfying – a trick of providence as Smith describes it. Or the way our desire for the good opinion of spectators clarifies and enforces morality. The veil of human ignorance about consequences sometimes helps us pursue the best course of economic action. He criticises the dangerous conceit of the "man of system" – the reformer who claims to know all connections and arrange things ideally – usurping the place of God. We may indeed as Smith says "admire the wisdom of God even in the weakness and folly of man".

For a privation theory of evil to be coherent, there has to be teleology which informs us about the goods that should be found. Alasdair MacIntyre's (1981: 51) view that Smith is a turning point in the banishment of teleology from Western thought is difficult to sustain. Instead Smith's analysis of commercial society in the *Wealth of Nations* is set in the framework of the evolution of society through stages, each with distinctive institutions and scientific understanding. His teleological virtue ethics is developed in the *Theory of Moral Sentiments*. The future hope has an important place in his system (more on these in the next section of this chapter).

Smith's ameliorative approach to economic suffering is consistent with a privation theory of evil. He describes and endorses human attempts at "bettering our condition", and the whole burden of the *Wealth of Nations* is to improve the functioning of economic systems so that all people can enjoy the goods of freedom and prosperity. We join with God as free individuals, conscious of our own limitations and imperfect knowledge, in realising these goods. Smith's Augustinian approach to evil warrants doing something about it, unlike some other approaches.

Conclusion on Adam Smith's theodicy

I am suggesting Smith has elements of a different type of Augustinian theodicy to that proposed by Anthony Waterman (2002). Waterman argued that Smith's idea in the *Wealth of Nations* that self-interested individual action in the context of appropriate market institutions generates good outcomes for society, may be read as Augustinian theodicy of markets without any claim by Waterman that Smith intended such a theodicy. The idea is that just as in Augustine's *City of God* government is providentially instituted for the benefit of sinful humans, so are market institutions. What I am suggesting is that Smith had another (though not necessarily opposed) Augustinian approach to theodicy stemming from a privation theory of evil.

Again, reading Smith theologically, especially utilising the British tradition of natural theology and the Augustinian/Calvinist tradition, has borne fruit. The next test case is Smith's writing on the future hope which connects to his idea of justice.

The future hope, nature and justice in Smith's system

Smith on the afterlife

Smith strongly affirms the afterlife, and everything he writes on the subject remains within the bounds of orthodoxy defined by the *Westminster Confession of Faith*. He develops ideas about the afterlife from his natural theological and moderate Calvinist backgrounds which serve his system of ethics and political economy. He particularly emphasises justice in the life to come and the natural-ness of belief in the afterlife alongside the scriptural warrant.[13] One of the many passages dealing with the afterlife illustrates this emphasis:

> Our happiness in this life is thus, upon many occasions, dependent upon the humble hope and expectation of a life to come: a hope and expectation deeply rooted in human nature; which can alone support its lofty ideas of its own dignity; can alone illumine the dreary prospect of its continually approaching mortality, and maintain its cheerfulness under all the heaviest calamities to which, from the disorders of this life, it may sometimes be exposed. That there is a world to come, where exact justice will be done to every man . . . is a doctrine, in every respect so venerable, so comfortable to the weakness, so flattering to the gran-deur of human nature, that the virtuous man who has the misfortune to doubt it, cannot possibly avoid wishing most earnestly and anxiously to believe it.
>
> (*TMS* III 2 34: 132)

The necessity of a naturally formed sense of justice leading us to a future hope comes out in another passage, where Smith discusses the famous case of the Frenchman Calas who was broken on the wheel and burnt for the supposed murder of his son to prevent his conversion to Catholicism, then posthumously declared innocent after a campaign led by Voltaire. Smith wrote:

To persons in such unfortunate circumstances that humble philosophy which confines its views to this life, can afford, perhaps, but little consolation. Everything that could render either life or death respectable is taken from them. They are condemned to death and to everlasting infamy. Religion can alone afford them any effectual comfort. She alone can tell them, that it is of little importance what man may think of their conduct, while the all-seeing Judge of the world approves of it. She alone can present to them the view of another world; a world of more candour, humanity, and justice, than the present; where their innocence is in due time to be declared, and their virtue to be finally rewarded: and the same great principle which can alone strike terror into triumphant vice, affords the only effectual consolation to disgraced and insulted innocence.

(*TMS* III 2 11–12: 120–1)[14]

In a similar vein Smith writes:

When we thus despair of finding any force upon earth which can check the triumph of injustice, we naturally appeal to heaven, and hope, that the great Author of our nature will himself execute hereafter, what all the principles which he has given us for the direction of our conduct, prompt us to attempt even here; that he will complete the plan which he himself has thus taught us to begin; and will, in a life to come, render to every one according to the works which he has performed in this world. And thus we are led to the belief of a future state, not only by the weaknesses, by the hopes and fears of human nature, but by the noblest and best principles which belong to it, by the love of virtue, and by the abhorrence of vice and injustice.

(*TMS* III 5 10: 169)

The afterlife is particularly important in Smith's system because of his (perhaps Calvinist) emphasis on the imperfections of the administration of justice in this present life. Even if correct judgments are made by those whose moral and intellectual capacities have been damaged by the fall, rewards and punishments in this life fall short of what justice demands. It matters greatly to Smith that there is another place where justice will eventually be done, for in both the *Theory of Moral Sentiments* and the *Wealth of Nations* he sees that justice is necessary to the proper functioning of economic system. For instance: "society cannot subsist unless the laws of justice are tolerably observed" (*TMS* II ii 3 6: 87). It is justice rather than benevolence which is necessary:

If there is any society among robbers and murderers, they must at least, according to the trite observation, abstain from robbing and murdering one another. Beneficence, therefore, is less essential to the existence of society than justice. Society may subsist, though not in the most comfortable state, without beneficence; but the prevalence of injustice must utterly destroy it . . . justice . . . is the main pillar that upholds the whole edifice.

(*TMS* II ii 3 3: 86)

If justice is necessary for the maintenance of society and the afterlife sustains our sense of justice, then the afterlife has an important role in Smith's system. As he suggests, we can even admire divine providence at work as this sense of justice arises within us.

Overall for Smith, judgment and future hope operate as a court of appeal where the wrongs of this world are righted and persons receive their just deserts. The justice of the divine court of appeal is continuous with and reinforces the natural sense of justice we have in this present life. There is no conflict between the two because for Smith the "great Director of nature" is providentially at work in both.

The future hope as an imaginative space

One of the themes of recent Smith scholarship has been the importance of the imagination in Smith's account of scientific progress, and in Smith's spectator mechanisms of morality (Griswold 1999; Otteson 2002). For Smith, the future state also operates as an imaginative space where morality can be negotiated under the gaze of the author of nature.

He uses passages about the future state to recommend an active life which bears practical fruit, as against the quiet monkish life recommended by some of his religious contemporaries. The best example is Smith's vigorous objection to the elevation of monkish virtues by Massillon, the French Catholic Bishop of Clermont. Smith writes:

> To compare, in this manner, the futile mortifications of a monastery, to the ennobling hardships and hazards of war; to suppose that one day, or one hour, employed in the former should, in the eye of the great Judge of the world, have more merit than a whole life spent honourably in the latter, is surely contrary to all our moral sentiments; to all the principles by which nature has taught us to regulate our contempt or admiration. It is this spirit, however, which, while it has reserved the celestial regions for monks and friars, or for those whose conduct and conversation resembled those of monks and friars, has condemned to the infernal all the heroes, all the statesmen and lawgivers, all the poets and philosophers of former ages; all those who have invented, improved, or excelled in the arts which contribute to the subsistence, to the conveniency, or to the ornament of human life; all the great protectors, instructors, and benefactors of mankind; all those to whom our natural sense of praise-worthiness forces us to ascribe the highest merit and most exalted virtue. Can we wonder that so strange an application of this most respectable doctrine should sometimes have exposed it to contempt and derision; with those at least who had themselves, perhaps, no great taste or turn for the devout and contemplative virtues.

> (*TMS* III 2 35: 134)

A further example is the famous passage added to the final edition of the *Theory of Moral Sentiments* where Smith writes of the connection between virtue and our sense of the benevolence of God. He writes:

> To this universal benevolence . . . the very suspicion of a fatherless world, must be the most melancholy of all reflections; from the thought that all the unknown regions of infinite and incomprehensible space may be filled with nothing but endless misery and wretchedness . . . All the splendour of the highest prosperity can never enlighten the gloom with which so dreadful an idea must necessarily overshadow the imagination.
>
> (*TMS* VI ii 3 2: 235)

Recall that Smith's father died early. I take this to be an eloquent statement of the imaginative power of future hope and of the destructive effects on the imagination of a Godless and thus hopeless future.

Cosmic utilitarianism?

Smith's linkage of the future life to happiness, and his emphasis on continuity between the present and future life might suggest that Smith adheres to a version of 18th-century "cosmic utilitarianism",[15] or even that Smith is a precursor of models in the contemporary economics of religious literature where heavenly and earthly utility are flatly traded off against each other.

While there are utilitarian elements in Smith, especially when he is giving policy advice, and he often comments that behaviour promotes happiness of the individual and the good order of society, his moral philosophy overall cannot be described as utilitarian. Smith strongly criticises utilitarian accounts of justice, and more generally accounts of justice, such as Hume's, which ground it in reason. There is a great distance between Smith and his utilitarian contemporaries Paley and Bentham.[16] No passage in Smith's writings describes such tradeoffs an individual makes between earthly and heavenly utility.

Teleology?

If there is a continuity between the present and future life, yet Smith resists the utilitarian flattening of moral discourse and rejects tradeoffs between present and future rewards, then what exactly is the relationship? How does the future life continue and complete the present life? Or to put it another way, what sort of teleology is operating in Smith's system?[17]

Teleology in Smith is perfectly consistent with his theological roots in the British tradition of scientific natural theology and the moderate Calvinism of the Scottish Enlightenment. Teleological elements in Smith, variously understood, have been identified in recent years by scholars such as Gloria Vivenza, Ryan Hanley, Richard Kleer and Deirdre McCloskey,[18] against a number of prominent authors who made Smith part of their larger stories of the banishment of teleology from modern science. For instance, Smith was a minor villain in Alasdair MacIntyre's (1981: 54) story of the abandonment of teleology in 18th-century moral philosophy, and Charles Taylor took Smith as a representative of the providential deism of the 17th and 18th centuries which lost the idea of God guiding society towards mutually beneficial ends (2007: 220). Knud Haakonssen adopted an intermediate position where teleological explanation in Smith is acknowledged, but inessential to his system, and thus able to be discarded. He writes:

> Nothing hinges on teleological explanations and thus on a guarantor of a teleological order. I think it is safe to say that whenever a piece of teleology turns up in Smith it is fairly clear where we have to look in order to find a real explanation in terms of what we may broadly call efficient causes.
>
> (Haakonssen 1981: 77)

In the literature there is some ambiguity over whether teleology means recourse to teleological explanation (in the sense of specifying final causes alongside or instead of efficient causes), or a full-blown Aristotelian-Thomist teleological framework for science and ethics. Economists, including historians of economics, tend to use teleological in the first weaker sense. There has not been much recent writing on economics within an Aristotelian-Thomistic teleological framework. Part of the reason for the disagreement in the literature over teleology in Smith is that scholars like Kleer find teleology in the weaker sense, while MacIntyre and Taylor are looking for it in the stronger sense.

Examining Smith's writings, it is clear that teleology in the weaker sense is present, though final causes are separated carefully from efficient causes. A key passage is:

> In every part of the universe we observe means adjusted with the nicest artifice to the ends which they are intended to produce; and in the mechanism of a plant, or animal body, we admire how everything is contrived for advancing the two great purposes of nature, the support of the individual, and the propagation of the species. But in these, and in all such objects, we still distinguish the efficient from the final cause of their several motions and organizations. The digestion of the food, the circulation of the blood, and the secretion of the several juices which are drawn from it, are operations all of them necessary for the great purposes of animal life. Yet we never endeavour to account for them from those purposes as from their efficient causes, nor imagine that the blood circulates, or that the food digests of its own accord, and with a view or intention to the purposes of circulation or digestion. The wheels of the watch are all admirably adjusted to the end for which it was made, the pointing of the hour. All their various motions conspire in the nicest manner to produce this effect. If they were endowed with a desire and intention to produce it, they could not do it better. Yet we never ascribe any such desire or intention to them, but to the watch-maker, and we know that they are put into motion by a spring, which intends the effect it produces as little as they do. But though, in accounting for the operations of bodies, we never fail to distinguish in this manner the efficient from the final cause, in accounting for those of the mind we are very apt to confound these two different things with one another. When by natural principles we are led to advance those ends,

which a refined and enlightened reason would recommend to us, we are very apt to impute to that reason, as to their efficient cause, the sentiments and actions by which we advance those ends, and to imagine that to be the wisdom of man, which in reality is the wisdom of God. Upon a superficial view, this cause seems sufficient to produce the effects which are ascribed to it; and the system of human nature seems to be more simple and agreeable when all its different operations are in this manner deduced from a single principle.

(*TMS* II ii 3 6: 87)

Smith is here insisting on specifying efficient causes, within a larger framework that leaves space for final causes. The discussion of the watch connects with his later discussion of the economic system in the *Wealth of Nations*. There the individual economic actors are like parts of the watch, lacking an intention to produce beneficial social ends, an intention which is supplied by the divine designer economic system.

But is there a stronger Aristotelian teleological framework in Smith? Answering this question is complicated by Smith's viscerally negative attitude to the degenerate Aristotelianism of his day, formed especially during his unrewarding years as a Snell scholar at Balliol College Oxford as discussed earlier in the chapter. The negative comments about scholastic Aristotelianism littered thorough his works may have provoked commentators to latch onto Smith as a turning point in the banishment of teleology from science. Another complication is that for Smith with his Calvinist roots, teleology tends to be expressed in providential language.

If Smith is working within such a larger teleological framework, then a telos needs to be identified. Smith is reasonably consistent about this, though also slightly evasive. In the *History of Ancient Physics*, he writes of science progressing to the point where the "Universe was regarded as a complete machine, as a coherent system, governed by general laws, and directed to general ends, viz. its own preservation and prosperity, and that of all the species that are in it" (*History of Ancient Physics* in Smith 1980: 113–4). In the passage cited above, the end is specified as the "support of the individual and propagation of the species", elsewhere it is "happiness of mankind" or the "happiness and perfection of the species" (*TMS* II ii 3 6: 87, *TMS* III 5 7: 166 and *TMS* II iii 3 2: 105). In both the *Theory of Moral Sentiments* and *Wealth of Nations*, the end is given as "bettering our condition", without any more specific guidance about its content (*TMS* I iii 2 1: 50 and *WN* II iii 27: 341).

Smith's acknowledgement of the ends of nature and admittedly vague specifications of these ends fits in with an Aristotelian framework, certainly more so than the utilitarian framework which came to dominate economics in the early 19th century. The ends have an earthy flavour which is entirely appropriate for a writer observing the beginning of the industrial revolution and seeing the possibilities for better material provision for his Scottish compatriots – of perhaps burying the English epithet that oats were the food of horses and Scotsmen. However, alongside the emphasis on provision of material goods, there are passages about how ultimately unfulfilling wealth is, for instance, his famous comparison of the happiness of the beggar beside the road with the rich man, and passages about how the baubles and trinkets of wealth are a divine trick played on human beings to drive the economic system (for example, *TMS* IV 1 10: 184–5). Material wealth, much discussed in the *Wealth of Nations*, is never specified as an ultimate end. It contributes in a complex and indirect manner to ultimate ends like the "happiness and perfection of the species".[19]

Smith's evasiveness about specifying ends comes I think comes from his Calvinist suspicion of our capacity to know these matters. God works providentially in ways that we cannot fully comprehend, and presumption about these matters is dangerous. In fact, Smith suggests that ultimate ends and connections between our actions and these ultimate ends are opaque to human beings for good reasons, leaving our God-given human nature rather than our rational powers to guide us towards beneficent ends. As he writes:

> Nature has directed us to the greater part of these by original and immediate instincts. Hunger, thirst, the passion which unites the two sexes, the love of pleasure, and the dread of pain, prompt us to apply those means for their own sakes, and without any consideration of their tendency to those beneficent ends which the great Director of nature intended to produce by them.
>
> (*TMS* II I 5 10: 77, footnote)[20]

In Smith's great idea that self-interested action in properly functioning markets generates beneficent economic outcomes, we have perhaps the strongest illustration of indirect achievement of ends. Smith disparages those who are "affected to trade for public good" and instead claims that the trader "by pursuing his own interest he frequently promotes that of the society more effectually than when he really intends to promote it" (*WN* IV ii 9: 456). The providential coordination of self-interested action achieves something that humans reflecting on ends and directing their actions towards them cannot.

The aspect of ends within an Aristotelian/Thomistic framework that is the focus here is the future hope, but other aspects such as his account of human nature and his account of virtue also show that Smith is not as far from this older view of science and ethics as most economist commentators assume. Smith's teleological framework provides intellectual space for his account of the future hope.

Conclusion

The cumulative biographical and textual evidence for the importance of Newtonian natural theology and moderate Calvinism of the Scottish Enlightenment, the illumination of key Smithian themes and texts provided by these theological backgrounds, and the fact that Smith was read theologically by his 19th-century followers, in my view makes the existing accounts of Smith which ignore the theological dimensions of his work untenable. The distortions caused by ignoring the theological background are especially dangerous for a writer like Smith whose works constitute a carefully planned (though admittedly incomplete) system.

If so, and Smith's influence on the development of political economy as a discipline is great, then theology has shaped political economy.

The argument will now be extended to Smith's 19th-century followers, but before doing so it is worth noting that Smith's work was read theologically by them. For instance, Richard Whately, holder of the first chair in political economy at a British university, interprets providentially Smith's assertion of unintended positive consequences of self-interested behaviour, writing: "Man is, in the same act, doing one thing by choice, for his own benefit, and another, undesignedly, under the care of Providence, for the service of the community" (Whately 1832: 94). Whately also places Smith's *Theory of Moral Sentiments* and *Wealth of Nations* above William Paley's works as natural theology. One of the most important 19th-century British popularisers of political economy, Thomas Chalmers, took Smith to be suggesting that the transformation of self-interested behaviour into the greatest economic good is providential, writing:

> Such a result which at the same time not a single agent in this vast and complicated system of trade contemplates or cares for, each caring only for himself – strongly bespeaks a higher Agent, by whose transcendental wisdom it is, that all is made to conspire so harmoniously, and to terminate so beneficially.
>
> (Chalmers 1833: 238–9)

Theological readings of Smith are common among the 19th-century pioneers of political economy as a discipline, and even more so in popular discussions of political economy.

Notes

1 This chapter draws on several articles: Oslington (2011b, 2012a, 2012b, 2015a) and the introduction to my edited book (Oslington 2011a).
2 The Viner quotation is from *The Role of Providence in the Social Order* 1972 pp. 81–82.
3 This chapter is about Smith's ideas as expressed in his writings, rather than Smith's personal faith or otherwise. For one thing, we cannot ultimately know about Smith's personal faith, but even if we could know, the information that Smith was or was not of orthodox Christian faith would not decide the issue of theological influences on his work. It is perfectly conceivable that Smith's various professions of religious faith were a sham, yet his works still be deeply influenced by theological ideas. It is equally conceivable that a writer could have intense personal faith, yet theological ideas leave no trace in his or her work. The latter possibility is more plausible for a writer living in a contemporary secular society than in 18th-century Scotland.
4 The atonement passage is discussed by Raphael and Macfie in their introduction and an appendix to the standard edition of *TMS*. It will also be discussed further later in this chapter.
5 Hanley (2010) argues that Smith took naturalism not skepticism from Hume. A naturalistic account of religious belief and religious institutions is perfectly compatible with religious belief and participation in religious institutions.
6 Here and elsewhere, Smith's published works will be abbreviated *TMS* and *WN*, with page references to the OUP/Liberty Fund Bicentennial Editions listed in the bibliography.

7 The appendix includes an N-gram of mentions of Adam Smith and the invisible hand in English books. The upsurge of interest in the invisible hand begins from the 1950s.

8 Jacob Viner, after writing his classic paper for the Chicago celebration of the 150th anniversary of the *Wealth of Nations*, published little else on the topic. Two post-humously published works (Viner 1972, 1978) give some indication of Viner's vast reading over subsequent decades as he pursued the question of the religious background of 18th-century political economy. The Mudd Manuscript Library at Princeton contains many kilograms of evidence of his pursuit. Two scholars who took up Viner's questions were Bitterman (1940), whose work reinforced Viner's conclusions, and Coase (1976) who disagreed. Coase's conclusion was "it seems to me that Viner much exaggerates the extent to which Adam Smith was committed to a belief in a personal God" (Coase 1976: 554), which, if correct, is about Smith's personal faith rather than the influence of theology in forming Smith's ideas, which was the more important question that interested Viner. As Viner stated in correspondence 3 November 1965, responding to questions from Alec Macfie about Smith's personal faith, "I am not really interested in Smith's views re religion except as items of intellectual history to be analysed if at all for their logical character and their relevance to his thought on other matters". Further discussion of Viner's reading of Smith and its reception may be found in Oslington (2012b).

9 Commentators have speculated about where Smith might have picked up the invisible hand language – ranging from straightforward associations with divine hands in the Bible to Emma Rothschild's (1994) suggestion that it could be the bloody and invisible hand of Shakespeare's Macbeth. A recent thorough investigation of previous usage by the historian of science Peter Harrison (2011b) shows that hidden and invisible hands were frequently discussed in sermons, devotional works and Biblical commentaries in the 17th century. The idea usually expressed is that God accomplishes his purposes in history in spite of the intentions of human agents. It is an expression of the Christian doctrine of divine providential care for humanity. Smith seems to be transferring the idea from history to the economy.

An intriguing discovery by Harrison is that the 1762 Glasgow edition of Calvin's *Institutes* translates Calvin's Latin in Book 1 84 as "But those things which appear to us to happen by chance, faith will acknowledge to have been owing to a secret impulse of God. I grant there doth not always appear the like reason, but doubtless we ought to believe, that whatsoever changes of things are seen in the world, are brought about by the direction and influence of God's invisible hand". Harrison suggests that Thomas Norton's 1561 translation "the secret sturring of the hand of God" is truer to the original Latin and that the 1762 editor seems to have been influenced by the providential associations of the invisible hand phrase. It is reasonable to suppose Smith was similarly influenced by the common providential associations.

Another intriguing suggestion about the source of the invisible hand image was made by Gloria Vivenza (2008). She notes that Adam Smith (at *WN* V ii h 3: 859) cites Dion Cassius on Roman inheritance law and mentions in a note the 1734 work of Burman de Vectigalibus. Examining this work, Vivenza found a discussion of the hidden activity of Jupiter interrupting the normal course of events that connects with Smith's use of the invisible hand image in his early essay *History of Astronomy*. As Vivenza points out, similar discussions in classical literature abound, and we cannot be sure this work was in fact Smith's source.

10 In the literature, the most important discussion of the *History of Astronomy* passage is by Macfie (1971), who finds the reference to the invisible hand in the *History of Astronomy* puzzling, especially the way irregular events are attributed to the gods, seemingly contradicting the other invisible hand passages which he believes are about providential activity in regular events. In the end, Macfie suggests this early and somewhat ambiguous reference should not overshadow the later "classic" expressions of the invisible hand idea.

11 Some of the interpreters who see the hand as divine were mentioned in the introduction, notably Viner (1927). The literature specifically on the invisible hand passage in *Theory of Moral Sentiments* is not extensive, with the two substantial treatments being Macfie (1970) and Brewer (2009). Macfie called attention to the natural theological background of the passage, then concentrated on Stoic natural theologies, though he ended up puzzled by the inconsistencies with the other invisible hand passages and called for further investigation of the natural theological background. Brewer's contribution was to examine the passage against the background of 18th-century debates about luxury, and argued the passage makes the point that while income and consumption may be unequal, the consumption of necessities such as food is equalised and perhaps the rich are no happier in the end than the poor. Brewer's interpretation is compatible with mine. Considering the theological background allows us to see how the equality-maintaining invisible hand fits into Smith's larger conception of divine activity.

12 It is incredible how often the passage is quoted to include "as if" by an invisible hand. Stiglitz (2002) is one among many examples.

13 A passage which some see as evidence of Smith straying from orthodoxy is one that he modified through different editions of the *Theory of Moral Sentiments*. The final version is "Nature teaches us to hope, and religion, we suppose, authorises us to expect, that it will be punished, even in a life to come . . . in every religion, and in every superstition that the world has ever beheld, accordingly, there has been a Tartarus as well as an Elysium; a place provided for the punishment of the wicked, as well as one for the reward of the just" (Smith *TMS* II ii 3 12: 91). Earlier versions included an exposition of the orthodox Christian doctrine of the atonement. Details of the changes are discussed by the editors Raphael and Macfie in footnotes and their appendix II to the standard OUP edition. It is commonly thought that the changes weaken the passage, but they may also be taken to generalise and naturalise belief in the afterlife, especially as some of the deleted theological material found its way into other passages added by Smith to this final edition. The most likely explanation of the changes remains a desire to avoid unnecessary controversy over the doctrine of the atonement.

   If nature teaches largely by analogy, then Smith is departing from Hume's position that such analogies are philosophically illegitimate, or at least suggesting that the fact that we learn about the afterlife by analogy is more important than a philosophical argument about the legitimacy of analogy. In keeping the reference to the afterlife fairly general, Smith avoids buying into controversies such as mortalism, the dispute between upholders of the traditional view that the soul is immortal, and others such as Hobbes in England and Hume in Scotland, who held that the soul is mortal, though God can grant eternal life.

14 The Calas case is discussed in Ross (1995: 201).

15 Cosmic utilitarianism is discussed by Waterman 1991a and Cole 1991. Paley's *Principles* 1785 epitomises this tradition, but even in his work there is nothing like the tradeoff between these worldly and future rewards we see in contemporary economics of religion. Instead, there is a harmony between creation, providence and eschatology because they are all expressions of the character of the one God.

16 One of the places where Smith criticises utilitarian accounts of justice is *TMS* II ii: 86–92. He departs substantially from Hume's position on justice. In relation to utilitarianism, Ian Simpson Ross concludes that "Smith is consistently hostile to utility as an explanation of the origin of moral rules, and as a principle to be applied routinely in day-today transactions. However, he does apply the criterion of utility". Ross describes Smith as a "contemplative utilitarian" (Ross 1995: 167). Young (1997) and Witzum and Young (2012) argue against a utilitarian reading of Smith, as do Campbell (1971), Raphael (2007) and Sayre-McCord (2010).

17 Discussing teleology in relation to economics, which has been intimately associated with utilitarian philosophy since the early 19th century, raises some terminological difficulties. In Catholic moral theology, a contrast is sometimes drawn between deontological and teleological moral philosophies, with utilitarianism classified as teleological. The more usual terminology in contemporary moral philosophy (and among economists) is deontological and consequentialist, with utilitarian theories classified as consequentialist. This reserves the term teleological for the Aristotelian-Thomist tradition of a teleological ethics. See Hausman and McPherson (2006).

18 Vivenza and Hanley's work on the relationship between Smith and Aristotle was mentioned earlier in the chapter. Also Kleer (1995, 2000) on teleology and McCloskey (2008) who reads Smith as an Aristotelian virtue ethicist. Ross (1995: 340) writes "His philosophy of social explanation involves final explanations, couched in terms of a purposeful nature or God, and this variety of theism is an integral part of his approach to social phenomena".

19 There is an interesting discussion of the issue by two of the greatest Smith scholars among economists, Alec Macfie and Jacob Viner, preserved in Viner's correspondence held by the Mudd Manuscript Library at Princeton University, New Jersey. Viner wrote on 4 April 1963 about their growing common interest in the theological dimensions of Smith's work. He considered the "question of what Smith regarded as the value of economic activity in view of his disparaging remarks about the value to the individual of wealth above a modest level" and speculated "The question for Smith, I think, is, what does God want? And his answer, an adequate level of living for as many persons as possible".

20 This raises questions about Smith's view of the relationship between divine and human agency, and essentially Smith's position is that God works mainly but not exclusively through the constitution of our human nature.

5   Natural theology and the emergence of political economy

Stewart, Malthus, Sumner and Chalmers

John Veitch expressed the view that "the internal history of Britain, during the past half century, is in great measure the record of the slow but secure prevalence of the political principles of Smith and Stewart".

Malthus was supposed to have begun what the historian Arnold Toynbee called "The bitter argument between economists and human beings" that raged throughout the 19th century.

Robert Southey was perhaps the most vicious of the many critics of Malthus, suggesting: "Break him on the wheel . . . you ought to set your foot upon such a mischievous reptile and crush him".

Marx sneered at both "Parson Malthus" and "Arch-Parson Chalmers".

Malthus praised JB Sumner for his "masterly development and completion of views of which only an intimation could be given in the Essay".

Malthus described Chalmers as his "ablest and best disciple".[1]

Introduction

The usual continuation of the story of political economy after Smith includes passing reference to Dugald Stewart's Edinburgh lectures on political economy attended by James Mill and others who brought Adam Smith's work to England, and then theoretical developments by Ricardo and other classical economists culminating in JS Mill's mid-century textbook.[2] Malthus is often treated as a somewhat confused and reactionary version of Ricardo. Jeremy Bentham rather than Paley's utilitarianism is regarded as providing the moral philosophical underpinning of the enterprise. JB Sumner and Thomas Chalmers, who also attended Dugald Stewart's Edinburgh lectures, have received much less attention from historians of economics despite making significant theoretical contributions and having a huge impact on popular thinking and economic policy.

Further Scottish background: Dugald Stewart

Before moving on to Malthus who is the central character in this chapter, it is worth lingering briefly to consider Dugald Stewart (1753–1828) who as a lecturer on political economy and philosopher influenced 19th-century English political economy more than is often recognised in standard histories of the discipline. Dugald Stewart's theoretical contributions were minimal, but his framing of the inquiry and influence on methodology of political economy was great.[3]

Dugald Stewart like Adam Smith worked in the theology-soaked environment of 18th-century Scotland. He was Smith's first biographer (Stewart 1795). He attended the lectures of Smith's successor as Professor of Moral Philosophy at Glasgow, Thomas Reid, on natural theology, ethics and politics in 1771–2, hoping like Smith for a Snell scholarship to Oxford which entailed taking Anglican orders, though Stewart was passed over though for this. Instead he devoted himself to mathematics and was elected Professor of Mathematics, and then Professor of Moral Philosophy at Edinburgh. According to Stewart, political economy was that part of philosophy that dealt with "the happiness and improvement of political society" (Stewart 1855, quoted by Winch 1983: 37) and philosophers were "fellow workers with God in forwarding the gracious purposes of his government" (Stewart 1855, quoted by Winch 1983: 41).

Dugald Stewart's famous Edinburgh lectures on political economy, first delivered in 1800–1 and continued until his retirement in 1809 were delivered as Professor of Moral Philosophy.[4] Smith's *Wealth of Nations* was used in his classes. Attendees included JR McCulloch, James Mill, George Pryme, possibly JB Sumner, Thomas Chalmers and the *Edinburgh Review* founders, Sydney Smith, Francis Horner, Francis Jeffrey and Henry Brougham, among many other important figures.

Much of the lectures was taken up with discussion of the "objects and province of political economy" along with its connection to law. When he turned to substantive doctrines, he focused on population, perhaps because Malthus' 1798 *Essay on the Principle of Population* was prominent in the minds of his hearers. Stewart was much more optimistic than Malthus about the prospects for society and saw no need to offer a theodicy. Next, he considered "national wealth" and the organisation of the lectures loosely followed Smith's *Wealth of Nations*, though not always agreeing with Smith's views. Then he turns to policy towards the poor, and a subject of great interest to almost all of the 19th-century natural theological political economists, "the education of the lower orders".[5] Throughout the lectures he stresses the possibilities of improving both science and society.

Besides the lectures on political economy, Stewart's philosophical works were important for their inductive methodology and emphasis on clarity of definitions of terms. They included his *Elements of the Philosophy of the Human Mind* (Stewart 1792–1827) and his *Philosophical Essays* (Stewart 1810). These works set the terms of methodological debates that will be considered in this and subsequent chapters. Pierro Corsi (1987, especially p. 132) suggests that the

Oxford economists Edward Copleston, Richard Whately and Nassau Senior took up the deductive side of Stewart's work but with greater reticence about drawing policy conclusions from economic theory, along with his emphasis on clarity of language, while their Cambridge opponents Richard Jones and William Whewell took up Stewart's revival of Baconian inductive methods. All shared the natural theological framing of political economy.

Malthus' *Principle of Population* and its theodicy

Alongside Adam Smith, Robert Malthus (1766–1834) was one of the "joint founders of the science" of political economy (Winch 1996: 373).[6]

As well as the importance of his own work on political economy, especially his *Essay on the Principle of Population* first published in 1798, Malthus was a major channel through which Smith influenced 19th-century English social and political discussion. Malthus was familiar with Adam Smith's *Wealth of Nations* and it was the basis of his teaching of political economy at the East India College Haileybury from 1805, as well as Malthus' own *Principles of Political Economy* published in 1820. He was a close friend of David Ricardo, and their correspondence from 1811 is an important testament to early theoretical and policy debate. JM Keynes (1933) hailed Malthus as the first of a line of Cambridge economists responsible for most of the theoretical advances in economics, as well as the first to see the possibility of failures of effective demand, or in Malthus' terminology "general gluts".

Malthus explicitly joined political economy with natural theology, raising important questions which he and others struggled with through the early decades of the 19th century. The biographical warrant for reading his works as natural theology is strong – Malthus was educated at the dissenting academy of Warrington, then University of Cambridge where he absorbed Paley's natural theological approach. In the *Essay on the Principle of Population* he states, "it seems absolutely necessary that we reason from nature up to nature's God and not presume to reason from God to nature" and goes on to speak of "the book of nature where alone we can read God as he is" Malthus (1798: 201). He is prepared to invoke the doctrine of providence in defending the existence of economic rents as a "bountiful gift of providence" (Malthus 1815: 122). His letters and sermons (Malthus 2004) display a commitment to Scriptural revelation which warrants a scientific natural theology.

Malthus followed Paley on natural theology and understood that his own works would be read in the context of Paley's then influential system. In correspondence, Malthus commented that "The proofs of design are indeed everywhere so apparent that it is hardly possible to add much to the force of the argument as stated and illustrated by Paley" (Malthus to Whewell 1833, in Todhunter 1876 I: 73).

The *Essay on the Principle of Population* was one of the most influential and controversial books of the early 19th century. It was intended, as Malthus signals in the subtitle of the work, as an attack on the utopian speculations of Godwin's 1793 *Political Justice* and Condorcet's 1795 *Outlines of an Historical*

View of the Progress of the Human Mind (translated from the 1794 *Esquisse d'un Tableau Historique des Progres de l'Espirit Humain*). In the words of Waterman (1991a: 7), Malthus' *Essay* was "an anti-Jacobin defence of property rights embedded in the religious worldview and theological framework of 18th-century Anglican Christianity".[7] Although the principle of population undermines the idea of the perfectibility of man, it does not imply that all attempts to improve the conditions of human life are in vain, just that we should focus our efforts on those which are achievable (Malthus 1798: 69).

Malthus drew on the writings on population and wealth of the Scots Hume and Smith, and especially of fellow Cambridge man Paley's *Principles of Moral and Political Philosophy*. The core argument was that population tends to grow more rapidly than the food supply, or as Malthus (1798: 71) puts it "Population, when unchecked, increases in a geometrical ratio. Subsistence increases only in an arithmetical ratio". Any discrepancy between population and the food supply is corrected by the checks of "misery and vice" (Malthus 1798: 72). Policies such as more generous support of the poor would thus increase population without increasing the food supply, increasing vice and misery rather than improving life for the poor.

Within his natural theological framework, a pressing issue Malthus felt he needed to deal with was the seeming conflict between his population theory and the goodness and power of God.[8] The final two chapters of the first edition of the *Essay* attempted to make theological sense of a world where misery and vice were necessary to keep the growth of population in line with the food supply. This is a nasty special case of the problem of why an all-powerful and good God allows suffering.

Malthus' theodicy began by rejecting the position of Butler and Paley that earthly life is a trial for the future life (Malthus 1798: 201–2), instead arguing that life is about developing the human mind. He invites us to:

> [c]onsider the world and this life as the mighty process of God, not for the trial, but for the creation and formation of mind, a process necessary to awaken inert, chaotic matter into spirit, to sublimate the dust of the earth into soul, to elicit an ethereal spark from the clod of clay. And in this view of the subject, the various impressions and excitements which man receives through life may be considered as the forming hand of his creator, acting by general laws, and awakening his sluggish existence, by the animating touches of the Divinity, into a capacity of superior enjoyment.
>
> (Malthus 1798: 202)

Malthus suggested that the human mind was initially inert and required some stimulus to development. So "evil seems to be necessary to create exertion, and exertion seems evidently necessary to create mind" (Malthus 1798: 204). The principle of population, though appearing evil, is in Malthus' view perfectly consistent with the goodness of God.

To furnish the most unremitted excitements of this kind, and to urge men to further the gracious designs of Providence by the full cultivation of the earth, it has been ordained that population should increase much faster than food. This general law undoubtedly produces much partial evil, but a little reflection may, perhaps, satisfy us, that it produces a great overbalance of good.

(Malthus 1798: 205)

He adds that just as Newton discovered general laws of planetary motion, the principle of population is a law of human society. Overall, "the acknowledged difficulties occasioned by the law of population tend rather to promote rather than impede the general purpose of Providence" (Malthus 1798: 206). He adds there is "no more evil in the world than what is absolutely necessary" (Malthus 1798: 216). What is particularly striking is his suggestion about our response to evil. "Evil exists in the world, not to create despair, but activity. We are not patiently to submit to it, but to exert ourselves to avoid it" (Malthus 1798: 217).

In setting out his position, the status of the traditional doctrines of original sin and eternal suffering in hell were left unclear.[9] His comments on eternal suffering are worth quoting in full:

When we reflect on the temptations to which man must necessarily be exposed in this world, from the structure of his frame, and the operation of the laws of nature and the consequent moral certainty that many vessels will come out of this mighty creative furnace in wrong shapes, it is perfectly impossible to conceive that any of these creatures of God's hand can be condemned to eternal suffering. Could we once admit such an idea, all our natural conceptions of goodness and justice would be completely overthrown, and we could no longer look up to God as a merciful and righteous Being. But the doctrine of life and immortality which was brought to light by the gospel, the doctrine that the end of righteousness is everlasting life, but the wages of sin are death, is in every respect just and merciful, and worthy of the great Creator. Nothing can appear more consonant to our reason and that those beings which come out of the creative process of the world in lovely and beautiful forms should be crowned with immortality, while those which come out misshapen, those whose minds are not suited to a purer and happier state of existence, should perish and be condemned to mix again with their original clay. Eternal condemnation of this kind may be considered as a species of eternal punishment, and it is not wonderful that it should be represented, sometimes, under images of suffering. But life and death, salvation and destruction, are more frequently opposed to each other in the New Testament than happiness and misery. The Supreme Being would appear to us in a very different view if we were to consider him as pursuing the creatures that had offended him with eternal hate and torture, instead of merely condemning to their original insensibility those beings that, by the operation of general laws, had not been formed with qualities suited to a purer state of happiness.

(Malthus 1798: 215)

Malthus dropped the two theological chapters from the 1803 second edition of the *Essay*. In a 1799 letter to the *Monthly Magazine* Malthus suggested, "I shall in deference to the opinion of some friends whose judgements I respect, omit them".[10] These unidentified friends we now know from recently discovered letters to be ED Clarke, Thomas Cautley and Bewick Bridge.[11] What still remains a mystery is which doctrines were at issue and the reason Malthus accepted the view of his friends and omitted the chapters. Perhaps the most likely reason was caution about expressing theological views not strictly necessary to the argument of the principle of population.

An addition to the 1803 edition of the *Essay*, which became infamous among critics of political economy, reads as follows:

> A man who is born into a world already possessed, if he cannot get subsistence from his parents on whom he has a just demand, and if the society do not want his labour, has no claim of right to the smallest portion of food, and, in fact, has no business to be where he is. At nature's mighty feast there is no vacant cover for him. She tells him to be gone, and will quickly execute her own orders, if he does not work upon the compassion of some of her guests. If these guests get up and make room for him, other intruders immediately appear demanding the same favour. The report of a provision for all that come, fills the hall with numerous claimants. The order and harmony of the feast is disturbed, the plenty that before reigned is changed into scarcity; and the happiness of the guests is destroyed by the spectacle of misery and dependence in every part of the hall, and by the clamorous importunity of those who are justly enraged at not finding the provision which they had been taught to expect. The guests learn too late their error, in counteracting those strict orders to all intruders, issued by the great mistress of the feast, who, wishing that all guests should have plenty, and knowing she could not provide for unlimited numbers, humanely refused to admit fresh comers when her table was already full.
>
> (Malthus 1803 Book IV, Chapter VI: 249)

Malthus was using a variation of a biblical parable to make the point about the compassionate nature of restraints imposed on the poor, but the controversy meant the passage did not make it into subsequent editions.[12]

There is nothing in these passages from the *Essay* which directly contradicts the Anglican 39 Articles of Religion, which Malthus was required to affirm as a clergyman.[13] It was rumoured that Malthus admitted to conditionalist sympathies, but views expressed in these chapters are vague enough to be consistent with both immortality of the soul and conditional immortality. Either view is in any case consistent with the Articles of Religion. Malthus came closest in these chapters of the *Essay* to denying Article IX on Original Sin, though in my view remains within the generous bounds of Anglican orthodoxy on this. He is not saying that mankind's inert state is a sinless state, or that exertion and growth of mind displace Christ's sacrifice in expiating sin, merely that exertion and growth of mind develop human capacities. Malthus is offering a theodicy not a soteriology in the *Essay*.

Recently discovered letters and sermons (Malthus 2004) provide no other evidence of theological unorthodoxy, instead they indicate Malthus' earnestness and biblical faith throughout his life as a clergyman and teacher at the East India College. Reason and revelation are used together and seen as mutually supporting.

Malthus' theodicy was complicated by another change to the second 1803 second edition of the *Essay*. Moral restraint was added as a check to population growth – essentially postponement of marriage by the labouring classes – contraception of course being unthinkable in Malthus' time. Before this addition, the human suffering associated with the principle of population was innocent suffering – coming from an inconsistency between the productivity of land and the natural urge to procreate. However, once moral restraint is added to the system, humans become culpable for not exercising this restraint.

Malthus introduced God's punishment for failure to exercise moral restraint into his further revised theodicy published in the 1830 *Summary View of the Principle of Population*. He comments:

> It has been thought, that a tendency in mankind to increase beyond the greatest possible increase of food which could be produced in a limited space, impeaches the goodness of the Deity and is inconsistent with the letter and spirit of the scriptures. If this objection were well founded, it would certainly be the most serious one which has been brought forward; but the answer to it appears to be quite satisfactory, and it may be compressed into a very small compass. First, it appears that evil[s] arising from the principle of population are exactly the same kind as the evils arising from the excessive irregular gratification of the human passions in general, and may equally be avoided by moral restraint . . . Second, is almost universally acknowledged that both the letter and the spirit of revelation represent this world as a state of moral discipline and probation. But a state of moral discipline and probation cannot be [a] state of unmixed happiness, as it necessarily implies difficulties to be overcome, and temptations to be resisted.
>
> (Malthus 1830: 271)

This revised theodicy places Malthus closer to Paley's state of trial and punishment for sin theodicy, though without denying the growth of mind theodicy from the 1798 *Essay*.

The main point to draw from this is that Malthus (and others) would only devote so much attention to theodicy if they were operating within a natural theological framework. Malthus' *Essay* was important to the debate over theodicy which shaped political economy in succeeding decades.

Development of Malthus' theodicy by JB Sumner

John Bird Sumner (1780–1862) is not prominent in the standard histories of economic thought, but is important for his development of the theodicy of Malthus' *Essay*.[14] Sumner moved in influential circles; educated at Eton and Kings College

Cambridge where he came under the influence of Charles Simeon, and later to become Bishop of Chester and Archbishop of Canterbury. His interest in political economy seems to have been aroused at Cambridge, with Waterman (1991a: 159) speculating that he was responsible for the College library purchasing the works of Smith and Malthus, and he may have attended Dugald Stewart's Edinburgh lectures on political economy. In the early decades of the 19th century, Sumner had considerable influence on economic policy through his membership of the Political Economy Club in the 1820s, articles on the condition of the poor (Sumner 1814, 1817) and work as Poor Law Commissioner from 1832.

David Ricardo, a fellow member of the Political Economy Club, lamented Sumner's decision to devote most of his energies to theology and church affairs rather than political economy: "I am sorry to hear that Mr Sumner does not intend writing any more on Political Economy . . . I very much regret the science will no longer be assisted by his distinguished talents" (Ricardo to Hutches Trower 1818, quoted in Waterman 1991a: 157).

Sumner's most substantial work is his *Treatise on the Records of Creation with Particular Reference to the Jewish History, and the Consistency of the Principle of Population with the Wisdom and Goodness of the Deity*. It appeared in 1816 and sold very well, going through five editions by 1833. Like Malthus, he operated within the framework of British scientific natural theology. The book developed from a Burnet Prize essay for which he was required to show that "Reason and Revelation mutually support and assist each other in contemplating the justice and goodness of the Deity" (Sumner 1816 vol I: xvii). Part of the role of natural theology is to "show the strong probability of that being true which revelation declares" (Sumner 1816 vol I: x). Without the relationship to scripture, "The God of natural theology will never be anything more than the dumb idol of Philosophy" (Sumner 1816 vol I: xi). In common with others in this tradition of scientific natural theology, he is adamant that scripture cannot be inconsistent with true natural philosophy (including political economy), noting "the absurdity of supposing, that the literal interpretation of terms in Scripture ought to interfere with the advancement of philosophical inquiry" (Sumner 1816 vol I: 325).

In the eyes of Sumner, the principle of population was not a theological problem, but rather additional evidence of the wisdom of the creator. Waterman (1991a: 151) records the opinion of the Oxford philosopher and political economist Edward Copleston that Sumner was an "able and ingenious expositor" who "dissipated the gloom" hanging over political economy since the publication of Malthus' *Essay*.

Sumner drew on the state of trial theodicy of Paley's 1802 *Natural Theology*, though continuing the developmental theme of the theodicy in Malthus' 1798 *Essay*.[15] His approach was to point, as Malthus had previously, to the way the principle of population enforces labour and discourages indolence, but Sumner added the argument that it gave mankind the best opportunity to develop virtues in this world. The inequality of ranks in Sumner's view gave mankind particular opportunity to develop virtues – the rich can exercise benevolence and the poor frugality (Sumner 1816 vol II: 31ff). "Man is inevitably placed in that condition which is most calculated to improve his faculties and afford opportunities for the exercise of virtue" (Sumner 1816 vol II: 113).

One of the richest parts of Sumner's work is where he breaks off the theological argument to consider collateral effects of the principle of population. It is an excellent example of theology stimulating the development of political economy. His discussion of scarcity flowing from the principle of population (Sumner 1816 II: 170ff) is particularly novel and insightful, suggesting that the division of labour is encouraged by scarcity, and therefore the pressure of scarcity is a spur to the creation of wealth. For Smith, by contrast, no such spur was necessary and the division of labour unfolded as markets expanded. Sumner goes on to discuss how scarcity produces communication and interchange between nations, leading to the transfer of arts and improvements, generating further wealth.

Alongside the encouragement of international trade, the principle of population was "prescribed by the Deity as an instrument of peopling the world" (Sumner 1816 II: 196), so that emigration to empty parts of the globe could be an alternative to vice and misery in reconciling the local population to the food supply. The search for an adequate theodicy has given rise here to a theory of international migration.

Sumner then returns to the main theological argument, picking up Paley's view that mankind is in a state of discipline and trial. This is also where the Smithian theme of the divine use of imperfections appears. There must be evils and suffering, including economic suffering, for the trial of mankind to be meaningful. However, "mitigation [of evils] is provided by the nature of happiness itself" and this is additional testimony of the goodness and wisdom of the Deity (Sumner 1816 II: 326–7).

One of the novel suggestions in the book is the providential role of political economy – arising at it did in Britain's time of need – in the economic troubles following the Napoleonic wars. For Sumner, as for Malthus, it is not the influence of political economy on government policy which is crucial, but the role of political economy in educating the public. If the labouring classes can be taught the principles of political economy, then they will be aware of the consequences of their choices and will exercise the moral restraint necessary to avoid the operation of the checks of vice and misery.

If "the fundamental cause of the greatest evils of the poor is ignorance" (Sumner 1816 II: 332) and ignorance is remediable, then "an indefinite capability of improvement opens before us" (Sumner 1816 II: 333). As he colourfully continues:

> [w]hen the good seed of religion is sown upon the soil prepared by education, to remind the growing generation that the object of the care bestowed upon them is not to raise them above their allotted condition, but to fit them for performing more adequately their duties both to God and man; then we have the prospect of general improvement, not chimerical and visionary, but approved by judgment and realized by experience.
>
> (Sumner 1816 II: 334)

This is an interesting development of Malthus' preventative check of moral restraint. Rather than the responsibility falling on the poor, the emphasis on education as a remedy shifts the responsibility to the potential providers of education – the church and the wealthy. God is certainly not responsible where he has provided attainable means of alleviating the evil: "where these advantages are attainable, shall the goodness of God be impeached?" (Sumner 1816 II: 338).

Sumner does not miss the opportunity to give us his view of how the evils of poverty are to be ameliorated: "the only true secret of assisting the poor is to make agents in bettering their own condition, and to supply them, not with a temporary stimulus, but with a permanent energy" (Sumner 1816 II: 338). Direct assistance to the poor "contains a mixture of good and evil" (Sumner 1816 II: 340) and he outlines a system of parish-based education and assistance. The scale of the problem calls for something more than individual acts of charity. Security of property rights, free mobility for the poor to take advantage of opportunities and access to capital are part of his system.

Revolution or even any levelling of existing social hierarchies are not on his agenda: "no preparatory dispensation could be more consistent with the divine goodness, than that which makes the general well-being of the members of society depend on the right performance of their respective duties" (Sumner 1816 II: 366–7).

Waterman's conclusion (1991a: 170) that Sumner "embedded the concept of moral restraint within a larger theodicy which included the beneficence of the market economy" is a fair statement of his contribution. Further, according to Waterman (2014: 107), "Sumner reassured the educated elite that political economy was not opposed to and was indeed positively supportive of Christianity". This assessment, however, is difficult to reconcile with the continuing anxiety about the theological interpretation of economic suffering in 19th-century Britain.

Malthus' Scottish disciple Thomas Chalmers

Thomas Chalmers (1780–1847) was immensely influential in Scotland and England as a preacher, Presbyterian churchman and economist.[16] After training in theology and mathematics at the University of St Andrews, he was exposed early to political economy, reading his fellow Scot Adam Smith's *Wealth of Nations* in 1796 and attending Dugald Stewart's lectures in 1800, where he seems to have first encountered Malthus' principle of population.

His study of Adam Smith, Dugald Stewart and Malthus, plus the provocation of Napoleon's 1806 Berlin decree which attempted to cut off British trade with Europe, led to a substantial work of economic theory, his *Enquiry into the Extent and Stability of National Resources* (Chalmers 1808).[17] This book was written in his leisure time in the rural Fife parish of Kilmany and argued that foreign trade was not essential to national wealth, and neither the cutting off of trade nor the raising of taxes could destroy Scotland because its most important resources "lie within the bosom of the island. There is a vigour within, that no revolutions of commerce can ever destroy, and that is entirely beyond the reach of his impotent policy" (Chalmers 1808: 298). Perhaps more important than the argument is his sophisticated three sector model of the Scottish economy, combining Smith's model of income distribution and growth with insights from Malthus, especially diminishing returns in agriculture.[18]

A serious illness then religious crisis in 1810 led him to evangelical Christianity. Chalmers re-emerged as preacher and writer, penning the article on "Christianity" for David Brewster's *Edinburgh Encyclopædia* (Chalmers 1813) and delivering a series of sermons at Glasgow's Tron church, published as *Discourses on Christian Revelation Viewed in Connection with the Modern Astronomy* in 1817 which sold over 20,000 copies within a year and went through nine editions. Then a series of *Discourses on the Application of Christianity to the Commercial and Ordinary Affairs of Life* (1821). These works established Chalmers' reputation as a scientific, natural theologian.

An appointment as minister to the new working class parish of St Johns in Glasgow in 1819 gave Chalmers the opportunity to put his economic ideas into practice. He organised a successful parish-based system of education and voluntary assistance for the poor. This experience led him to campaign against government poor relief, though he argued that the government should fund the church's efforts at alleviating poverty, especially educational efforts. The St Johns' experience was the basis of his *Christian and Civic Economy of Large Towns*, completed in three volumes from 1819 to 1826.

From 1823, Chalmers was Professor of Moral Philosophy at the University of St Andrews, then from 1828 Professor of Divinity at the University of Edinburgh. He wrote a great deal on political economy over this period with his most substantial work being *On Political Economy* (Chalmers 1832) based on his Edinburgh lectures in political economy.[19] The analytical structure was still that of his *National Resources*, and he drew extensively on *The Christian and Civic Economy of Large Towns*. Chalmers views had hardened on the necessity of moral restraint by the poor, the corrosive effect of government administered poor relief and the importance of the church diffusing the principles of political economy aided by state funding. Chalmers writes of the "intimate alliance which obtains between the economical and the moral" and "for the economic well-being of a people, their moral and religious education is the first and greatest object of national policy" and necessary to banish the "moral leprosy" of pauperism (Chalmers 1832: iv). In Chalmers' view, the clergy were best placed to deliver this education, and so:

> Each several clergyman, who labours piously and conscientiously in the home-walk of his own parish, helps forward this great consummation, till, by means of a universal blessing, peace and plenty will become alike universal throughout the families of a regenerated world.
>
> (Chalmers 1832: 458)

The stress on education picks up Adam Smith's discussion of religious education in the *Wealth of Nations* (Smith 1776). These kinds of statements were repeated many times in Chalmers' economic writings and sermons; perhaps why Malthus described Chalmers as his "ablest and best disciple" (Malthus' letter to Chalmers 21 July 1822, quoted by Winch 1996: 372) though Malthus' own statements on these matters were much more guarded.

Chalmers, like Adam Smith and David Hume, was interested in the economics of church establishment.[20] His *On the Use and Abuse of Literary and Ecclesiastical Endowments* (Chalmers 1827) made the economic case for church establishment on the basis that an established church can best inculcate morality and self-restraint which the principle of population indicates is necessary for the maintenance of a reasonable standard of living of the poor and thus avoiding ineffective and costly poor relief.

An invitation to write the first of the Bridgewater Treatises,[21] *On the Power Wisdom and Goodness of God Manifested in the Adaption of External Nature to the Moral and Intellectual Constitution of Man* (Chalmers 1833) allowed Chalmers to further develop the natural theology of his article on "Christianity" and his *Astronomical Discourses*, and connect them with his political economy.[22] In this period, he corresponded with other political economists operating in a natural theological framework, including Malthus and Whewell. I will concentrate on this work of Chalmers as it is his deepest theological engagement with political economy.

The preface to the Bridgewater Treatise lauded Butler as Chalmers' authority on natural theology, and saw Paley, Smith, Malthus and Whately as natural theological political economists. Natural theology was perfectly consistent with Chalmers' evangelicalism, as it was with JB Sumner's evangelical Anglicanism.[23] Evangelicals saw natural theology as grounded in the Scriptural doctrines of creation and providence, and emphasised the limitations of natural theology flowing from our fallen state. Chalmers, like Smith with a Calvinist background, emphasised the role of natural theology as a prompter of enquiry (for instance, Chalmers 1833 II iv article 13: 414), and that salvation in Christ could only come through Scriptural revelation (for instance, Chalmers 1833 II iv article 24: 423–5, and almost all of Chalmers 1813 was devoted to proving the trustworthiness of scripture, and he explicitly ruled out rational proofs of the doctrine of salvation in Christ).

Chalmers enlarged the subject on which he had been commissioned to write his Bridgewater Treatise to include political economy by defining "external nature" as "external to the individual mind" and by including interactions of individuals with others as interactions of "mind and mind", in addition to interactions with the material world (Chalmers 1833 Introduction article 2: 2). Chalmers writes that his focus is on the implications of the moral constitution of man (which is established by observation), and distinguishes his work of natural theology from moral philosophy (Chalmers 1833 Introduction article 4: 3–4).

The preface of the Bridgewater Treatise alludes to the large amount of existing work deploying natural science to illustrate the goodness and wisdom of God, but suggests that there is a "much larger territory . . . unexplored" and that he will take the opportunity of "tracing the marks of a divine intelligence in the mechanism of human society, and in the framework of the social and economical systems" in which men "follow the impulses of those affections which God has bestowed on them" (Chalmers 1833 Preface p. xl). Man is a "microcosm of the divine art" (Chalmers 1833 Introduction article 11: 12).

Before considering the market economy, he offered an account of private property as grounded in human nature, which was the product of creation. The proof was in observing children:

> [t]he desires or notions of property, and even the principles by which it is limited, spring up in the breasts of children, without the slightest apprehension, on their part, of its vast importance in the social economy of the world. It is the provision, not of man, but of God.
>
> (Chalmers 1833 I vi article 8: 180)

In children, we see both the claim of long and undisputed possession and the claim that arises from their own labour, and the recognition of these claims by their playmates (Chalmers 1833 I vi article 11: 183). If this is true of private property, the only role of government is as an arbiter of disputed property rights, and government should seek to strengthen rather than overturn these two sources of claim to property (Chalmers 1833 I iv article 14: 187).

Chalmers offered a providentialist reading of Smith's idea of unintended beneficial outcomes in a market economy:

> The greatest economic good is rendered to the community . . . by the spontaneous play and busy competition of many thousand wills, each bent on the prosecution of his own selfishness, than by the anxious superintendence of a government, vainly attempting to medicate the fancied imperfections of nature.
>
> (Chalmers 1833 I vii article 15: 238)

As with Smith, this conclusion assumes properly functioning institutions, such as property rights, and a reasonable degree of honesty and trust.

Chalmers concludes about this economic provision:

> Such a result, which at the same time not a single agent in this vast and complicated system of trade contemplates or cares for, each caring only for himself – strongly bespeaks a higher Agent, by whose transcendental wisdom it is, that all is made to conspire so harmoniously, and to terminate so beneficially.
>
> (Chalmers 1833 I vii article 15: 238–9)

Furthermore:

> The whole science of political economy is full of these exquisite adaptions to the wants and comforts of human life, which bespeak the skill of a master-hand, in the adjustment of its laws, and the working of its profoundly constructed mechanism.
>
> (Chalmers 1833 I vii article 16: 240)

Also, "When we look at the effect . . . of a thousand reciprocities of mutual interest in the world – we see in this the benevolence and comprehensive wisdom of God" (Chalmers 1833 I vii article 15: 240).

Interestingly, Chalmers tried to construct an appropriately pious Adam Smith to go with the Smithian natural theology. It was well known that Smith removed a passage about the atonement from the later editions of his *Theory of Moral Sentiments*.[24] Chalmers takes it upon himself to quote the atonement passage (Chalmers 1833 II iv articles 30–31: 431–2) and to put the blame for removal on David Hume:

> [o]ne fears lest, under contagion of a near and withering intimacy with him [Hume], his [Smith's] spirit may have imbibed of the kindred poison; and he at length have [sic] become ashamed of the homage that he once had rendered to the worth and importance of Christianity.
>
> (Chalmers 1833 II iv article 32: 433)

These statements are fanciful, but Chalmers must have felt he needed a pious Smith to support his own natural theological reading of Smith's work. Chalmers added that Smith's passage "notwithstanding remains one of the finest examples of the way in which Nature bears on Christian theology" (Chalmers 1833 II iv article 32: 433).

Chalmers deployed his natural theological political economy in support of two particular policies (Chalmers 1833 I vii: 214–24). He strongly opposed the tithe system which provided for the English clergy from the produce of landowners. The issue is not the provision for clergy but the way it is achieved, for the tithe system violates landowners' property rights, and he argued the tithe should be commuted to a general tax. Chalmers' opposition to the English Poor Laws is even stronger. They too violate property rights, but more importantly are undermined by the principle of population and morally damaged the poor. The unnaturalness and hence wrongness of Poor Laws, Chalmers claims, is evident even to paupers themselves.

Chalmers was completely convinced of the principle of population from the time he first encountered it around 1800, and the principle was an essential component of Chalmers' attacks on the government administered poor relief.

> However obnoxious the modern doctrine of population, as expounded by Mr Malthus, may have been, and still is, to weak and limited sentimentalists, it is the truth which of all others sheds the greatest brightness over the earthly prospects of humanity – and this in spite of the hideous, yet sustained, outcry which has risen against it. This is a pure case of the adaption between the external nature of the world in which we live, and the moral nature of man.
>
> (Chalmers 1833 I vii article 22: 249)

It is only when population is of "restrained and regulated numbers" that society can achieve "blissful consummation in the virtue of the people; carried into sure and lasting effect by the laws of political economy", which is an "alliance between the moral and physical" (Chalmers 1833 I vii article 22: 250).

Chalmers also offers a natural theological defence of free trade and free capital movements. While he does not go back on the argument of *National Resources* that free international trade is not essential to wealth, he argues in the Bridgewater Treatise that it is nevertheless natural and beneficial. In relation to saving, prices and capital movements he states, "capital ever suits itself . . . so as to leave uncalled for any economic regulation by the wisdom of man; and that precisely because of a previous moral and mental regulation by the wisdom of God" (Chalmers 1833 I vii article 20: 247).

In general, Chalmers sees economic education of the public rather than government policy as the most powerful influence on outcomes.[25] Foolish policy can frustrate improvement, but good policy is not the driver of improvement. This is a theme repeated constantly in his economic writings, and the emphasis on the education of the public sits uneasily with contemporary economists. We tend to think of change coming from economic research which is then embodied in policy advice, implemented by a well-informed rational government (provided "special interests" can be resisted) using its powers to tax, spend and coerce individuals. This emphasis of Chalmers and other natural theological political economists including Smith, Malthus and Whately, is both more respectful of individuals and more democratic than our reflex of getting the government to do something about problems. Theologically, the difference arises because Chalmers emphasises God's role in creating human nature, and locates God's providence in the market interactions, rather than in government activity.

Now to theodicy. Given Chalmers' reliance on the principle of population and his awareness of theological controversy it had aroused, he devotes considerable space in the Bridgewater Treatise to defending the consistency of the principle of population with God's power and goodness. There is something of Malthus' theodicy of the 1798 *Essay*, as well as something of Butler's and Paley's state of trial theodicy in his description of humanity as being in a "state of pupilage and probation" (Chalmers 1833 I viii article 5: 258) and his comment that part of God's purpose is to "prepare the disciples of a probationary state for their final destinations" (Chalmers 1833 I viii article 6: 259).

His main theological defence of the principle of population is that natural theologians take too narrow a view of the goodness of God, and that goodness includes justice:

> If apart from the equities of a moral government, we look to God in no other light than mere tasteful and sentimental religionists do, as but a benign and indulgent Father whose sole delight is the happiness of his family – there are certain stubborn anomalies which stand in the way of this frail imagination, and would render the whole subject hopeless and [an] utterly intractable mystery.

> (Chalmers 1833 I x article 3: 287–8)

He reinforces this by asking whether we would consider an earthly Father good who did not instruct and discipline his children.

Chalmers resists taking refuge, as some other natural theological political economists including Smith and Paley had done, "in the imagination of a future state – where it is assumed that all the disorders of the present scene are to be repaired" (Chalmers 1833 I x article 5: 288). This seems to be related to his desire to emphasise the continuity between this world and the next, consistent with his continued attachment to the theodicy of Malthus' 1798 *Essay*. The next world is described later in the chapter as unfinished business from this world (Chalmers 1833 I x articles 13–18: 300–8).

An idea he shares with JB Sumner is the role of sound political economy in mitigating evil. "Those evils which vex and agitate man, emanate, in the great amount of them, from the fountain of his own heart; and . . . a distempered political economy" (Chalmers 1833 I x article 8: 294). His defence of the principle of population concludes with a plea not to judge the goodness of God on the actual miseries of the world, but on the means God has provided to make a virtuous species happy.

Overall, his attempt to reconcile economic suffering with the goodness and power of God is lengthy, spirited, but not in my view entirely successful. Especially his attempt to redefine goodness. If the more usual and narrower moral understanding of goodness is retained, then Chalmers merely is transferring some of the blame for economic suffering from God to the poor who fail to exercise moral restraint,[26] as well as to those with a responsibility to diffuse the principles of political economy among the public.

These economic views remain fairly constant in his later writings, including an article "The Political Economy of the Bible" published near the end of his life (Chalmers 1844). He continued to see economics and theology as separate but mutually supporting: "They who would divorce Theology from Science, or Science from Theology, are, in effect if not intention, the enemies of both" (Chalmers 1844: 3). The article then continues with a lengthy defence of the principle of population. He maintains his providential interpretation of markets. For instance:

[l]et us not be surprised, that while man seeks after one object, and by his efforts succeeds in obtaining it – such is the constitution of things, that by these very efforts another and wholly distinct object is secured, of which he may be altogether unseeing, and which therefore he does not seek after. This is altogether of a piece with the order of nature, and with the economy of God's providential administration in the world.

(Chalmers 1844: 28)

Furthermore:

Political Economy is full of such examples – insomuch, that a Natural Theology, of which Archbishop Whately has given some specimens, might be founded on the phenomena, and the laws which this science places before us.

(Chalmers 1844: 28)

And further:

> Thus it has been found that the maximum of a nation's commercial prosperity is best realized by each individual being left to the busy and sharp-sighted, though, in reference to the general result, short-sighted prosecution of his own interests – so that, while his single view is the advancement of his own fortune, he, without any express design on his part, along with thousands of others who are similarly situated, contributes each his share towards the best economic condition of the country in which he lives.
>
> (Chalmers 1844: 29)

He concludes that:

> [i]n the philosophy of free trade, the essence of which consists in leaving this mechanism to its own spontaneous evolutions, a striking testimony to the superior intelligence of Him who is the author both of human nature and of human society.
>
> (Chalmers 1844: 29)

As with his earlier writings on political economy, he struggles to offer an adequate theodicy.

Conclusion

This chapter has added to the number of important political economists who operated within a natural theological framework. However, neither Malthus nor JB Sumner nor Chalmers were any more successful than their predecessors in dealing with economic suffering, and the problem remained for the political economists who followed them.

Notes

1 Veitch's view is from his memoir in Stewart's *Collected Works volume* X 1858. Toynbee's remark is from his *Lectures on the Industrial Revolution* 1882, quoted by Winch (1996 p. 6). Southey's disparagement of Malthus is in an 1803 letter to John Rickman, quoted by Winch (1996 p. 288). Malthus view of Sumner is quoted from Waterman (1991a p. 150). His description of Chalmers is recorded in a letter of 21 July 1822, quoted by Winch (1996 p. 372)
2 Standard histories of economic thought tend to be theologically blind, and the attention to figures is proportioned to 20th-century theoretical concerns rather than to the significance of figures in their time. We do not have to go as far as Waterman (1991a: 14): "Christian Political Economy was the mainstream of Anglo-Scottish social theory in the early 19th century, and Philosophic Rationalism was a backwater" to recognise that the standard accounts are in need of correction. Comparing the Google N-grams for Ricardo with those of Malthus and natural theological political economists is instructive (see Appendix).
3 Dugald Stewart's life is covered by MacIntyre (2003) and Phillipson (2008).

4 The Edinburgh political economy lectures were revised by Stewart after his retirement with clear intention to publish, but they did not appear until 1855 in conjunction with Stewart's *Collected Works* edited by William Hamilton in 1855. Unfortunately, his revisions were lost and the published text is based on the 1809 lectures, though the editor also provides Stewart's plan of the original 1800–1 lectures. They are discussed by Corsi (1987), Rashid (1985, 1987) and Winch (1983, 1996).

5 Norman (1976 ch. 2) discusses the reasons for the switch in Anglican social thinking from suspicion towards education for the poor as unnecessary and possibly troublesome, to education for the poor becoming a major concern in the early 19th century.

6 Malthus biography is covered by Otter (1836), Bonar (1885), James (1979), Pullen (1987a, 1987b, 2004a) and Cremaschi (2014). For Malthus library, see Gray (1983). For his economics, see Winch (1987, 1993, 1996), Waterman (1991a, 1998), Pullen (1981, 1998) and Groenewegen (1999).

7 If the animating force of the Christian political economy of Malthus, Sumner, Chalmers and others considered by Waterman (1991a) was simply anti-Jacobinism, then his explanation for the decline of Christian political economy in the 1830s that the need for such polemic no longer existed would be difficult to dispute. However, if the larger and more longstanding concerns of British scientific natural theology described in Chapter 2 were important to these writers, then Waterman's explanation loses much of its force. Chapters 3 and 4 suggested the interest in economic theodicy existed before the Jacobinism Malthus was confronting, and Chapters 6 and 7 will suggest it lasted past the mid-1830s.

8 Malthus' theodicy is discussed by Pullen (1981), Le Mahieu (1979), Harvey-Phillips (1984), Rashid (1984) and Waterman (1991a). Pullen's view (1981: 39) is that that "his principle of population cannot be properly understood if it is excised from its theological context". This has several components according to Pullen (1981: 40–4): (1) reconciliation of the principle of population with evil and divine benevolence; (2) and (3) rejection of the view that life was a trial in favour of life as an opportunity for growth of mind; (4) reinterpretation of divine omnipotence; (5) divine plan for replenishment of earth; (6) recognition of the pleasures of this world; (7) reinterpretation of original sin as state of torpor; and (8) commitment to conditionalism/annihilationism (in other words that immortality is conferred as a benefit of salvation, so that the souls of the unsaved perish with their bodies at death). Waterman (1991a: 59) regards the theological chapters as "an essential part of Malthus's argument and may not be detached as irrelevant appendices".

9 Malthus' theodicy follows Irenaeus' "soul making" theodicy rather than Augustine's in John Hick's (1977) classification of Christian theodicies. In the years since Hick's attempt at rehabilitation, conditionalism and soul making theodicies have experienced a revival in theological circles, even in evangelical circles. It seems to me that theologians interested in economics are particularly attracted to these views, but further study would be needed to determine whether this is a robust pattern and what the reasons are. My guess would be that these views about evil and the eschaton are attractive because they make our present life of more enduring significance.

10 This letter is quoted in Rashid (1984).

11 The 1798 letter which identifies Malthus' friends is reproduced in Malthus 2004 vol I: 73–4. The comments reported by ED Clarke include that the two chapters "do not seem a necessary appendage" and "the public will admit no apology for sending forth arguments on doctrinal points which have not been digested" and "A neat casual reader would swear he is a materialist . . . [and] might also think he admitted the doctrine of annihilation – and yet I firmly believe he has no intention to excite such an opinion". If caution was the reason Malthus omitted the chapters, this brings to mind Smith's earlier omission of theological material from later editions of his work. In both cases, abandoning the views omitted is not the only explanation available, nor a very plausible explanation.

12 The allusions to various feasts prepared by God for his people and especially to Jesus' parable of the wedding feast in Mt 22 and Lk 14, are obvious, but seem to have escaped attention in the recent literature on Malthus. One of the points of the parable is the choice of the guests about whether to respond to the invitation to the feast, which may be linked to the introduction of moral restraint as a check on population in the 1803 second edition, discussed later in this chapter.

13 Waterman (1991a: 110–2) argues that Malthus' theodicy was inconsistent with the Articles of Religion. In particular, he argues that Malthus' statement: "Evil exists in the world, not to create despair, but activity. We are not patiently to submit to it, but to exert ourselves to avoid it" (Malthus 1798: 217) represents a denial or at least an avoidance of salvation in Christ. Malthus however is not offering a soteriology but a theodicy. Waterman also argues that Malthus denies divine omnipotence in that God needs time to achieve his purposes and that God appears to make mistakes "some beings which come out of the creative process . . . misshapen" (Malthus 1798: 215). This seems to me similar to Adam Smith's idea of human failings serving God's purposes, which has ample scriptural warrant. I cannot see that there is any basis for Waterman's conclusion that Malthus theodicy violates Articles IV and VIII on the resurrection, Article II on the incarnation, Articles XV XXI and IX on salvation in Christ, and Article I on Divine omnipotence. As Waterman notes, Malthus' theodicy was not at the time attacked as heretical, even though the *Essay* was at the centre of fierce controversy. The subsequently discovered letters and sermons (Malthus 2004) where he outlines a conventional soteriology are further evidence that this is not what is being offered in the *Essay*. As well as being inconsistent with the Articles of Religion, Waterman believes Malthus' theodicy to be confused, for instance "the cogency of the theological portions of the first Essay is weakened by self-contradiction and confusion" (Waterman 1991a: 107) and "Malthus was obsessed with the heuristic power and efficiency of natural theology" and so "betrayed into a non-solution of the problem of evil" (Waterman 1991a: 108). However, the alleged confusions seem to be inconsistencies with Waterman's interpretations of certain other doctrines, which are not the only interpretations of these doctrines within mainstream Christian theology through the centuries.

14 JB Sumner is discussed at length by Waterman (1991a). Biography is in Scotland (1995, 2004).

15 In my view, Waterman (1991a) overstates the advance Sumner made on Malthus' theodicy. For instance, he neglects the discussion of creation in the first chapter of Sumner's work, where he restates the view of Malthus that in the Garden of Eden development of mind was still needed (Sumner 1816: 3ff).

16 Chalmers' life is detailed in Hanna (1852), Cheyne (1985) and Brown (1982, 2004). His economics is discussed by O'Brien (1987), Waterman (1991a, 1991b), Hilton (1985, 2006), Winch (1996), Mochrie (2008) and Dixon and Wilson (2010). Hilton (1985: 55) writes of Chalmers "his influence was enormous – and not just in Scotland" and quotes eminent contemporaries who had the same view.

17 Waterman (1991b) discusses the *Enquiry into the Extent and Stability of National Resources* and reconstructs Chalmers' model with the aid of mathematics. According to Waterman (1991a: 228), it is a work of "originality and sustained analytical brilliance".

18 O'Brien (1987) suggests that Chalmers preceded Malthus with a theory of effective demand, though this is disputed by Waterman (1991b). My reading of Chalmers (1808) is that he raised the possibility of demand shortfalls, but lacking a theory of demand he operated with an assumption of full employment. It is significant that later he devotes a chapter of his book on political economy to a vigorous denial of the possibility of general gluts (Chalmers 1832 ch. 5: 37ff).

19 Waterman (1991a) notes these Edinburgh lectures were the first lectures to be offered under the label of political economy in Scotland (Stewart's being moral philosophy), and only narrowly missed being the first lectures in political economy offered in a British University. Chalmers lectured on political economy to divinity students,

believing they should be acquainted with the subject, and maintained this view throughout his life (see, for instance, Chalmers 1846).

20 Hume (1759) argued for church establishment, but Smith (1776 Book V i g: 788–814) was concerned about the tendencies of monopoly religion in alliance with the state to corruption and violence, and argued that free competition between religious groups would be led to better outcomes. Smith and Chalmers particularly stressed the educational role of the churches. Smith's and Chalmers' writings on religious education and the wisdom of state financing are discussed in the earlier work of Anderson (1988) and Leathers and Raines (1999). The issues are similar to church involvement in state-funded social services (Oslington 2015b).

21 The Bridgewater Treatises "On the Power, Wisdom and Goodness of God, as manifested in Creation" were commissioned in the 1830s to place the latest science in a natural theological framework – see Brooke (1991a) and Topham (1992, 1998).

22 Waterman (1991a) argues that Chalmers' political economy was largely independent of his theology, because his political economy developed little in his view from his 1808 *National Resources*. This may be true of his core model, but the meaning and impact of his political economy depended on its theological framing. Without being connected to theology, it is difficult to see how his political economy could have made such an impact on early 19th-century Britain. Waterman does not have a high view of Chalmers as theologian and economist: "the Bridgewater Treatise, like Chalmers writing in political economy, is crassly oblivious of the subtler difficulties of the subject and of the attempts of his predecessors and contemporaries to deal with them" (Waterman 1991a: 250).

23 Topham (1999) discusses evangelical natural theologies.

24 The passage and circumstances of its removal are discussed at length in Smith (1759 appendix II: 383–401). JB Sumner (1816 vol II: 275) makes similar comments to Chalmers on Smith's removal of the atonement passage. Smith's atonement passage is discussed in Chapter 4.

25 This emphasis on education is also highlighted in a recent article by Dixon and Wilson "In Thomas Chalmers's work the moral and the economic are integrated to form the basis of what he saw as a viable social order. The moral was essential to the proper implementation of political economy while, also, participation in a free market was the ground for the formation of moral conduct" (Dixon and Wilson 2010: 723). This develops Anthony Waterman's suggestion that "Chalmers was a moral paternalist but an economic individualist" (Waterman 1991a: 222).

26 Waterman (1991a: 246–51) considers Chalmers' theodicy inadequate, following criticisms of Chalmers' theology from his own Anglican standpoint. He wrote of "serious weakness in Chalmers' theology: his failure to understand the nature of the church. Second, his insistence on economic benefits of moral and religious habits undermines the distinction between wealth and virtue so important to ethical discourse at that time. And thirdly, his willingness to see the hand of God in day-to-day economic events" (Waterman 1991a: 240).

6   Progress and tension
Richard Whately and William Whewell[1]

Richard Whately made a rare move straight from a Chair of Political Economy to an Anglican Archbishop's palace. As Archbishop of Dublin, he took a great interest in the faraway colony of New South Wales, threw a boomerang for the amusement of guests and composed a much-anthologised poem There is a Place in Distant Seas *about the colony.*

Whewell described science as a "Hymn in honour of the Creator . . . which is filled into a richer and deeper harmony by the greatest philosophers of these later days, and will roll on hereafter as a perpetual song in the temple of science".

Whewell's natural theological Bridgewater Treatise of 1833 was quoted on the title page of Darwin's Origin of Species: *"But with regard to the material world, we can at least go so far as this – we can perceive that events are brought about not by insulated interpositions of Divine power, exerted in each particular case, but by the establishment of general laws".*

Charles Lyell said of Whewell that "a more wonderful variety and amount of knowledge in almost every department of human inquiry was perhaps never in the same interval of time accumulated by any man", though Sydney Smith remarked "Science is his forte, omniscience is his foible".[2]

Introduction

We now move from Malthus and other figures such as Chalmers of enormous popular impact in early 19th-century Britain to the economists who established the study of political economy in the English universities.

The first Professorship of Political Economy in an English University was the Drummond Chair at Oxford, established in 1825 by Henry Drummond (1786–1860), the English banker, politician and religious eccentric. At Cambridge, George Pryme was Professor of Political Economy from 1828. The other early English chairs were at University College London where JR M'Culloch was Professor of Political Economy from 1826, and Kings College London, where Richard Jones was Professor of Political Economy briefly from 1833. Malthus taught political economy at the East India College, Haileybury. Dugald Stewart's

Edinburgh lectures from 1800 were as Professor of Moral Philosophy, as were Thomas Chalmers' lectures at St Andrews from 1823.[3] The work of Malthus' friend David Ricardo, who never held a university position, was in the background of some of these contributions.[4]

Political economy at Oxford: Nassau Senior and responses by Richard Whately and JH Newman

At Oxford, there was considerable suspicion of political economy, with one influential Oxonian Sydney Smith suggesting that "A set of lectures on political economy would be discouraged in Oxford, probably despised, probably not permitted" (Mallet 1927: 215). Even the founder of the Chair, Henry Drummond, "was anxious to have it understood that he relied on the University to keep the study in its proper place" (Mallet 1927: 215).

Nassau Senior's inaugural lecture

The first Drummond Professor at Oxford was Nassau Senior from 1826–29, who was close to Richard Whately and the Oriel logicians.[5] His inaugural lecture (Senior 1827) is a key moment in the development of political economy as a discipline. Senior was less of a natural theologian than many of the others who built political economy as a discipline, but his work was read in this context. I will examine his inaugural lecture through the lens of JH Newman's commentary on it in *Idea of a University* (Newman 1873)[6] and the review of the lecture by his teacher Richard Whately (1828).

Senior began by predicting that political economy will soon "rank among the first of the moral sciences in interest and in utility" (Senior 1827: 1),[7] and proceeded to define it as the science of wealth which is divided into "theoretic and practical" branches (Senior 1827: 7). The theoretic branch:

> [r]ests on a very few general propositions, which are the result of observation, or consciousness, and which almost every man, as soon as he hears them, admits, as familiar to his thoughts, or at least, as included in his previous knowledge.
>
> (Senior 1827: 7)

These propositions are listed later in the lecture and are (1) A definition of wealth as "those things . . . which are transferable; which are limited in quantity; and which, directly or indirectly produce pleasure or prevent pain"; (2) "That every person is desirous to obtain, with as little sacrifice as possible, as much as possible of the articles of wealth"; (3) "That the powers of labour . . . may be indefinitely increased by using their products as the means of further production"; (4) "That, agricultural skill remaining the same, additional labour employed on the land within a given district, produces a less than proportional return"; and (5) "That the population of a given district is limited only by moral or physical evil, or by deficiency in the means of obtaining those articles of wealth" (Senior 1827: 35–6).

He adds that the second proposition "is a matter of consciousness; the others are matters of observation" (Senior 1827: 36).

A striking feature of Senior's lecture is his assessment of certainty and universality which attaches to political economy:

> I hope in the course of these lectures to prove the truth of my statement, that the theoretic branch of the science, that which treats the nature, production and distribution of wealth – is capable of all the certainty that can belong to any science, not founded exclusively on definitions; and I hope also, to show that many conclusions, and those of the highest importance, in the practical branch, rest so immediately on the conclusions of the theoretic branch as to possess equal certainty and universality.
>
> (Senior 1827: 11)

Newman's critique of Senior

Newman's views on political economy were presented to the public in his own inaugural lectures as Rector of the Catholic University of Ireland in 1852, later published as the *Idea of a University* (Newman 1873).[8]

Within the lectures, the context of Newman's discussion of political economy was a larger argument about how the sciences, including theology, are part of a circle of knowledge which should be reflected in the structure of a university. This is explained at the beginning of the lecture in which he discusses political economy:

> In order to have possession of truth at all we must have the whole truth; and no one science, no two sciences, no one family of sciences, nay, not even all secular science, is the whole truth; revealed truth enters to a very great extent into the province of science, philosophy, and literature, and to put it to one side, in compliment to secular science, is simply, under colour of a compliment, to do science great damage.
>
> (Newman 1873: 72–3)

The image of the circle of knowledge is used frequently by Newman to emphasise the complementarity between different pieces of knowledge – how they all fit together into something greater.

Newman begins his specific comments on political economy by affirming that there is nothing wrong in principle with a science of wealth, describing it as "a science simply lawful and useful, for it is no sin to make money" Newman (1873: 83). He agrees with Senior's description of political economy as a moral science and accepts Senior's proposed method of logical deduction from a set of premises. Newman then traces its moral character to Senior's second premise: that every person desires as much wealth as possible with as little sacrifice as possible. While it is true that this premise only states that wealth is sought rather than ought to be sought, the context indicates that wealth is evaluated positively. This positive evaluation of wealth seeking is one of the reasons Senior considers political economy to be a moral science, and Senior's comments elsewhere in the lecture about wealth leading to virtue and true religion will be considered later. If it is accepted that the wealth seeking premise is given moral significance by Senior, the crucial issue then is its ethical authority. Newman argues that Senior's attribution of the premise to introspection gives it no ethical authority, neither does Senior's suggestion that the premise is consistent with observation, and no other argument is offered for its ethical force. Newman also considers Senior's reliance on introspection as a source of moral premises defective as it leaves no room for theological restraints and balances on the moral content of political economy.[9] Thus Senior's claim for a moral character for political economy on the grounds of morally authoritative premises obtained through introspection is problematic.

As well as having moral premises, Senior claimed a moral quality for political economy on the grounds that it assists the pursuit of wealth, and that wealth is a source of moral improvement and promoter of religion. This draws sharp criticism from Newman.[10] The passage is worth quoting in full:

> He [Senior] says the "endeavour to accumulate . . . is, to the mass of mankind, the great source", not merely a source, but the great source, and of what? of social and economic progress? – such an answer would have been more within the limits of his art, – no, but . . . "of great moral improvement".
>
> (Newman 1873: 88)

And he continues:

> But it is not enough that morals and happiness are made to depend on gain and accumulation; the practice of Religion is ascribed to these causes also, and in the following way. Wealth depends on the pursuit of wealth; education depends on wealth; knowledge depends on education; and Religion depends on knowledge; therefore Religion depends on the pursuit of wealth.

Newman's point is that Senior's claim for a moral quality for political economy as a promoter of wealth goes beyond the proper bounds of political economy, straying into the domains of ethics and theology. Political economy lacks appropriate tools for dealing with such issues and goes beyond its proper domain in asserting that moral benefits flow from the practice of political economy.

There are some interesting remarks by Newman about the false humility of political economy. Senior pleads that the pursuit of wealth (and the science of political economy which studies it) is "one of the humblest of human occupations, far inferior to the pursuit of virtue" Senior (1827: 11–12). Newman (1873: 86–7) objects that deciding its own place among the sciences is something political economy cannot do, and pretending it can is dangerous. Its proper scope can only be determined in conjunction with other disciplines, like philosophy and theology, which have tools appropriate to such questions.

The common threads which run though all of Newman's particular criticisms of political economy are false self-sufficiency and a tendency to go beyond its proper bounds. His critique is summarised with characteristic eloquence towards the end of his discussion of political economy:

> There is reason and truth in the "leading ideas", as they are called and "large views" of scientific men; I only say that though they speak the truth, they do not speak the whole truth; that they speak a narrow truth and think it is a broad truth; that their deductions must be compared with other truths, which are acknowledged to be truths, in order to verify, complete and correct them. They say what is true . . . true, but not the measure of all things; true, but if thus inordinately, extravagantly, ruinously carried out, in spite of other sciences, in spite of Theology, sure to become but a great bubble and burst.
>
> (Newman 1873: 89)

Before assessing Newman's critique, some possible misunderstandings of his position must be dealt with. It is important to recognise that Newman's criticisms do not come from ignorance of political economy or lack of appreciation of its value as a science. Some previous writers (e.g. Checkland 1951) who discuss Newman's influence on the formation of political economy dismiss him this way, wrongly associating him with the extreme anti-scientific views of some other leaders of the Oxford movement.

There is evidence of Newman's familiarity with political economy. His library contained works by Malthus, Ricardo, Senior and Whately. All these works seem to have been acquired before his remarks on Senior's lecture, but afterwards his reading in the subject seems to have been less. Scattered through Newman's letters are positive comments about the value of economic analysis, together with a healthy reluctance to pronounce judgment on technical issues beyond his competence.[11]

Another possible misunderstanding of Newman's criticisms of political economy's self-sufficiency and tendency to go beyond proper bounds, would be that he saw no distinction between political economy and theology. Some of his contemporaries in the church were suspicious of political economy and wanted it, if carried on at all, to be carried on as a branch of moral philosophy or theology. Newman clearly rejects this position, assigning it a place alongside the more established sciences and describing political economy as "a science simply lawful and useful" (Newman 1873: 83). Newman stresses that theology as well as political economy must respect its proper bounds:

> The enemies of Catholicism ought to be the last to deny this [the possibility of sciences exceeding their proper bounds] – for they have never been blind to a like usurpation, as they have called it on the part of the theologians; those who accuse us of wishing, in accordance with Scripture language, to make the sun go round the earth, are not the men to deny that a science which exceeds its limits falls into error.
>
> (Newman 1873: 74)

Later in the *Apologia* he remarks that in spite of its divine origin, "the Bible does not answer a purpose for which it was never intended" (Newman 1864: 220).[12] There is no suggestion in any of his writings that the content of economic science can be derived from theology or that theology makes scientific investigation redundant.

Having cleared up some possible misunderstandings of Newman's position, its substance can now be assessed. The first issue is the validity of theological knowledge alongside economic knowledge. Unlike many of his fellow churchmen, Newman was not content merely to appeal to revelation as the justification of religious knowledge, and felt it important to clarify the structure and grounds of both religious and scientific knowledge. In *Idea of a University* we get a few sketches of an argument that was later to be presented more fully in his *An Essay in Aid of a Grammar of Assent* (Newman 1870).

Newman's argument begins from the observation that little of what we know comes from logical deduction from a set of premises, because sure premises are difficult to find. Instead, it typically comes through an accumulation of probabilities, which point to truth, to which we then assent. Discerning truth from the probabilistic evidence is a skill that Newman calls the illative sense, which in Newman's philosophy is related to the Aristotelian notion of *phronesis* or judgment. Granting assent to a discerned truth is an act of the will, and assent is individual and has a moral dimension. While Newman's main purpose in *An Essay in Aid of a Grammar of Assent* was to clarify and justify religious belief, he showed through a number of examples that the same process of accumulating probabilistic evidence leading to assent applies in other areas, including the sciences. For instance, to give his most famous example, we believe that Great Britain is an island, without having circumnavigated it, or even having met people who have, and certainly without it having been proved from a set of indubitable premises. We see maps showing Great Britain as an island and accept this as a basis for action even though the evidence is imperfect. Similarly, for theological knowledge, there is an accumulation of imperfect evidence (including conscience, observation of the nature of the world and humanity, the testimony of others) for accepting theological truths. If both scientific and religious knowledge consists of assents given to truth recognised through evidence that can never be perfect, then the sciences cannot claim that their knowledge rests on superior foundations to theology.

If all knowledge is one, and assents have the same structure, this does not imply that the method of accumulating the probabilistic evidence that precedes assent is the same in all areas. Different types of judgment are needed for different types of evidence; a scientist has a well-developed illative sense in his or her field. Deciding appropriate methods for physics was a task for physicists, and they may differ from the methods used in other sciences. Newman refrained from commenting on appropriate methods for accumulating evidence that lead assent in political economy, leaving this for Senior and his fellow political economists to resolve.

Having now presented Newman's argument for the validity of theological knowledge, the second issue is the relevance of theology to political economy.

Here Newman is not entirely clear. At some points he appears to be suggesting that the role of theology is to supply moral premises from which the political economist can then reason. A position more consistent with his general views would be that theology, along with other disciplines like moral philosophy which have appropriate tools, produce evidence and argument about the moral principles which guide the political economist and others. Moral principles guide all aspects of the practice of political economy rather than merely supplying moral premises for deductive arguments. Part of the inconsistency in Newman's position can be explained by tensions between his acceptance, for the sake of argument, of Senior's method of deduction from certain premises to certain economic conclusions, and Newman's own inductive view of science.[13] It must nevertheless be acknowledged that Newman is not completely clear and consistent about how theology actually affects the practice of political economy.

To summarise Newman's model of the relationship between political economy and theology:

1   All knowledge is one, and economic truth cannot contradict theological truth.
2   Economic knowledge and theological knowledge are both well grounded.
3   Different branches of knowledge are distinct and have their own tasks. The task of economics is to understand how the economy operates, while the task of theology is to supply an ethic for the political economists, and to balance and ethically guide the work of political economists.
4   While distinct, the different branches of knowledge form a circle and depend on each other. Economics is of limited use without ethics and theology.

Whately's response to Senior

In view of the importance of Richard Whately's writings on the relationship between political economy and theology, it is worth comparing his response with Newman's. As emphasised by Waterman (1991a, 1994), Whately's writings on political economy emerged in a particular polemical context – he was seeking to show (against widespread opinion in the church) that political economy was not in conflict with theology and (against the utilitarians) that political economy was unable to generate policy conclusions without some additional ethical input.

Whately's views are contained in his review of Senior's lectures (Whately 1828) and also his Drummond Lectures (Whately 1832), to be considered in more detail later in this chapter. The relevant aspects of Whately's model of the relationship between political economy and theology (as summarised by Waterman 1994: 57–8) are:

1   Scientific or secular knowledge is sharply distinct from theological or sacred knowledge.
2   Scientific knowledge comes by experience: that is to say, through the interpreting of observational data by theory.

3   Theological knowledge comes by faith: that is to say, by the spiritual discernment of the strictly religious truths contained in revelation and which are, and must be, beyond the reach of unassisted reason.
4   Reason may make use of scientific knowledge in corroborating religious knowledge. This is natural theology.
5   Reason cannot be at variance with faith because the latter generates knowledge where the former cannot operate.
6   Political economy is the scientific study of the nature, production and distribution of wealth.
7   Because the science of political economy abstracts from ethical aspects of its subject matter, political economy can provide guidance only with respect to the means of obtaining certain social ends, and none at all about whether those ends ought to be pursued.

It is not surprising, given Newman and Whately's close intellectual and personal links in the years leading up to Senior's lecture, that they share many views on the relationship between political economy and theology. Both men held the unusual view for churchmen of their time that political economy was valuable and distinct from theology. Both believed that political economy and theology could not contradict each other. Both also rejected the view that political economy could generate its own ethic. There are, however, important differences between Newman's and Whately's models of the relationship between political economy and theology. While Whately's position was powerful in its polemical context, Newman offers something more general (in the sense of being appropriate beyond the original polemical context) and better grounded.

Whately's polemical task of making political economy "safe" for the church (Waterman 1991a,1994) was well served by his sharp epistemological dualism expressed in points 1 to 5 above, but this dualism has dangers in other contexts. Political economists can be discouraged by this supposed sharp epistemological separation from bringing scientific and ethical/theological considerations together in ways that are fruitful. The enduring philosophical necessity of such a sharp epistemological dualism was not demonstrated by Whately. By contrast, Newman distinguishes political economy from theology while maintaining that all knowledge is attained in essentially the same way and has the same epistemological status. The philosophical arguments supporting his position were suggested in *Idea of a University* and more fully developed in the *Grammar of Assent*. With no epistemological gulf to bridge, economics and theology and ethics can be more readily brought together in relation to practical problems by economists, theologians and others. Newman's philosophy provides grounds for questioning the marginalisation of theology in mainstream writing on economic issues since the mid-19th century.

Related to Whately's epistemological dualism is his identification of theological knowledge with normative questions and exclusion of theology from what we would now call positive economics. The sharpness of Whately's distinction is clear from points 6 and 7 of Waterman's summary above. For Newman, theology has a broader role in guiding the practice of economics, in providing a framework in which political economy operates and offering critical perspectives on the content of political economy. None is purely normative. It must be acknowledged that Newman's discussion of the role of theology is less precise than Whately's, and questions remain about how exactly theology influences the practice of economics.

Richard Whately

Richard Whately (1787–1863) followed his pupil Nassau Senior as the second Drummond Professor of Political Economy at Oxford.[14] Whately accepted the Chair in 1829 because of recognition of the growing importance of political economy and its potential usefulness in Christian apologetic. To an unnamed correspondent he wrote:

> Religious truth . . . appears to me to be intimately connected at this time especially with the subject in question [political economy]. For it seems to me that before long, political economists of some sort must govern the world . . . Now the anti-Christians are striving very hard to have this science to themselves, and to interweave it with their own notions.
>
> (Whately 1886: 66–7)

According to Waterman (1991a: 10–11), political economy was seen to be "hostile to religion", and was used by Bentham and James Mill to promote "their own unashamedly atheistic program of reform".

> It was the single-handed achievement of Richard Whately to defeat the philosophical radicals by showing that a defensible demarcation is possible between scientific and theological knowledge, thereby insulating each from illegitimate encroachment by the other . . . by safeguarding the integrity of each, it validated the ideological alliance of political economy and Christian theology that Malthus and his colleagues attempted to create.

Whately saw no conflict between political economy and religion, suggesting in his inaugural lecture:

> [t]hat Political Economy should have been complained as hostile to religion will probably be regarded in a century hence with the same wonder, almost approaching to incredulity, with which we of the present day hear of men's having opposed on religious grounds the Copernican system.
>
> (Whately 1832: 25)

An earlier signal of the importance Whately placed on political economy was his invitation to Nassau Senior to contribute an addition to the appendix to his *Logic* (Whately 1826) on definitions in political economy, commencing

"The foundation of Political Economy being a few general propositions deduced from observation or from consciousness, and generally admitted as soon as stated" (Whately 1826: 230). This work offers a vision of a deductive political economy where the pressing need is to clarify definitions of key terms.

Whately revealed in correspondence that he was thinking "of making a continuation of Paley's *Natural Theology*, extending to the body-politic some such views as his respecting the natural" (Whately 1886: 66–7). Such project is consistent with his proposed deductive approach, although as we will see later in the chapter, Jones and Whewell regarded it as dangerous.

Although prefigured in his review of Senior's Drummond Lectures, Whately's project of extending the design argument to society began in his own *Introductory Lectures on Political Economy*. "In nothing perhaps will an attentive and candid inquirer perceive more of the divine wisdom than in the provisions made for the progress of society" (Whately 1832: 84). He then illustrates this by describing the remarkable way a city like London of a million inhabitants can be supplied each day, observing that "no human wisdom directed to that end could have conducted so well the system by which that enormous population is fed from day to day" and that this bears "the same marks of contrivance and design, with a view to beneficial end, as we accustomed to admire (when our attention is drawn to them by the study of Natural Theology) in the anatomical structure of the body etc" (Whately 1832: 90). He draws an analogy between the circulation of blood and the circulation of commodities, but observes the latter is more wonderful because it is not the circulation of inert matter but circulation induced by rational free agents with a variety of motives (Whately 1832: 91). The conclusion to which he is led is that:

> Man, considered not merely as an organised being, but as a rational agent, and as a member of society, is perhaps the most wonderfully contrived, and to us the most interesting specimen of divine wisdom that we may have knowledge of.
>
> (Whately 1832: 91)

Whately makes no particular analytical economic contribution in developing this argument, and leans heavily on Adam Smith's *Wealth of Nations*. Whereas Smith was reticent about linking the idea of unintended benefits of self-interest in a market economy to the doctrine of providence, Whately is explicit: "Man is, in the same act, doing one thing by choice, for his own benefit, and another, undesignedly, under the care of Providence, for the service of the community" (Whately 1832: 94).

In one of his later works there is an even stronger providentialist reading of Smith:

> You will have observed that it is as a writer on the evidences of natural and revealed religion that I consider Paley to be especially eminent. Though there is nothing of his that is not worth an attentive perusal, I would place

Adam Smith's *Theory of Moral Sentiments* and *Wealth of Nations* (though not regarding either as infallibly right throughout) higher than Paley's works on the same subjects.

(Whately 1859: 39)

As was noted in Chapter 4, we may have doubts about Smith's intentions, but there is no doubt that the dominant interpretation of the *Wealth of Nations* in the years when political economy took shape was providentialist and naturally theological.

Whately's concern for educating the poor in sound principles in political economy was clear during his time as Archbishop of Dublin, the appointment which followed his tenure in the Drummond Chair at Oxford. He established the Whately Chair of Political Economy at Trinity College Dublin in 1832.[15] More important for the general public were his hugely popular *Easy Lessons on Money Matters* (Whately 1833) written for schoolchildren[16] because "next to sound religion, sound Political Economy was the most essential to the well-being of society" and that "the sort of thing wanted most now for children and the poor, is some plain instructions in Political Economy".

In relation to the problem of reconciling Malthus' principle of population with the power and goodness of God, Whately referred his readers to Sumner's *Treatise on the Records of Creation*, but added his opinion that a satisfactory account cannot be given of this problem of the existence of evil, and that it is a problem which "we more and more perceive to be the only difficulty in theology" (Whately 1832: 96). This suggests that despite the efforts of Malthus, Paley and Sumner, one of the core ideas of political economy, the principle of population, created insoluble difficulties for natural theology.

Political economy at Cambridge: Richard Jones and William Whewell

William Whewell is best known among economists as an early contributor to mathematical economics, mainly for papers delivered to the Cambridge Philosophical Society in 1829 and 1831. However, this is a small and relatively unimportant episode within his much wider influence on the development of political economy as a discipline. Jones' and Whewell's economic writings are part of an immensely influential scientific project with its British natural theological background. Both Jones and Whewell struggled with the problem of theodicy and this ended up undermining the plausibility of the natural theological framework for political economy and contributing to the separation of the disciplines in the middle years of the 19th century.

Political economy in Jones' and Whewell's lives and writings

To understand the work of Whewell and Jones on political economy, it is helpful to place their economic writings within the context of their own lives and writings.

Richard Jones was born in 1790 and studied at Gonville and Caius Cambridge from 1812–16, developing an interest there in political economy.[17] The only substantial work he published was his *Essay on Distribution: Rent* 1831, which will be discussed further later in this chapter. He was appointed by Kings College London as their inaugural Professor of Political Economy, but moved on in 1835 to succeed Malthus at the East India College, where he remained until his death in 1855. His idleness and reluctance to publish frustrated many of his friends, including Whewell. Various papers eventually appeared in Jones' *Literary Remains* published in 1859, edited by Whewell and John Cazenove.

William Whewell was born in 1794 in Lancashire.[18] Despite modest origins his ability in languages and mathematics, support of teachers who recognised his ability, plus Whewell's commitment to hard work took him to Trinity College Cambridge on a scholarship. He graduated as second wrangler in 1816, and was offered a Fellowship at Trinity the following year. It was at Trinity that he developed close friendships with Richard Jones, the astronomer John Herschel and the mathematician Charles Babbage. Whewell was very active during this period: founder of the Cambridge Philosophical Society in 1818, Fellow of the Royal Society in 1820 and a major figure in the British Association for the Advancement of Science from 1831.

Whewell's interest in political economy had developed in the 1820s in conversation with his Cambridge friend Richard Jones, evidenced by 1822 correspondence where he seeks information about the progress of political economy and asks Jones' advice about books on political economy. In these years, controversy was continuing over Malthus' writings on population, especially their theological implications. The controversy was heightened by the publication of Ricardo's *Principles of Political Economy and Taxation* 1817 which modified and further developed Malthus' idea of diminishing returns in agriculture. Ricardo combined diminishing returns with a particular understanding of rent to derive stark conclusions about conflict between social classes over the distribution of income and the path of the British economy to a stationary state where growth would cease. For Ricardo, this modelling was partly directed towards the abolition of the Corn Laws, for allowing the importation of foreign corn would postpone the stationary state. Whewell and Jones recognised more general implications about social conflict and the aspersions Ricardo's view cast on the adequacy of divine provision for the British population.

Whewell's ordination as Priest in 1825 led to a series of sermons delivered at St Mary's Cambridge in 1827 where he attempted to reconcile contemporary science with theology. These unpublished sermons will be discussed more fully in the next section, including the 28-page text of the undelivered fifth sermon which is crucial to understanding why he thought the currently dominant forms of political economy could not be reconciled to Christian theology, and that political economy needed to be redirected along theologically framed inductivist lines. This fifth sermon is the earliest textual evidence of Whewell's lifelong engagement with political economy.

During the 1820s, political economy was establishing itself as a distinct field of enquiry, evidenced by Malthus' lectures at the East India College, lectures in political economy delivered at Cambridge by George Pryme and the establishment of the Drummond Chair in Political Economy in 1825 which was occupied first by Nassau Senior and then by his mentor Richard Whately. One of the pressing questions, evident in the early political economy lectures of Senior and Whately at Oxford, was the appropriate method for the new field. This question was recognised by Whewell and Jones, and most of the other participants, to have moral and theological dimensions.[19]

Whewell's Cambridge Philosophical Society papers of 1829 and 1831 *Mathematical Expositions of the Doctrines of Political Economy* have been the focus of economists' interest in his work, often seeing him as a pioneer of mathematical economics. They are better seen as a reluctant resort to mathematics to rebut Ricardo on his own terms.

Richard Jones was uneasy about the approach of his friend Whewell, believing that his friend's mathematical approach granted a false legitimacy to Ricardo's assumptions.[20] Jones pursued a different strategy of detailed empirical investigation of the different types of rent, attempting to undermine empirically the simplified view of rent that was the basis of Ricardo's reasoning. According to Jones, Ricardo's analysis was based on just one of four types of rent, and not the most prevalent type. Jones' book was published in 1831 and reviewed by Whewell in the *British Critic*. Whewell wrote that "The work before us places the subject of Rent in a new point of view, and connects it with a multitude of problems and researchers which had not been previously understood to bear upon it" (Whewell 1831b: 41). Arguing against Ricardo and the early work of Malthus, Whewell emphasises this new point of view is especially moral and theological:

> The "bounteous earth" . . . yields to the cares which educe its fruits more than is sufficient to support the cultivators. There is a surplus produce, a subsistence for others who do not cultivate . . . This superfertility, this fruitfulness is beyond the bare necessary limit, is a remarkable and universal blessing which we owe to him who created the earth, and man, and their powers.
>
> (Whewell 1831b: 41)

Repeating the argument of his 1827 sermons, Whewell wrote that Ricardian political economy is "the most glaring example of false method of erecting a science which has occurred since the world had any examples of the true method" (Whewell 1831b: 52). So:

> [p]olitical economy . . . must be a science concerned with actual facts and daily observations; its general propositions, if they are true at all, must be so by being verified in particular cases of human affairs . . . Political economy in short must be a science of induction and not of deduction.
>
> (Whewell 1831b: 52)

Whewell wrote of the "vices of their method" (Whewell 1831b: 53).

A new stage of the debate over political economy came when Whewell received a letter from Jones[21] about Nassau Senior's appendix to Whately's *Logic* on definitions in political economy and Whately's Drummond inaugural lectures published as *Introductory Lectures on Political Economy*. Senior's 1827 Drummond inaugural lectures seem to have escaped their scrutiny. Whewell and Jones were horrified by the deductive method of Whately and the Oxford logicians, which was especially dangerous because, unlike Ricardo, the Oxford men shared Jones' and Whewell's commitment to Christianity and a natural theological intellectual framework. Jones makes the significant suggestion in correspondence that his friend Whewell publish a work on inductive reasoning.[22]

The debate was somewhat clouded by misunderstanding between Whewell and Malthus. Robert Malthus was initially dismayed by an 1832 paper by Whewell criticising the fixation of political economists with definitions of terms, but subsequent correspondence clarified that the attack was on Senior's appendix to Whately's *Logic* on definitions in political economy, not Malthus' 1827 work on definitions.[23] Malthus' approach is complicated because the first edition of his *Essay on the Principle of Population* 1798 was a tight deductive argument, but the increasingly lengthy subsequent editions of the *Essay* from 1803 sought to justify his assumptions and conclusions empirically. As we shall see in the next section, the first edition of Malthus' *Essay* was criticised in Whewell's 1827 sermon, but Malthus by that time was at odds with Ricardo over method and had moved closer to Jones' and Whewell's position.[24]

Whewell's rise to fame was both marked and assisted by the invitation to write a Bridgewater Treatise *Astronomy and General Physics Considered with Reference to Natural Theology* published in 1833. His work was positively reviewed and became the bestseller of the series.[25] Despite the topic of "Astronomy and General Physics", Whewell found space for discussion of human society and morality, suggesting that these topics were of continuing interest to him and an integral part of his wider scientific project.

It is possible that Whewell's lack of success in the 1827 sermons in reconciling political economy with theology, in contrast to his feeling he had achieved success with the physical sciences, led him in the 1833 Bridgewater Treatise to separate the manner of God's government of the social world from that of the physical world. Such a separation would help insulate his reconciliation of the physical sciences with theology from any difficulties of reconciling the political economy with theology. As he wrote in the Bridgewater Treatise, "There can be no wider interval in philosophy than the separation which must exist between the laws of mechanical force and motion, and the laws of free moral action . . . by which God governs his moral creatures" (Whewell 1833: 374–5). He also attempted to reassure readers of his Bridgewater Treatise that any lack of satisfaction they might have about the reconciliation should not interfere with Christian devotion:

> [i]f, in endeavouring to trace the tendencies of the vast labyrinth of laws by which the universe is governed, we are sometimes lost and bewildered, and can scarce, or not at all, discern the line by which pain, and sorrow, and vice

> fall in with a scheme directed to the strictest right and greatest good, we yet
> find no room to faint or falter.
>
> (Whewell 1833: 380–1)

Significantly, the sources of possible bewilderment are identified as "pain, sorrow and vice" which were precisely the stumbling blocks Whewell identified in 1827 in attempting to reconcile political economy with Christian theology. Furthermore, Whewell called his readers to take comfort from the way the advances of other sciences such as physics and astronomy had shown nature to be harmonious and beneficent in their domains, even though the problems of pain sorrow and vice "are the darkest and most tangled recesses of our knowledge" into which "science has as yet cast no ray of light" (Whewell 1833: 381).[26]

Whewell's fullest discussion of the sciences is in his multivolume *History of the Inductive Sciences* published from 1837 and *Philosophy of the Inductive Sciences* from 1840.[27] Political economy is dealt with in chapter 23 of the volume *On the Philosophy of Discovery* as an immature science and one of somewhat "mixed character" where "observations and ideas are mingled together, and act and react in a peculiar manner" (Whewell 1860: 292). Political economy is here argued to be separated methodologically from the physical sciences (because its object of study is human behaviour) and not just because of its immaturity as a science.

Whewell's rise continued with his appointment as Master of Trinity College Cambridge, and then as Knightsbridge Professor of Moral Philosophy from 1845. The moral philosophy appointment signalled a concern with the state of that discipline, especially the growing dominance of the utilitarian philosophy of Paley and Bentham, and the connections between the sciences and moral philosophy. Whewell's *Elements of Morality, Including Polity* (1845a) was written as a replacement text at Cambridge for Paley's *Principles of Moral and Political Philosophy* (1785), drawing instead on the moral philosophy of Joseph Butler's *Sermons* (1726). As a reforming Cambridge Vice Chancellor from 1842–3 and 1855–6, Whewell played a major role in establishing the Natural Sciences Tripos and the Moral Sciences Tripos from 1848.

The death of his friend Richard Jones in 1855 meant that any hope was gone of Jones publishing sequels to his 1831 *Rent* volume and thereby of establishing a foundation for the inductive political economy that Whewell sought. My own sense from the correspondence is that a desire to avoid invading Jones' territory precluded Whewell from undertaking substantive work on political economy. Jones' anxiety about Whewell publishing on matters they discussed together is evident in correspondence, as is Whewell's increasing frustration with Jones' lack of progress with his work on political economy and with Jones' reluctance to publish.[28] What Jones was able to produce was published as *Literary Remains* 1859, largely edited by John Cazenove, but including a lengthy introduction by Whewell which picked up many of the themes raised in his 1827 sermons and his 1831 review of Jones on *Rent*.

Whewell's *Lectures on Political Economy* 1862 are of less interest than they might appear, being a record of lectures prepared for the Prince of Wales (the future Edward VII) who was taking classes in political economy at Trinity College Cambridge in 1861. They were intended as a summary of existing "opinions" on "leading questions belonging to the subject by successive eminent writers". Whewell explicitly declaimed propounding any system of his own (Whewell 1862: 1). There is, as one might expect, considerable discussion of Jones' work on rent, commendation of Jones and Malthus on political economy (but not Malthus on population), and criticism of Ricardo. Whewell returned often to Smith as a figure of authority, emphasising that the *Wealth of Nations* is "a book full of actual facts, and not of mere hypothetical cases" (Whewell 1862: 2).

Not many years after this, in 1866, Whewell died in a horse riding accident, and his statue stands alongside Bacon and Newton in Trinity College chapel.

Whewell's attempt to reconcile political economy with Christian theology

I will now return to consider in detail the neglected but crucial sermons on the consonance of science and Christian theology Whewell delivered at St Marys Church at the University of Cambridge in February 1827. According to Todhunter, these sermons "attracted great attention" at the time but were never published.[29] [30]

While preparing the sermons, Whewell wrote to his friend Hugh Rose, explaining his view that the sciences must harmonise with religion:

> What I do hold is that inductive science is a good thing, and, as all truth is consistent with itself, I hold that if inductive science be true it must harmonize with all the great truths of religion; nor do I see how anyone can persuade one's self to believe that all this tempting system of discoverable truths is placed within our reach, as it were on purpose, while it is at the same time tainted with the poison of irreligion – a sort of tree of knowledge and of death, both in one, without the merciful prohibition attached to it.[31]

This assurance of the harmony between science and religion was characteristic of scientific natural theology, and similar statements can be found in the writings of Malthus, Whately and others.

Whewell wrote to Jones that his topic would be "benevolent design in the moral frame of society". He was behind in writing the sermons, but:

> [w]ith time enough I should not fear the greater part of the work – all the argument about the activity and omnipresence of the Deity, but when I come to the indications of benevolent design in the moral frame of society I have not such an habitual familiarity with the view of the subject in its details as merits with the confidence and vehemence which would be becoming. I have no doubt I should get on better if I had you at my elbow.

What is interesting here is the emphasis Whewell puts on benevolent design in society in a series of sermons that was to cover the relationship between all the sciences and theology.[32] For Whewell, political economy was the study of society.

When Whewell came to preach the sermons in February 1827, only the first four of the five he prepared were delivered. As he wrote to Jones:

> I have got through them without getting quite up to the moral part of my subject . . . No population and in short nothing but one or two analogies from the natural world to illustrate the probability of our being very fairly ignorant of the non-general laws of the moral world.

Whewell described the sermons as "an attempt to make science fall in with a contemplative devotion which I don't think was difficult though people seem from the notion they had of scientific men to have thought it must be impossible". "I forgot to say that I doubt much about publishing. I wrote at last in haste and believe I'd better wait" and that "my plan altered much in shape"[33] from that which he had previously discussed with Jones.

After the sermons, he encouraged Jones to carry on the attack on false political economy, writing that Jones had a:

> [g]reat deal of work to do in the world of which the execution is yet to begin? That you have got to trouble the shortwitted, rotten, pseudo-political-economists; and to yoke history, & morals, & natural characteristics, and practical experience to that chariot of science which they have hitherto been driving tandem with one jack-ass before another.[34]

Why was the fifth sermon on political economy not delivered? Todhunter (1876 I: 330) suggests Whewell was concerned about premature disclosure of views his friend Richard Jones was planning to publish in a book which eventually appeared in 1831 as *Essay on Distribution: Rent*. The reasons are more likely to have been Whewell's lack of success in reconciling political economy with Christian theology (as suggested by Yeo 1993: 194) and the continuing difficulty of constructing an adequate economic theodicy. Whewell's lack of success might also explain why he was so keen for Jones to carry forward his own work on political economy, especially the attack on the Ricardian theory of rent.

Consider now the content of Whewell's 1827 Cambridge sermons. The first sermon took the text Isaiah 33:6 "wisdom and knowledge shall be the stability of thy times, and strength of salvation: the fear of the Lord is his treasure". Whewell argued that theology is deductive, beginning from scriptural revelation and the irresistible evidence of sense. As such it leaves "room for the love of knowledge without expelling the love of God" as exemplified by the natural theologically framed inductive science of Bacon and Newton.

The second sermon was on Romans 1:20 "For the invisible things of him from the creation of the world are clearly seen, being understood by the things that are made". This sermon carries on the argument about the proper place of science in relation to theology; that scientific knowledge cannot save us but does gratify the intellect and can give us a taste of heaven.

Next was a sermon on Proverbs 3:5–6 "Trust in the Lord with all thine heart; and lean not on thine own understanding. In all thy ways acknowledge him, and he shall direct thy paths". Again there is much said about the value of the sciences, but the emphasis is on the imperfect state of scientific knowledge, and how the natural world which the sciences study remains in God's hand. In the end, the natural world:

> [s]hall expire in the throes and agonies of some sudden and fierce convulsion; and the same hand which plucked the elements from the dark and troubled chaos, shall cast them into their tomb, pushing them aside that they may no longer stand between His face and the creatures whom He shall come to judge.

The fourth sermon, and the last to be actually delivered, was on Job 36:3 "I will fetch my knowledge from afar". This sermon, like the third, has a more devotional tone than the philosophical arguments of the earlier two sermons. Whewell here describes how Job and his friends struggle for an adequate explanation of events, how Job in spite of this does not curse God for the misfortunes he has suffered, and how God answers not with an explanation of evil but with a reminder in the whirlwind of who has created the world and has the power over nature and the fortunes of human beings. According to Whewell, our response must be awe of creation and worship.

The ground that Whewell had prepared was to lead into his fifth sermon on political economy. His text was James 3:13 "Who is a wise man? Let him shew out of a good conversation his meekness of wisdom".

Whewell began by announcing that he will "speak now . . . of those who have reasoned concerning the moral nature and prospects of man and societies of men" (p. 1 of the manuscript) and observes that "they do not lead us, through their teaching, up to an admiration of the beneficent wisdom and ever-good producing contrivance of the great Creator". The reference seems to be specifically to David Ricardo and his followers, because of the following comment about "founders and idols of sects and schools" and the suggestion that if this was the intention rather than the effect of the writing, then the author must be considered "among the most abandoned and degraded of the bondsmen of error, with tongues and hearts vile and hardened enough for such a cursed and unhallowed work" (p. 1). This could hardly be said of Malthus who did not have followers in the same way as Ricardo, and was a fellow clergyman rather than Ricardo, the Jew turned Unitarian. It is too early to refer to Senior's and Whately's work on political economy, to which Jones seems to have first drawn Whewell's attention in 1831 correspondence.[35]

Having politely ruled out the horrible possibility that these political economists intended to cast doubt on the character of God, Whewell speaks only:

> [o]f the effect produced on men's minds by the doctrines of these teachers. I speak of the manner in which their views and opinions of the laws which influence human events fit themselves with our views, and the believers' views of a God of mercy and justice presiding over the world which he has made and ordered all things for good.

(p. 2)

He asks to consider particularly the effect of this new science of political economy "which in these modern times has won the largest share of applause" on the "humble believer" (p. 2) and suggests that it has caused "something of seeming disturbance, some struggle and conflict, between the spirit of prayer and praise, of trust and thanksgiving to the wisdom that orders all things well" (p. 2) particularly in relation to evils and imperfections. Whewell points to a "want of harmony perceived between the views of the Reasoner and the Believer" (p. 2), noting that he means by Reasoner the speculative or deductive reasoner, a figure regularly mocked in his other writings.

He then explores why these political economists have fallen into error. He suggests "this discord, this struggle arises from too narrow a view which their philosophy has taken of the moral structure of this world and of man" (pp. 2–3) and goes on in somewhat florid language to suggest it is because the world and human beings are not regarded by these political economists as part of creation and therefore sources of knowledge of a creator God in the manner of natural theology. As Whewell puts it:

> [t]heir wings are leaden, their flight is crippled, their strength is broken by some inward infirmity, some disease of falsehood and mistake . . . their sight is imperfect in that they discover not the door that leads out of their difficulties and doubts of their systems into the regions of religious truth, and they are like blind insects beating their wings against the walls of their self-chosen prison to see the opening by which they might emerge into the wider and clearer air of heaven.
>
> (p. 3)

At this point, the specifics of political economy with which Jones was assisting him[36] seem to fail him and he evades the task with the suggestion that:

> To sift and examine all the erroneous doctrines by which men may have been shaken and disturbed in their contemplation of the goodness and holiness of God is too vast a task for one man, and not for this place or for this occasion.
>
> (p. 3)

He adds that in any case, "how could the preacher find language suited to his lips" (p. 3) in relation to these political economists.

Nevertheless, he will offer "a brief and general indication at some of the forms of error, its causes and the grounds of its refutation" (p. 4) for there is:

> [n]o higher subject than showing that the motives and actions of men and the frame of society has marks of benevolent contrivance as strong as that the eye was made to give the pleasures of sight and the ear of sound.
>
> (p. 4)

The reference to the eye suggests Whewell is calling for an extension of Paley's natural theological project to human society – the task that the political economists he is criticising have rejected. Whewell at this point discusses the greater complexity of the natural theological project in the social world, and our present lack of understanding of laws in the social world. He writes of the "tangled and multifarious texture of questions relating to man" (p. 7). Without our imperfect understanding of social or economic laws, we struggle to see God's government in this domain.

The sermon then switches focus to Malthus' principle of population, which Whewell summarises as follows:

> It has, for instance, been maintained, and this doctrine has produced and does still produce a powerful impression and manifest tendency in the speculations of those who even now reason concerning the laws which regulate the prosperity and riches of human societies, that the fiat of His will by which the Creator ordained the increase and multiplication of men, impelled them in a career leading by a course not to be stopped or deflected, to want and degradation, to vice and misery. It has been passed from pen to pen and from lip to lip as a great discovery, that the tendency of mankind to replenish the earth ever pushes them on till the sharp discipline of pain, the iron hand of want and its deadly concomitant crime, drive them back or at least forbid their further progress. That however the large bounty of nature opens some new supply, pours out some new store of nutriment, this fierce and indomitable property of human societies springs forth instantly upon the offered food and devours it with wolfish rapidity, leaving the spot that seemed thus enriched as bare and hungry as it had been. That thus the more depressed of the orders of mankind, those portions of society that win their bread by the labour of their hands and eat it in the sweat of their brows are destined to eternal and irredeemable degradation – fated to increase in numbers as the fruits of the earth allow of their increase, and as it were condemned to become more numerous lest they should become more happy. That this, or something like this, is the representation often given of the necessary course of states and nations by those who most loudly call our attention to their success in speculation most will recognize and know. That the proclamation of such a doctrine, represented as a demonstrated truth and the fruitful source of many truths besides, shook and startled the minds of pious and benevolent men, and seemed like an oppressive and disquieting thought forced in among their belief and trust in God's goodness, like a funereal and menacing light thrown upon the fair face of nature, many who bear in mind the youth and first appearance of these doctrines and their operation on the minds of men, will still recollect.
>
> (p. 9)

The accuracy of Whewell's summary is debatable, and seems to correspond most closely to the initial 1798 edition of the *Essay on the Principle of Population*. This is also the edition of the *Essay* which included Malthus' later abandoned attempt to reconcile the principle with Christian theology, arguing that the struggle for existence in the face of limited food supply was a necessary spur to the full development of human capacities.

Whewell's diagnosis of the problem with Malthus' *Essay* is "rushing headlong on with abstract generalisation of a principle without considering the limitations and exceptions with which in human affairs truth is clothed" (p. 10). This is more true of Malthus' 1798 *Essay* than the later editions from 1803 which included moral restraint as a less gruesome way of reconciling population with the food supply than starvation (or vice and misery), was more modest in its claims and included many more facts to support the argument.

Whewell's position on Malthus' theodicy is not clear. He suggests that what is going on is not "vice or misery, in any reasonable application of such terms" and that the uncertainty and struggle of daily life strengthens religion and allows mankind to "ennoble and exalt his being, promoting affection and friendship without which his character would be selfish and savage" (p. 11). Whewell added a comment in the margin in pencil:

> It is obvious that I am not here attempting to account for all the vice and misery in the world, but to show that one of the systems it represents as the source of laws of human existence is logically false.
>
> (p. 11)

Drawing together Whewell's discussions of Ricardian political economy and Malthus' principle of population, his diagnosis is that premature deduction undermines science and faith. Premature deduction is especially problematic in political economy because of the greater complexity of human nature and society, compared to the subject matter of other sciences. With unclear or erroneous laws we then struggle to see God's government in political economy, and our faith can be undermined. Particularly dangerous in Whewell's view was the way both the Ricardian theory of rent and the principle of population underestimate the bounty of nature, overstate the degree of conflict between social classes and fail to generate the sorts of evidence which allowed the natural theologian scientists to construct plausible theodicies in other domains.

Some of these points in Whewell's 1827 fifth sermon find their way into Whewell's (1831b) review of Jones' *Essay on Distribution: Rent*, and recur in Whewell's later writing on political economy. The sermon is not just significant as the original statement of Whewell's views, but because it offers insight into the formation of his views on scientific method.[37]

Whewell's political economy as scientific natural theology

Whewell's work on political economy coheres well with his project of science within a natural theological framework. Consider how Whewell's economic work exemplifies the non-demonstrative functions of natural theology discussed in Chapter 2:[38] promoting science, especially to those who saw it as a threat to religion. This is exemplified most strongly in Whewell's 1827 fifth sermon on political economy where he argues for the importance of the science, and this importance is the reason it must be pursued using appropriate methods. The associated function of:

1 Rebutting attacks of sceptics, scoffers and deists is exemplified by his attack on Ricardo in the 1827 fifth sermon.
2 Mediating between religious groups in the pursuit of science. Whewell regarded the Ricardians as antireligious and so mediation was not appropriate, while the other participants, Malthus, Jones, Senior and Whately, shared Anglican religious commitments.
3 Unifying science and religion in the minds of clerical participants. Whewell was one of these religious participants and the natural theological framework enabled him to bring together his political economy, his moral philosophy, his other scientific work and his clerical vocation.
4 Suggesting scientific theories and supplying teleological regulative principles for the interpretation of the natural world. The teleological principle operates in his discussion of different views of humanity in the fifth sermon and in his discussion of the principle of population as being in conflict with his understanding of the purposes of God in creation and the eschaton.
5 Political resource. Whewell used natural theological arguments against Ricardo's suggestion that conflict between the social classes was inevitable over the distribution of income, as well as Ricardo's and Malthus' fears about the stationary state and food shortages. The threat to this function of natural theology seems to be the reason for the ferocity of Whewell's arguments against Ricardian political economy. An important political function was supressing religious enthusiasm in favour of rational religion. Whewell's advocacy of reason is not as strong in his work on political economy as it is in his work on moral philosophy. This may be because his work on political economy was criticising the erroneous use of deductive reasoning by Ricardo and other political economists.

How theological problems rendered political economy ineffective as natural theology

As discussed in previous chapters, Malthus offered a theodicy in the 1798 first edition of his *Essay* where the struggle over limited food supplies was necessary to awaken human potential. This growth of mind theodicy was withdrawn from later editions of the *Essay*, though the ideas survived to some extent alongside a more orthodox state of trial theodicy articulated in Malthus' later writings. Few contemporaries considered Malthus' theodicy adequate. Chalmers had little to offer in the way of a theodicy other than enthusiasm for education of the poor to ameliorate the problem. JB Sumner was considered by some to have developed a more successful theodicy than Malthus in his *Treatise on the Records of Creation* 1816. Richard Whately as we saw earlier in the chapter considered the problem insoluble.

It is clear from the undelivered 1827 sermon that Whewell was unable to harmonise political economy with theology, regarded the problem of economic suffering more difficult than similar problems thrown up by the other sciences, and was particularly troubled by the lack of an adequate economic theodicy. If Whewell had anything further to offer on theodicy, it was the hope that progress in the science of political economy would render it more able to be reconciled with theology, as had been the case with older sciences.

For Whewell, economic evils such as poverty and starvation and the lack of an economic theodicy cast doubt not just on the natural theological framing of political economy but on the whole scientific natural theological project. Wider doubts about natural theology stemming from his 1827 fifth sermon are evident in his Bridgewater Treatise *Astronomy and General Physics Considered with Reference to Natural Theology* 1833 and his *Sermons on the Foundations of Morals* 1837a. If a man such as Whewell, the greatest scientific authority of his age, ordained clergyman and Master of Trinity could not reconcile political economy with Christian theology, then what hope was there for lesser mortals? Reconciling theology and political economy must surely be impossible.

The lack of an economic theodicy affected particular functions of natural theology discussed earlier. Without an economic theodicy, natural theology's capacity to perform function 5 "Political resource" was severely limited. By the time we get to the 1840s, political economy is hugely popular and questions about economics suffering pressing. The lack of an economic theodicy also limited natural theology's capacity to perform function 7 and supply teleological regulative principles.

Conclusion

Theological impetus for the study of political economy is clear for both Whately and Whewell. Theology affected the method and perhaps substance of both Whately's and Whewell's political economy. Whately considered the problem of evil insoluble. Whewell was more hopeful about the problem of evil in relation to the other sciences, but his own failed attempt to reconcile political economy with Christian theology stemming from his neglected 1827 sermons undermined the wider natural theology project, contributing to its collapse in mid-19th-century Britain. The story of the death of natural theology will be taken up in the next chapter.

Notes

1 This chapter draws on Oslington (2001) and a paper "William Whewell's Writings on Political Economy in their Scientific and Theological Contexts" presented at the Centre for the History of Political Economy at Duke University in 2015.
2 The poem is anthologised in Les Murray's *New Oxford Book of Australian Verse* Oxford University Press 1986 and many other places. Whewell's comment about science as a hymn may be found in his *Indications of a Creator* (1845b) pp. 51–52. Lyell on Whewell is recorded in Todhunter (1876 I p. 1)

3 The story of the development of political economy in British universities is told by Checkland (1951) and Winch (1971). At Cambridge, there were early efforts by Professors of Modern History John Symonds from 1771–1807 and William Smyth from 1807, who associated regularly with David Ricardo. George Pryme lectured on political economy from 1816 (see Pryme 1816) and was eventually made a Professor of Political Economy in 1828. Perronet Thompson of Queens College Cambridge wrote on rent, opposing Ricardo. George Poulett Scrope also lectured on political economy at Cambridge in this period.

At Oxford political economy was pioneered by Professors of Modern History Henry Beeke from 1801–1813 and Nares who lectured on political economy in 1817. The main impetus came from revival of interest in logic centred at Oriel College, led by Edward Copleston, Richard Whately, Thomas Arnold and John Henry Newman. Edward West of University College Oxford published his work on rent in 1815. Oxford political economy was dissipated by Copleston's appointment as Bishop of Llandaff from 1827 and Whately's appointment as Archbishop of Dublin from 1831.

The London based Political Economy Club from 1821 is discussed by O'Brien (2004). The Roll of Members and Questions Discussed 1821–1920 and Minutes of the Club from 1899–1920 were published in 1921 by Macmillan.

4 David Ricardo is discussed by Schumpeter (1954), King (2013) and De Vivo (1987) among many others.

5 The Oxford Oriel logic background to political economy is discussed by Moore (2013). Edward Copleston's economics writings (for example, Copleston 1819) are discussed by Brent (2004a) and Waterman (1991a).

6 The interactions between Senior, Whately and Newman are described in more detail in Oslington (2001). Newman probably attended the lecture, and his letters indicate that he possessed a copy in May 1827, mentioning it among his papers in a letter to his sister Jemima (Ker and Gornall 1979: 17). If Newman was among the "relatively large assembly, including a number of distinguished Oxonians" sitting in one of the Schools of the Bodleian Quadrangle as the lecture began (Levy 1970: 52–3), he may also be among those who "walked out one by one, leaving him [Senior] only with the Vice-Chancellor" (Levy 1970: 52–3). Hardly an auspicious start for the first lecture by an economics professor at an English university, although Levy suggests the walkout was due to Senior having a "weak voice" and being difficult to hear. It may not be a coincidence that Newman's quotations come exclusively from the first part of the lecture.

7 Senior saw science as disciplined enquiry which required theoretical clarity, to be contrasted with the collection of practical maxims about economic life. He followed convention in calling it a moral science and did not have well-developed views on moral philosophy. Senior says in an 1845 letter "I am no metaphysician, and a very ill-read moralist. I have never read Locke or Stewart, or Brown or Reid, or indeed anything on these subjects, except Aristotle, Paley and Adam Smith" (Hilton 1988: 45).

8 Newman's lectures were given in 1852 and published shortly afterwards, and revised by Newman in 1873. The situation surrounding the lectures was difficult, as Newman had to maintain the support of the Irish bishops for the University, yet give his newly appointed and future Professors the control of curriculum and running of the University that he felt was necessary.

9 This objection, that political economy excludes theology by its method, also comes up in a letter written in 1840 to his sister Jemima, where Newman laments "Political Economists, who cannot accept (it is impossible) the Scripture rules about almsgiving, renunciation of wealth, self-denial, etc" (Ker and Gornall 1979 vol VII: 244–5).

10 There is a similar sharp exchange in 1841 between Newman and Sir Robert Peel on the question of whether opening a public reading room would lead to moral improvement. Newman concludes that "taking human nature as it is actually found" and Sir Robert's Peel's suggestion "that grief, anger, cowardice, self-conceit, pride, or passion,

can be subdued by an examination of shells or grasses, or inhaling of gasses, or chipping of rocks, or calculating the longitude, [or we might add the labours of the political economist] is the veriest of pretences which sophist or mountebank ever professed to a gaping auditory" and that we must seek virtue "in graver and holier places than libraries or reading rooms". These comments on the Tamworth reading room can be found in Newman (1989: 306–12, with the quotations coming from p. 310).

11 A good test of Newman's attitude towards political economy is his treatment of the subject as Rector of the Catholic University of Ireland. Among the first group of Professors recruited for his University was a Professor of Political Economy, John O'Hagan, whom Newman vigorously defended from clerical interference. In an 1854 letter to Archbishop Cullen, he points out that his Professors (including O'Hagan) "have their own sufficient sphere, in which I should not think of interfering" (Ker and Gornall 1979 vol XVI: 263). After Newman resigned as Rector, O'Hagan wrote expressing appreciation for Newman's support, and later visited Newman several times at Birmingham. If political economy failed to flourish at the Catholic University, lack of support from Newman was not the cause. Furthermore, on the distinctness of political economy from theology, it is worth noting that at Newman's Catholic University political economy was established within the Faculty of Arts (the others being medicine, law and theology). Newman feared proposals that would lead to the University becoming "priest ridden. I mean, men who do not know literature and science will have the direction" (Ker and Gornall 1979). One of Newman's letters of 1855 mentions a payment of five pounds due to O'Hagan for the inaugural lecture (Ker and Gornall 1979 vol XVI: 194). The Almanack of the Catholic University gives an outline of John O'Hagan's *Introductory Lectures in Political Economy*. The four topics covered are "1. The good of the individual, the end of society. 2. General view of the distribution of wealth. 3. Theories of socialism. 4. Theories of progress". Among the Almanacks and Calendars held at the Birmingham Oratory, I have been unable to locate the text of O'Hagan's inaugural lecture, if it was published. Some idea of the possible content of the lectures can be gained from an article O'Hagan wrote for the journal associated with the University, *Atlantis*, in 1860: "Views Preliminary to the Study of Political Economy". There is no record of textbooks at that time, but in 1863 the calendar lists Mill's *Principles of Political Economy* as the primary reference for students of political economy. Taking all this evidence together, the course in political economy at Newman's University does not seem to be an appendage of theology. From the limited evidence we have of the content of the lectures on political economy at the Catholic University, they do not differ radically from those of the Whately Professors at Trinity College Dublin, and the differences are not clearly attributable to Newman's influence.

12 There are similar statements in Whately. After giving examples of astronomy and geology, Whately (1832: 28) comments "Historical or physical truths may be established by their own proper evidence" and although "A Christian will indeed feel antecedently a strong persuasion that conclusions inconsistent with the Bible never will be established . . . it is not a sign of faith – on the contrary, it indicates rather a want of faith, or else a culpable indolence – to decline meeting any theorist on his own ground, and to cut short any controversy by an appeal to the authority of Scripture".

13 Newman's First University Sermon of 1826 (Newman 1873: 9) preached just before Senior's lecture indicates a strong preference for the inductive method in scientific investigation.

14 Whately's biography is covered by EJ Whately (1886), Brent (2004b), Akenson (1981) and Collison Black (1987).

15 The Whately Chair at Trinity College Dublin was occupied from 1832 by Mountifort Longfield, Isaac Butt, JA Lawson and W Neilson Hancock. It is discussed by Collison Black (1960).

16 The *Easy Lessons* competed with the *Conversations* of Jane Marcet (1816) and *Illustrations* of Harriet Martineau (1832–34) as popular expositions of the new science

of political economy, ostensibly for schoolchildren and women, but read much more widely. They are discussed more fully by Goldstrom (1966).

17 Jones' biography is discussed in Whewell's preface to Jones (1859), Pullen (2004b) and Tribe (1995).

18 Whewell's biography is discussed in Todhunter (1876), Stephen (1899e) and Yeo (2004). The existing literature on Whewell's economics such as Schumpeter (1954: 448–50), Rashid (1977a), Campanelli (1987) and Henderson (1996) concentrates on his early mathematical papers. Becher (1991), Snyder (2006, 2011) and Maas (2008) connect his economics to his wider project. Whewell is strangely not discussed at length by Waterman (1991a).

19 The moral and theological dimensions of the debate about methods of political economy are discussed by Corsi (1987, 1988) and Waterman (1991a).

20 Letter from Jones to Whewell 18 April 1829 Whewell Papers Add.Ms.c.52/16. Another letter from Malthus to Whewell 26 May 1829 Whewell Papers Add.Ms.a.209/10 offers qualified support for Whewell's attempt to apply mathematics to political economy: "particularly with a view to determine the different degrees in which certain objects are affected, under different hypotheses. The grand difficulty however, with a view to practicability, is the getting data to work upon, sufficiently near the truth; and such as can be stated distinctly in mathematical language". This is published as Letter I in De Marchi and Sturges (1973).

21 Jones to Whewell 24 February 1831 Add.Ms.c.52/20.

22 The suggestion is in a letter from Jones to Whewell 24 February 1831 Add.Ms.c.52/20. Jones suggested "that some popular views of inductive reasoning such as I shall sketch would be a good thing to publish, when you see them decide whether you will keep them & use them yourself or send them back for me to enlarge. If either of us do it must not be with a reference to natural philosophy exclusively or I think mainly – But mind if you insist on German phraseology or anything like it I wash my hands of the job". This is perhaps the seed of Whewell's later volumes on the history and philosophy of the sciences.

23 Malthus to Whewell 1 April 1833 Add.Ms.a.209/12. This is Letter IV in De Marchi and Sturges (1973).

24 For instance, Malthus to Whewell 28 February 1831 Add.Ms.c.53/2 where Malthus writes after reading Jones *Rent* "I am most gratified that he agrees with me on almost every point on which I differ from Mr Ricardo". Also Malthus to Whewell 31 May 1831 Add.Ms.a.209/11 where Malthus expresses appreciation of Whewell's support of his argument against Ricardo. These are published as Letters II and III in De Marchi and Sturges (1973).

25 The Bridgewater Treatises on the "Power, Wisdom and Goodness of God as Manifested in Creation" are discussed by Brooke (1991a) and Topham (1998).

26 Whewell seems to have completely ignored the work of Thomas Chalmers. There is a brief correspondence following Chalmers' Bridgewater Treatise *On the Power Wisdom and Goodness of God Manifested in the Adaption of External Nature to the Moral and Intellectual Constitution of Man* (1833), but Chalmers' early work on political economy was deductive in the spirit of Malthus' first *Essay*, and Chalmers' later popular writings on the subject dealt only superficially with the problem of theodicy. More surprising is his neglect of the work of JB Sumner (1816) who dealt with theodicy.

27 These volumes have a complex publication history. The dates given above are the first of several editions, complicated by publication of selections from *History* and *Philosophy* which "bear on theology" as *Indications of the Creator* 1845 then revised 1846, volumes often referred to as the third edition of the *History* entitled *History of Scientific Ideas* 1858, and companion volumes often referred to as the third edition of the *Philosophy* entitled *Novum Organon Renovatum* 1858 and *On the Philosophy of Discovery* 1860.

28 Evidence of Jones' anxiety includes Whewell to Jones 15 December 1826 Add. Ms.c.51/33, published in Todhunter (1876) I: 81: "I never intended to publish, and I do not think that I shall preach anything which will brush the most delicate bloom of novelty off your plums". There are many examples of Whewell's frustration with Jones' delays, including Whewell to Herschel 4 December 1836 "I am going to stay with him [Jones] in the Christmas vacation. The only misfortune is, that he is less and less likely to write the books he owes the world. He professes that he shall still do much in that way, but I confess I doubt it: and I doubt with grief, for in certain branches of Political Economy I am persuaded he is a long way ahead of anybody else, and might give the subject a grand shove onwards".

29 Todhunter (1876) I: 323. The 1827 sermons are mentioned by Brooke (1991b: 151), Yeo (1993: 194), Henderson (1996: 94) and Snyder (2006: 24). The manuscripts of the sermons are in the Whewell papers R6.17 at Trinity College Cambridge. The handwriting of the 28-page manuscript of the undelivered draft of the fifth sermon is indecipherable in places, which is perhaps part of the reason it has escaped detailed analysis. One can only speculate why the handwriting of the fifth is so poor – Whewell may have had a heavy night with the Trinity College port – which might also explain the florid language.

30 Sermons have been neglected as a source by historians of economics. Francis (2012) emphasises the reach of sermons both through the number of hearers, and the popularity of volumes of printed sermons in 18th- and 19thcentury Britain. Sermons delivered by clergymen economists and by influential non-economist preachers would seem to be particularly illuminating about the popularisation of political economy during this period. For the scholar, though, there is much dull reading involved in examining sermons, without the sometimes juicy discoveries from reading economists' private papers and correspondence.

31 Whewell to Hugh Rose 12 December 1826 R.2.99/27. Published in Todhunter (1876 II: 78).

32 Whewell to Jones, 10 December 1826 Add.Ms.c.51/32. Published in Todhunter (1876 II: 79). It seems from his letter to Jones 15 December 1826 Add.Ms.c.51/33 published in Todhunter (1876 II: 81), that he sought Jones' advice on the content of the lectures and even sent an early version to Jones, as suggested by Todhunter (1876 I: 330).

33 Whewell to Jones 26 February 1827 Add.Ms.c.51/34 published in Todhunter (1876 II: 82–3).

34 Whewell to Jones 10 September 1827 Add.Ms.c.51/41.

35 Jones draws Whewell's attention to the Oxford men's work on political economy in letters of 24 February 1831 Add.Ms.c.52/20 and 1 June 1831 Add.Ms.c.52/38.

36 Jones' assistance with the details of political economy is requested in several letters, for example Whewell to Jones, 15 December 1826 Add.Ms.c.51/33 (Todhunter 1876: 81), where he asks for assistance so that in the sermons "I shall talk confidently of that which I do not prove and assent loudly that a good deal more may be known".

37 Whewell associates deductive methods with atheism as they are joined in Ricardo's political economy. This association between deductive methods and atheism was also noted by Yeo (1993), Henderson (1996: 91–6) and Maas (2008: 144) who wrote, "Whewell's rejection of Ricardianism was motivated by methodological concerns. These were in their turn rooted in his theological convictions". The situation with Malthus is complicated because the 1798 *Essay* was anonymous, though authorship was soon widely known, and Malthus modified both his methods and his theodicy in subsequent editions. The correspondence between Malthus and Whewell, which began two years after these sermons, suggests that Whewell would probably have regretted public criticism of Malthus alongside Ricardo. Malthus saw Whewell as an ally in his disagreement with Ricardo, and Whewell later unsuccessfully attempted to recruit Malthus as a public supporter in his fight with Senior and Whately over appropriate

methods for the new science of political economy. The undelivered 1827 fifth sermon supports the argument that Whewell's reaction to Ricardian political economy shaped Whewell's advocacy of induction as the appropriate scientific method. Speculation and deduction came to be regarded as dangerous through their association in Ricardian political economy. Whewell's mature position (for instance, in his 1849 essay on JS Mill's *Logic*) was a softened version of this where induction did not exclude theory (induction was in fact an almost dialectical interplay between evidence and theory), and deductive methods were appropriate in the more developed sciences which did not of course at that time include political economy. This mature position distanced him from Jones' and Herschel's more extreme Baconian version of inductivism. The literature on Whewell attributes the shift to learning from his own scientific work such as on tides, his reading of Kant and other German philosophers, but the influence of his deepening engagement with political economy, especially Malthus' developing moderate position, cannot be discounted.

38 These functions of natural theology were discussed in Chapter 2, and originally identi- fied by Brooke (1991b: 149–50) in his study of Whewell's sermons.

7 The demise of natural theology and separation of economics from theology

Introduction

Previous chapters have shown how natural theology shaped political economy as a discipline in Britain in the 18th and early 19th centuries. I would now like to explore their relationship later in the 19th century, and will argue that the extension of natural theology to political economy contributed to the death of natural theology, and that this loss of natural theology as an integrating framework was the separation of theology from political economy.

I will begin by briefly reviewing existing explanations of the separation of political economy from theology, and explanations of the demise of natural theology.

Explaining the separation of economics from theology

Ecclesiastical and academic politics

Anthony Waterman (1991a, 1994, 2001) has argued that the alliance between Christianity and political economy in the early decades of the 19th century represented by Malthus, Sumner, Chalmers and Whately was intimately connected with English ecclesiastical and academic politics of this period. He observed that political economy was seen to be "hostile to religion", associated with Jacobinism, and was used by philosophical radicals Jeremy Bentham and James Mill to promote "their own unashamedly atheistic program of reform". However, "It was the single-handed achievement of Richard Whately to defeat the philosophical radicals by showing that a defensible demarcation is possible between scientific and theological knowledge, thereby insulating each from illegitimate encroachment by the other". Furthermore, "by safeguarding the integrity of each, it validated the ideological alliance of political economy and Christian theology that Malthus and his colleagues attempted to create" (quotations from Waterman 1991a: 10–11).

Waterman's explanation of the separation between economics and theology was that changes in ecclesiastical and academic politics after the 1830s rendered Christian political economy obsolete, and so the alliance collapsed.[1] "The ideological purpose of Christian Political Economy was to refute Jacobinism and to justify the ancien regime. By the mid-1830s both Jacobinism and the ancien regime were dead" (Waterman 1991a: 257). He notes that the death of Malthus and the appointments of Copleston and Whately as bishops also contributed.

This account of the rise of Christian political economy is in my view persuasive, but the account of its demise somewhat less so. The interactions between Christian theology and political economy in this period were not confined to Waterman's cast of Christian political economists, and so for my purposes the story needs to be broadened.

Maturing of economics as a science

For many economists, the explanation of the separation is straightforward. Theology and ethics are unnecessary baggage that economics needed to discard on the path to becoming a mature science, just as with other sciences.[2] A variant of this story that is particularly attractive to contemporary economists is that a separation between theology and economics is called for by the intellectual division of labour and that an efficient solution will therefore eventually emerge in history.

The supposed philosophical and sociological necessity of separation of economics from theology calls for supportive historical narratives. Many economists would point to the publication of Adam Smith's *Wealth of Nations* as the decisive moment in such a narrative; the composition of a work of economics as distinct from the moral philosophy of his earlier *Theory of Moral Sentiments*. However (as argued in a previous chapter, and also by Ross (1995, 2004a), Skinner (1996) and others), both the *Wealth of Nations* and *Theory of Moral Sentiments* were part of a larger Smithian system of which natural theology is an integral part.

In the history of economics literature, Schumpeter (1954) is an example of this narrative of throwing off ethics and theology as the science of economics or "economic analysis" matures. Similarly, TW Hutchison (1988). Even Jacob Viner's (1950) somewhat mournful account of the necessary marginalisation of what he calls "scholarship" in the economics profession, though he seems less sure of the separation in his unfinished great work on the history of the relationship between economics and Christian theology (Viner 1978). Mark Blaug's (1996) technically excellent history of economics does not even bother with the theological and ethical prehistory of the discipline.

Secularisation

Both Waterman's account of the obsolescence of Christian political economy and the explanation of the separation of economics from theology as the inevitable maturing of a science can be fitted into a larger narrative of secularisation. There is a huge literature on secularisation, and I will comment only on Charles Taylor's work as the major contemporary account and because he pays particular attention to the role of political economy.[3]

Charles Taylor (2007: 2–3) suggests there are three distinct meanings of the secular. First, that of a public square emptied of religion, at least officially. Second, a decline in religious belief and participation in religious institutions. Third, the conditions of belief and religious practice. What Taylor calls the "providential deism" of the 18th century is the turning point in his story of the transition to the modern secular world. Secular in his third sense of it now being intellectually plausible, and socially possible, to abandon traditional Christian religious belief and practice. The idea of the economy as an objectified reality and designed for mutual benefit is central to providential deism (Taylor 2007: 176–81). The doctrine of providence at this time takes an anthropocentric shift from being about God's purposes to being about human benefit, with political economy an important element in this shift. (Taylor 2007: 220–42).

This coheres somewhat with the account in of 18th-century English thought in Chapter 3 and Adam Smith's natural theological economics in Chapter 4, though I would resist the description of Smith as a deist because of his commitment, following his scientific hero Isaac Newton, to a God who was active in the cosmos and human affairs. None of my major figures from Chapters 3 and 4 feature prominently in standard histories and anthologies of deist writings (such as Gay 1968). Taylor's account also differs from mine in that he sees the idea of mutual benefit as a secularising force, whereas in my account it is an outflow of progress in the natural theologically framed discipline of political economy, and is not necessarily secularising. The separation of economics and theology comes from the collapse of the natural theological framework, for various reasons including the failure to produce an adequate economic theodicy. There is nothing inevitable about this process, or about the collapse of natural theology which separates economics from theology.

Explaining the demise of natural theology

A variety of stories have been told about the death of natural theology in Britain in the middle years of the 19th century.

Hume refuted natural theology

A popular story is that Hume's *Dialogues on Natural Religion* at the end of the 18th century mortally wounded the design argument that was central to natural theology, though natural theology managed to stagger on wounded for a few more decades before its inevitable death in the middle years of the 19th century.

There are a number of problems with this story:

- It assumes the most important function of natural theology was demonstrative, and so subject to refutation. This was not the case with British scientific natural theology; it was an intellectual framework which performed various mostly non-demonstrative functions as argued by Brooke (1991a) and others.
- It is puzzling that Hume is read so often as destroying a work which was not yet written; William Paley's *Natural Theology* was published in 1802.

- It misreads Hume's *Dialogues*. Hume was certainly highlighting short-comings of the design argument as a rational demonstration of the truth of Christianity, but the real force of his critique of Christianity was moral, in particular the inability to reconcile God's power and goodness with suffering (Brooke 1991a; Swinburne 1991, 2011; Newlands 2016).
- It struggles to explain how a mortally wounded natural theology was able to continue for so long, and why Paley was seemingly able to ignore Hume even though he wrote several decades after the publication of the *Dialogues*. Paley was aware of Hume's arguments and his *Natural Theology* was constructed to avoid their force (Le Mahieu 1976; McLean 2003).[4]

Darwin destroyed natural theology

Another common story is that the publication of Darwin's *Origin of Species* in 1859 killed Paley's design argument and natural theology with it. For instance, Anthony Waterman sees the death of natural theology as subsequent to and largely unconnected with the demise of Christian political economy, and identified Darwin publishing his account of evolution by natural selection as the critical event: "Natural theology continued to flourish in nineteenth-century Britain and America, undisturbed by Hume's posthumous *Dialogues Concerning Natural Religion* until the appearance of *Origin of Species*" (Waterman 2001: 57). To support the view that "all of a sudden Paley's reputation slumped" (Waterman 2004: 6), he presents evidence of the decline of new editions of Paley's *Natural Theology* after 1859.

Problems with the view that Darwin destroyed natural theology are:

- The evidence of a sudden death of Paley's design argument after the publication of the *Origin of Species* is unpersuasive. An examination of references to Paley in English books over the period 1750–2000 indicates the decline in Paley's reputation began in the 1830s, well before the publication of the *Origin of Species* and there is no obvious downturn after 1859.[5]
- It is not clear that Darwin's theory of evolution by natural selection was seen as incompatible with Christianity. Christian theological reactions to the *Origin of Species* were mixed, and were particularly positive among evangelicals (Moore 1979; Livingstone 1987; Brooke 1991a ch. 8; Ruse 2001). Some theologians welcomed Darwin's theory as showing the mechanisms of design to be more complex and wonderful than had been previously recognised. The great conflict between Darwinian science and religion was a partisan invention by TH Huxley and others later in the 19th century. "Creation science" is even more remote from the context of Darwin's Britain, being an early 20th-century American disease.[6]
- Natural theology was more than Paley's design argument. Even to the extent that natural theology had a demonstrative function, the design argument was only one argument among others such as the ontological and cosmological arguments. Darwin changed the terms of the debate about natural theology rather than ended it.

Professionalisation and natural theology

Increasing professionalisation of science is perhaps the dominant explanation in the contemporary history of science literature for the decline of natural theology. According to Young (1985), the natural theological context for science became redundant as the sciences became more professionalised and specialised through the 19th century in Britain. In his view, natural theology worked at too high a level of abstraction to continue to be of use to practising scientists, and fragmented for this reason. Turner (1974, 1978, 1993) argues the tension over science and religion in Victorian Britain was a debate about jobs, prestige and authority between increasingly professionalised scientists and religious amateurs. Natural theology became the focus of disagreement, and to oppose natural theology was to oppose church influence on appointments. As Turner notes, it was not just opposition from outside the established Anglican church that undermined natural theology; the church itself turned inward after the Oxford movement, becoming less interested in wider projects like natural theologically framed science. By the 1850s, clerical scientists faced ridicule from professional scientists and suspicion within the church. Such processes operated for the science of political economy as powerfully as they did for other sciences.

Natural theology undermined itself

The historian of science and religion, John Hedley Brooke (1991a ch. 6), supplements the professionalisation explanation with a consideration of the changing emphasis on the various functions of natural theology. In 19th-century Britain, natural theology was increasingly asked to demonstrate God's existence and goodness, a function for which Brooke considers it was ill-equipped. By the 1840s, Brooke suggests this became too heavy a burden, both scientifically and religiously, contributing to the decline of natural theology.

The demise of natural theology as the separation of economics from theology

The death of natural theology and the separation of political economy from theology need to be connected. My argument is that the death of natural theology deprived political economy of the framework that integrated it with theology, and the loss of this integrating framework was the separation of economics from theology. This supplements rather than replaces the arguments discussed earlier in this chapter about the role of ecclesiastical and academic politics in the demise of Christian political economy (offered by Waterman), and the professionalisation argument about the decline of natural theology (offered by Young and Turner). It is closest overall to John Hedley Brooke's arguments about natural theology being asked to carry too heavy a demonstrative burden, and the non-demonstrative functions becoming problematic in the 19th century.

In my account, an important factor in the death of natural theology in mid-19th-century Britain was its inability to deal with economic suffering, in other words its inability to provide an adequate theodicy. This difficulty was exacerbated by the extension of scientific natural theology to the economy. Why does economic suffering create particularly difficult problems for natural theology, and why did the problem of economic suffering only begin to do serious damage to natural theology in the 19th century?

The rise of political economy in the 19th century changed the way economic suffering was seen. Rather than being seen as an inevitable feature of society, it was now both explicable and remediable in a way it had not been in centuries past. It was now the responsibility of the science of political economy. The extension of natural theology to political economy connected economic suffering more clearly with divinely designed human nature and the economic system built around this human nature.

With the increasing emphasis on demonstrating the existence and goodness of God, a natural theological political economy was in deep trouble unless it could come up with an adequate theodicy.[7] As we have seen in previous chapters, political economists from Smith through Malthus, Paley, Sumner and Whewell struggled unsuccessfully to construct an adequate economic theodicy. Some such as Chalmers tried to ignore the problem. Whately openly acknowledged it was insoluble.

Extending natural theology to the economy affected the types of theodicies offered. The increasing sophistication of political economy in the 19th century meant that social ills like poverty could be linked to human choices in a way that natural ills like earthquakes could not, allowing the classical free will defence of divine power and goodness to be used with greater effect.[8] Political economy showed how humans could intervene to remedy economic suffering.

According to our natural theological political economists, government had some influence on economic suffering, but moral education of the poor informed by political economy had an even more powerful influence. We saw this emphasis on popular education in political economy to ameliorate economic suffering in Adam Smith. Also, Whately with his *Easy Lessons on Money Matters* 1833, Chalmers with his Glasgow pastoral work and *Political Economy: In Connection with the Moral State and Moral Prospects of Society* 1832, and Whewell with his *Lectures on Political Economy* 1862 delivered to the future King, were similarly keen on education.

As well as an acute and particularly nasty version of the problem of suffering and evil, extending natural theology to political economy caused other problems. Natural theology became much more politically charged when extended to political economy, undermining another of the functions of British scientific natural theology identified by Brooke (1991a). Arguments by theological political economists about inequality of ranks, land rents as a bountiful gift of nature and starvation of those at the bottom being part of God's design, stirred up political controversy in a way that arguments about the arrangement of the planets could not. This was why Whewell took particular exception to the Ricardian vision of unavoidable conflict of interest between economically defined classes as undermining the 18th-century vision of social harmony.

Another of the functions of British scientific natural theology that was threatened by extension to political economy was its capacity to unite different groups of scientists in the pursuit of truth. As we have seen in previous chapters, the natural theological background of political economists like Malthus, Whately, Jones and Whewell brought them into conflict with other political economists, rather than uniting them in a common cause as natural theology had done with those pursuing other sciences in earlier times. Natural theology became less and less scientifically useful to political economists through the 19th century.

Contrast the use Adam Smith (1776) made at the end of the 18th century of divinely ordained characteristics of human nature and doctrine of providence in his theory of the beneficial effects of individuals pursuing self-interest in a market economy, to the almost complete uselessness of natural theology to Whewell (1829–50) in theorising about the basis and gains from international trade. Becoming less useful in such a prominent science as political economy reinforced the wider decline in its fruitfulness in other sciences discussed by Young (1985).

The growing cultural importance of political economy in 19th-century Britain makes it plausible to attribute a large role in the demise of natural theology to these problems arising from the extension of natural theology to political economy.

One other dimension of the concurrent rise of political economy and national wealth in the 19th century was the way a rhetoric of prosperity took over some of the integrating functions of natural theology in British culture. The shared quest for wealth, guided by political economy, gradually displaced the quest for truth guided by Christian theology at the heart of British culture.

Evolution as a lost opportunity to renew natural theology

In my view, a lost opportunity for natural theological political economy in the middle years of the 19th century was connecting with evolutionary thought. In the previous section, I suggested the idea that Darwin's *Origin of Species* killed natural theology is problematic because Paley's version of the design argument is not the only version of the design argument, and the design argument is not all of natural theology. Indeed, as Brooke (1991a) has discussed, part of the problem with natural theology in the 19th century was its overemphasis on the design argument in demonstrating the truth of Christianity.

What if natural theological political economists had bypassed Paley's static version of the design argument in favour of engaging with early 19th-century British evolutionary thinking? An example of this thinking is Jones' and Whewell's old Cambridge friend Charles Babbage's unofficial *Ninth Bridgewater Treatise* (1838).[9]

Babbage's *Bridgewater Treatise* criticised and supplemented the previous works in the series, as he explains in the Preface: "One of the chief defects of the Treatises above referred to appears to me to arise from their not pursuing the argument to a sufficient extent" (Babbage 1838: vii). Whereas Whewell had attempted to push beyond Paley by arguing that scientific laws revealed God more clearly than contrivance, Babbage suggested that it was even more wonderful to consider a God who had in view all past and present instances of scientific laws, and the principles which control their development.[10] His aim was no less than "to show that the power and knowledge of the great Creator of matter and of mind are unlimited" (Babbage 1838: ix).

Babbage began by comparing nature to his famous calculating machine which operates in a changeable lawlike manner, under the control of its designer (Babbage 1838: 34–8). Consider a machine generating numbers according to what appears to be a rule, which then suddenly generates an unexpected number. Babbage suggests that the observer in this instance fails to appreciate the machine was operating under a more general law, and argues that it is a much greater machine (with a greater designer) that is able to adjust the rule it seems to be operating under, than a machine that can only change its apparent rule through the intervention of its operator. God as designer of the world would of course have much greater skill and foresight than Babbage had as designer of a calculating machine. Moreover, the extinction and rise of animals is a demonstration of divine "power and of knowledge of a far higher order" than a single instance of adaption (Babbage 1838: 45–6). So a natural or social system able to change itself reveals a much more wonderful God than revealed by the static design argument.

In a chapter "On the Nature of a Superintending Providence" added to the second edition of his *Ninth Bridgewater Treatise*, Babbage defended this view of design against charges that it is incompatible with the doctrine of providence, in particular the charge that it made God too passive.[11]

> Some of the readers of the former edition of this work, whilst they have admitted the exalted view of the Creator, which arises from considering his will as the development of laws of unbounded generality, have expressed regret that those views appeared to them, in some measure, to imply that we are less immediately the objects of his protecting care – that he seems thus less constantly and less directly, our watchful Guardian and Protector.
>
> (Babbage 1838: 141–2)

His reply is that:

> The inference from which the objection has arisen, is that the superintendence of Providence is remote, not immediate; the answer that I shall endeavour to make to it is, that the value of benevolence is not diminished by the distance of time at which its exertion arises.
>
> (Babbage 1838: 144)

The charge of inconsistency with the doctrine of providence seemed to particularly annoy Babbage, for as well as concluding in relation to geology that "there exists no fatal collision between the words of Scripture and the facts of nature" (Babbage 1838: 65), he wrote, "We must not . . . step forward Bible in hand to check the inquiries of the Geologist, the Astronomer, or the Political-economist, from an apprehension that the cause of religion can be endangered by them"

(Babbage 1838: 174).[12] The main point for our purposes is that Babbage was sketching a theologically framed evolutionary theory two decades before the publication of Darwin's *Origin of Species*.

Political economists in the 18th and early 19th centuries were showing how much the structure of society had changed over time, and was continuing to do so. The changes associated with the industrial revolution in late 19th-century Britain were a vivid contemporary illustration of this. Malthus' principle of population rested on designed human dispositions and the productivity of agricultural land, which could be argued to fit better with Babbage's thinking about design than Paley's. Much of the force of Richard Jones' work on *Rent* discussed in Chapter 6 was that the institutional arrangements which gave rise to rent varied greatly by country and over time, and were continuing to change. A large part of Whewell's criticism of Ricardo's rent theory was of its claimed universality – and he preferred the modest claims of Jones' historical approach taking account of diversity and change in institutional arrangements.

Whewell's own scientific work is complicated. There are evolutionary elements of his science,[13] but yet he was distinctly cold towards Babbage's *Ninth Bridgewater Treatise*. Aside from the work being partly directed against Whewell, it would not have helped that Babbage's book was extensively quoted in Robert Chambers' notorious evolutionary *Vestiges of the Natural History of Creation* 1844, which Whewell had attacked savagely as poor science and a religious threat. These personal and religio-political black marks against evolutionary thinking perhaps contributed to Whewell's reluctance to embrace Darwin's *Origin of Species* when published in 1859. If so, it is a great pity that these personal and religio-political accidents hampered the 19th-century natural theological political economist who was best equipped to connect political economy to evolutionary thought and who had the scientific and religious standing to promote an evolutionary approach to natural theological political economy.

Such a reorientation of natural theology was urgently needed because rapid change and new scientific thinking had reduced the appeal of traditional versions of the design argument which were based on analogies from an unchanging natural world. Paley's static clock–clockmaker analogy for divine design was beginning to lose its force even when it appeared in his *Natural Theology* in 1802. Something more was needed to sustain natural theology, especially as natural theology now embraced the troublesome new science of political economy.

Even without Babbage's contribution there were resources within political economy for an evolutionary reorientation; for instance, Adam Smith's stage theory of the evolution of commercial society described in Chapter 4, or Adam Ferguson's theory, or even Marx' theory of the evolution of economic arrangements. A natural theological political economy grounded in the Scottish Enlightenment conception of historical evolution may even have been stronger than one which took up Babbage's work or later Darwinian evolutionary theory. Could such a political economy have been the basis of a new alliance between political economy and natural theology for the 1860s?

An evolutionary natural theological political economy would have still struggled with the problem of economic suffering. Babbage's answer that God had designed the system which controlled the evolution of economic arrangements may take God away from the scene of the crime but does not relieve God of responsibility for economic suffering. It just moves the problem of explain economic suffering and evil back to a deeper level. One novel twist to theodicy that evolution offers is the possibility that while we currently suffer, the system may evolve in such a way that economic suffering will disappear, or possibly get worse, for humans cannot easily foresee the destination of the evolutionary process. The doctrine of the fall of course precludes the possibility of evolution eliminating suffering and makes a theodicy taking advantage of the unforseeability of the evolutionary process suspect for theologically orthodox political economists.

This is a way of thinking about design and providence that political economists should have found congenial. As well as possible benefits in relation to theodicy, evolutionary natural theological political economy may have better fulfilled the function of buttressing the established order, given that by the mid-19th century this order was reformist. Such an evolutionary natural theology may even have been theoretically fruitful for political economists. We can only speculate because it was a path not taken by political economists in the 19th century.

Subsequent developments in Britain, continental Europe and North America

Britain

However the various causes of the separation of political economy from Christian theology are weighted, the separation was well entrenched in Britain by the later decades of the 19th century.[14]

An instructive case is Phillip Wicksteed, a strong Unitarian whose economics arose from an underlying religious vision, and who made significant theoretical contributions to the discipline.[15] Developing an interest in economics at the end of the 19th century, he did not consider it appropriate to deploy theology in support of his economics or to discuss the relationship of his economics to theology in his *Common Sense of Political Economy* 1910. All the time while continuing to write on theological matters.

Alfred Marshall, whose *Principles of Economics* 1890 set the tone of British economics well into the 20th century, was instrumental in the formation of the Economics Tripos at Cambridge from 1903. He introduced his *Principles* with the statement that "the two great forming agencies of the world's history have been the religious and the economic" then made little reference to religion, dealing with what he saw as the separate realm of economics.

JM Keynes, who was writing well after the separation, identified the 1860s as "the critical moment at which Christian dogma fell away from the serious philosophical world of England, or at any rate of Cambridge" (Keynes 1933: 168).

His comment reflects the personal experience of Keynes and his Cambridge circle rather than the wider historical reality.

Although theology retreated from, or was pushed out of mainstream economics, economic questions continued to be discussed in the churches. An influential strand of the continuing church discussion of economic issues was the Christian socialism of FD Maurice, Charles Kingsley, JM Ludlow and others from the 1850s.[16] If anything gave this movement coherence, it was opposition to "the application of what they took to be the main tenets of classical political economy" (Norman 1987: 4) and the Christian socialists offered various amateur analyses of economic issues. None, aside perhaps from their practical influence on the co-operative movement and adult education, has been lasting. The original group was followed by a succession of academics in other fields such as RH Tawney and Anglican churchmen such as William Temple, who were increasingly divorced from mainstream economic discussion. Other movements such as the distributivism of the Roman Catholic writers GK Chesterton and Hilaire Belloc were even less engaged with mainstream economics.

The position of the Anglican church as an established church licenced attempts to bring theologians and economists together to discuss policy in England – for example, the Oldham groups and Oxford Conferences of the early 20th century – but the lack of an integrating framework and growing gap between the ways theologians and economists viewed the world made such gatherings less and less fruitful. The felt need to bring the two groups together is a reflection of how much things had changed since the early 19th-century alliance of political economy with theology.

Continental Europe

The story of economics and theology in continental Europe is outside the scope of this work, but a few brief comments here will help set the scene for the discussion in the next chapter of the contemporary relationship between economics and theology.

In the 18th century political economy was an international affair. Developments in France, the Netherlands, Germany and Italy were important to the formation of the discipline in Britain, and likewise had strong theological connections. The story in each country is different, shaped by local conditions and especially by major political developments such as the Revolution in France at the end of the 18th century.[17]

To begin with France, there is an important argument,[18] which runs parallel to my own argument for Britain, about theological influence on political economy through the Jansenists Jean Domat and Pierre Nicole, and Pierre Boisguilbert at the beginning of the 18th century, carried through Richard Cantillon and Bernard Mandeville to Adam Smith and key figures in the formation of political economy as a discipline. Later, and somewhat independently, in the 19th century JB Say and Frederic Bastiat offered theologically based defences of the market in France, but the dominant strands of French economics in the 19th century, especially those associated with the churches, were sceptical about markets.

Italy is an interesting case with Bruni and Zamagni (2007, 2014) arguing that the 18th-century Neapolitan Antoni Genovesi and others had a theologically based theory of markets, which they called the civil economy tradition, and suggesting it was superior in some ways to the British tradition.

Across Europe, the 1890s was a time of new developments in the relationship between religion and politics and economics. In the Catholic church, the "social question" arising out of increasing industrialisation and urbanisation was addressed by a series of Papal statements on social and economic matters beginning with Leo XIII's 1891 encyclical *Rerum Novarum*. The Popes were distinctly cold towards political economy, which was associated with British liberalism and perhaps even more dangerously with ways of thinking that had led to the French Revolution. Instead, the Popes drew on more familiar European political economy and earlier Scholastic natural law thinkers on economics.[19] Partly stimulated by this line of Papal encyclicals, a number of Catholics familiar with mainstream economic thinking made thought provoking contributions to the debate over the relationship between Christian theology and economics: Lonergan (1999, written in the 1940s), Noonan (1957) and Dempsey (1958).[20] Each of these writers was shaped in different ways by the revival of interest in the philosophy of St Thomas Aquinas in Catholic circles from the 19th century.

Also in the 1890s, the Dutch churchman and politician Abraham Kuyper was attempting to renew Calvinism for the 20th century.[21] One reading of Kuyper is that he was reasserting theological control over science, including political economy (for instance, Waterman 1987; Marsden 1989) but other readings emphasise his inclusive practice and theology of common grace (for instance, McGowan 2009; Oslington 2010). Kuyper's work became the basis of late 20th-century attempts to reconstruct economics on Christian foundations, which will be discussed in the next chapter.

Relationships between economics and theology in continental Europe from the 18th century were complex and varied, and the above merely highlights some developments relevant to my argument.

North America

The Enlightenment in America was strongly religious, more like the Scottish Enlightenment than the English Enlightenment, and in sharp contrast to the hostility to religion of the continental European Enlightenment (May 1976; Himmelfarb 2004). American economics from the late 18th to mid-19th centuries was heavily dependent on British writers, especially Scottish common sense philosophy, the economics of Adam Smith, with the addition of large doses of optimism linked to the growing American economy.[22]

In this period, economics was typically part of capstone courses in moral philosophy taught by the college president or another figure of sufficient moral standing, in a period where the major colleges were associated with churches. These teachers and textbook writers regarded Adam Smith's economics as harmonising perfectly with their theological commitments, and saw disseminating economics to be a religious task. Natural theology was part of this thought world, though the language was different to Britain as one would expect in the different scientific and political context of America. Confidence in the robustness of this harmony allowed American writers to freely investigate economic questions, just as had Smith, Paley and Malthus in Britain.

A good example is the Episcopalian clergyman John McVickar who was appointed Professor of Moral Philosophy and Political Economy by Columbia University in 1817. He has a reasonable claim to be the author of the first economics textbook published in America (McVickar 1825), built around JR McCulloch's *Encyclopædia Britannica* article on political economy, though often preferring Adam Smith's views to McCulloch's. A feature of the book is his sketch of "The Development of Economical Science in America" where "In tracing the history of Political Economy, some reference is due to the claims of our own country; though it must be acknowledged we have understood the subject much better in practice than in theory" (McVickar 1825: 44).

McVickar was convinced of the harmony between economics and theology: "That science and religion eventually teach the same lesson, is a necessary consequence of the unity of truth, but it is seldom that this union is so early and satisfactorily displayed as in the researches of Political Economy" (McVickar 1825: 69). This statement could have come from any of the British natural theological political economists of this period. His hopes for political economy in America were high:

> The language of Political Economy is the language of reason and of enlarged experience . . . Without incurring the charge of enthusiasm, it may be maintained to be the redeeming science of modern times – the regenerating principle that in connexion with the spirit of Christianity, is at work in the civilized governments of the world, not to revolutionize, but to reform . . . The high principles which this science teaches, entitle it to be regarded as the moral instructor of nations.
>
> (McVickar 1825: 186)

One important difference with the British economists is that McVickar is untroubled by questions about population and theodicy that absorbed Malthus' followers. He gives an accurate summary of the second edition of Malthus' *Essay* (McVickar 1825: 145) and is aware of the theological issues, but believes that the United States' rapidly growing population allows it to avoid the Malthusian problem. If the Malthusian preventative checks are not needed, neither is a theodicy. He is also sensitive to another problem raised by Malthus, that of potential shortfalls of effective demand, a problem over which Malthus and Ricardo disagreed sharply. Again, though, McVickar sees the problem as irrelevant to his American situation:

> Whatever may be thought of this principle [large unproductive consumption is necessary to stimulate industry, and prevent the overloading of the market], in relation to such a country as England, it is altogether inapplicable to us. So long as we in America have forests to subdue and canals to open, there

can be no injurious surplus of capital, labor, or commodities. The gradual improvement of the country will absorb, for centuries to come, all that is redundant, and population increasing in the same ratio as the means of support, be constantly affording a wider market and more varied consumption.

(McVickar 1825: 168)

No need for theodicy here either.

Another example is Francis Wayland, Baptist minister, President of Brown University and author of two of the most popular textbooks in 19th-century America, *Elements of Moral Science* first published in 1835, and *Elements of Political Economy* 1837. In a statement much quoted by writers after the separation of economics from theology in America, Wayland argued "economical questions on economical grounds" and "has not thought it proper to intermingle them with moral philosophy and theology" (Wayland 1837: iv). What is passed over by subsequent writers is that this statement must be read in the light of his natural theological convictions about harmony between political economy and the teachings of scripture.

Wayland defines political economy in Smithian terms as the "Science of Wealth" and adds:

[b]y Science, as the word is here used, we mean a systematic arrangement of the laws which God has established, so far as they have been discovered, of any department of human knowledge. It is obvious, upon the slightest reflection, that the Creator has subjected the accumulation of the blessings of this life to some determinate laws. Every one, for instance, knows that no man can grow rich, without industry and frugality. Political Economy, therefore, is a systematic arrangement of the laws by which, under our present constitution, the relations of man, whether individual or social, to the objects of his desire, are governed.

(Wayland 1837: 15)

This is reinforced later when he presents production theory as the explication of "the blessings which God has in reserve for man" (Wayland 1837: 59) and investigation of production must be conditioned by his understanding of the created order, for instance that "God has created man with physical and intellectual faculties, adapted to labor", that "the Creator has affixed several penalties, which those who disobey this law of their being, can never expect to escape" (Wayland 1837: 105–6).

As well as a harmony between political economy and scripture, there is a theologically based theory of harmony of interests, which he finds is amply vindicated by his investigations into political economy:

[i]n political economy, as in morals, every benefit is mutual; and we cannot, in the one case, any more than in the other, really do good to ourselves, without doing good to others; nor do good to others, without also doing good to ourselves.

(Wayland 1837: 171)

Like McVickar, there no anxicty about population. In his discussion of population and wages:

> [t]his subject illustrates the connexion between capital and population. Population always follows capital. It increases as capital increases; is stationary when capital is stationary; and decreases when capital decreases. And hence, there seems no need of any other means to prevent the too rapid increase of population, than to secure a correspondent increase of capital, by which that population may be supported.
>
> (Wayland 1837: 305)

And further:

> If the considerations which have been adduced above be correct, there is no need of seeking any further for the cause of that distress among the lower classes, of which we hear so frequently in Europe. If the capital which a bountiful Creator has provided for the sustenance of man, be dissipated in wars, his creatures must perish for the want of it. Nor do we need any abstruse theories of population, to enable us to ascertain in what manner this excess of population may be prevented. Let nations cultivate the arts of peace. Let them reduce the unnecessary expenses of governments. Let them abolish those restrictions which fetter and dispirit industry, by diminishing the inducements to labor. Let them foster the means by which the productiveness of labor may be increased, and the annual gifts of the Creator will so accumulate, that the means will be provided for the support of all the human beings that are annually brought into the world.
>
> (Wayland 1837: 307–8)

Again, with no population problem, at least if the government stays out of the way and allows capital to flow, then there is no need for a theodicy.[23]

I have lingered over these examples of early 19th-century American economics because of the connections with the British natural theological political economists of the same period. As the 19th century went on, American economics went its own way, but some of the forces that operated in the separation of economics and theology in Britain, such as increasing professionalisation of science, were certainly operating in America. Natural theology was weaker and expressed in a different language, and theodicy was not the same pressing issue that it was in Britain, so these other forces I emphasised in the previous section for Britain were not as strong. Was there a mid to late 19th-century separation of economics and theology in America? It is hard to say and more investigation is required, which could be quite illuminating in comparison to the British case.

We need more than a remark constantly quoted by historians of American economics as evidence of secularisation in this period. William Graham Sumner, sometime clergyman, Oxford educated long-time teacher of political economy and many other things at Yale, infamous in certain circles as a "social Darwinist" when asked about his religious beliefs quipped: "I never consciously gave up a religious belief . . . it was as if I had put my beliefs into a drawer and when I opened it there was nothing there at all".[24]

The often-told tale of the religious foundation of the American Economic Association in 1885[25] is certainly not the beginning of religious contributions to American economic thought. It is better seen as an attempt by Richard Ely and economists associated with the Social Gospel movement to legitimate their version of economics, against secular critics like Simon Newcomb and religious critics like Arthur Latham Perry. Bateman (2011) argues that the collapse of the progressive movement after WWI was the decisive event in the secularisation of American economics, and is sceptical about the creeping, unintentional secu-larisation arguments of Marty (1969) and Marsden (1990). Bateman's argument works if the Social Gospel and Progressive movement was the dominant frame-work holding American economics and theology together, but this does not seem to be the case in light of the earlier 19th-century history.[26]

Another popular tale of this period which must be rejected attributes the separation of American economics from theology to John Bates Clark.[27] The tale opens with the early Clark basing his economics on religious sentiment in *Philosophy of Wealth* 1886, then abandoning this for secular scientific reason in *Distribution of Wealth* 1899. Alongside Clark's own transformation is a trans-formation of the American Economic Association as Ely and his supporters were displaced. However, close examination of Clark's transformation by Everett (1946) and Henry (1982) does not support this tale. There seems to be little change in Clark's theological commitments, his anthropology or view of pri-vate property – just his attitude to competition. Many of the differences between the two books are of rhetoric rather than substance, as Clark accommodates his style to the different situation of the 1890s where appeals to religion are less persuasive. If the tale is false, then so too is the moral of the tale that is so much a part of the self-identity of American economists: that religious influences are inevitability cast aside in the march towards scientific economics, and that this is a good thing.

Whatever the true story of the separation of economics and theology in America, it is probably more complicated than the story for Britain, and has received much less attention. My guess is that it will be a story of strong but changing religious associations, consistent with a much less secular American culture than Britain. If Nelson (1991, 2001) is right about religious dimensions of economics up until the late 20th century at least, then the American story is even more complex. Settling this debate is well beyond the scope of the present work.

Conclusion

I have suggested in this chapter that the extension of natural theology to political economy, as well as nourishing political economy, helped to undermine natural theology. In my view, the death of natural theology is, with some help from politi-cal economy, the much-debated separation of economics from theology.

A theme that has recurred in the demise of scientific natural theology in 19th-century Britain is the increasing emphasis on its demonstrative functions, in contrast to other non-demonstrative functions natural theology was better equipped to perform. This emphasis on the demonstrative functions is largely why the problem of suffering was so damaging for natural theology – in political economy as much as the other sciences. Scientific natural theology misconstrued as a rational demonstration of God's existence and goodness was fragile.

A digression to the main argument of the chapter speculated on whether an evolutionary turn in natural theological political economy may have rescued it in the middle years of the 19th century. Finally, some brief comparisons were made of Britain with other places, and filling in some later parts of the story in preparation for reflections on the contemporary scene in the next chapter.

Notes

1 Waterman also suggests the demarcation between economic and theological knowledge is philosophically well founded, related to the positive/normative distinction, and justifies an enduring separation between economic and theological discourse (for instance, Waterman 1991a: 260, 1994, 2003).

2 This argument about sciences throwing off religion as they mature is demolished by Brooke 1991a ch. 2. The relationship to Max Weber's (1905) argument about certain forms of Calvinism contributing to the rise of capitalism, and then the original religious impulse falling away, is debatable. Durkheim (1893) is another sociological version of this argument.

3 The thesis of inevitable secularisation is still advocated by some sociologists of religion (for instance, Steve Bruce 2011), though heavily criticised (for instance, Stark 1999; Smith 2014) and abandoned by many previous advocates (including Peter Berger 2005). Charles Taylor (1989, 2007) describes a much more complicated process. Gregory (2012) connects secularisation to the Reformation. Hunter (2015) offers another account of the concept of secularisation in 19th-century cultural disputes, especially in Germany.

4 Paley's awareness of Hume's arguments is clear from the explicit references to "Mr Hume, in his posthumous dialogues" discussed by Murdith McLean (2003: 170). Paley's design argument is a cumulative argument that order educes wonder that can be satisfied by God, which is subtly different to the rational demonstration of God's existence that Paley is often taken to be offering. In McLean's view, "a number of Paley's arguments should be accorded a measure of success as rejoinders" to Hume even if not a refutation (2003: 186).

5 Google N-grams for Paley are presented in the appendix.

6 Brooke (1991a) examines the famous 1860 "confrontation" between TH Huxley and Bishop Wilberforce. The rise of creation science in 20th-century America is discussed by Numbers (1993).

7 An N-gram in the appendix shows rising occurrence of theodicy in English books from the 1840s, peaking around 1850, consistent with growing controversy over theodicy, partly related to political economy. The peak of interest in theodicy coincides with declining occurrences of natural theology.

8 Waterman 1991a: 64–82 discusses this in terms of the transition in the late 18th and early 19th centuries of economic suffering from being seen as a natural evil to being a moral evil.

9 Charles Babbage wrote his unsolicited and unofficial *Ninth Bridgewater Treatise* in response to Whewell's own Bridgewater Treatise *Astronomy and General Physics*

Considered with Reference to Natural Theology 1833, and out of a desire to defend recent work in geology against charges that it was incompatible with the Genesis account of creation. Lyell's *Principles of Geology* 1830–33 is clearly in view. A quotation from Whewell's Bridgewater Treatise appears on Babbage's title page and his preface indicates his concern about Whewell's pessimism about the possibilities of mathematical sciences contributing to natural theology. This connects to debates about Cambridge mathematics flowing from Babbage's founding of the Analytical Society and connection to French mathematicians. Babbage explains "I have again read, with much attention, the chapters in Mr Whewell's Bridgewater Treatise, which bear upon the question of the effect of the pursuits of science on our belief in natural religion, and I confess that I am unable to alter the opinion I have already expressed upon that subject – that they give support to those who maintain that the pursuits of science are in general unfavourable to religion". He authored a work on political economy (Babbage 1832) but is much better known as a mathematician and pioneer of computing than political economist. Maxine Berg (1980, 1987), Boyd Hilton (1988), William Ashworth (1996) and Laura Snyder (2011) discuss Babbage's ideas in relation to political economy.

10 Babbage's is not very clear about what exactly he means by a law of nature and by laws changing. He seems to have in mind different laws applying in different situations and an evolution of our understanding of the laws of nature, rather than the laws of physics changing. Besides the calculating machine example, the emphasis is on divine foresight rather than divine intervention.

11 This is similar to the debate between Leibniz and Newton over special providence mentioned in Chapter 4, with Smith following Newton in allowing an active providence, expressed in my view in Smith's invisible hand passages.

12 Whewell was only expressing doubts in his own Bridgewater Treatise about mathematics advancing the cause of religion, not claiming that there was a conflict with religion. By 1838, Whewell and Babbage (then Lucasian Professor at Cambridge) were at odds over many issues. Babbage in a footnote here references the "First Lecture on Political Economy", doubtless Whately's, and this reference was perhaps calculated to annoy Whewell.

13 Darwin (1859) on his title page quotes Whewell's *Bridgewater Treatise* "But with regard to the material world, we can at least go so far as this – we can perceive that events are brought about not by insulated interpositions of Divine power, exerted in each particular case, but by the establishment of general laws". The quotation is from p. 356.

14 There is a large literature on relationships between economics and theology in early 19th-century Britain, but thin on subsequent developments, and even thinner on developments outside Britain. Emmett (2014) discusses economics and theology after the separation. The edited volumes of Brennan and Waterman (1994) and Bateman and Banzhaf (2008) deal mostly with the connections between the faith of individual economists and their economics.

15 Wicksteed and his contributions to political economy are discussed by Ian Steedman (1987, 1994).

16 Edward Norman (1976 ch. 6, 1987) discusses the key 19th-century Christian socialists, and Preston (1993) the broader movement. FD Maurice came very close to being elected to the Drummond Chair at Oxford, but this was perhaps the last serious contact of the movement with mainstream economics.

17 Nineteenth-century developments in continental Europe are discussed in much more detail by Teixeira and Almodovar (2008, 2012), Force (2003), Facarello (2014) and Bruni and Zamagni (2014). The argument about the importance of the Jansenists and Boisguilbert for the development of political economy is made by Viner (1978) and Faccarello (1999), with comments by Groenewegen (2002) and Waterman (2008a). JB Say is covered by Forget (1999) and Bastiat by Hebert (2008). Genovesi and the Italian civil economy tradition is discussed by Bruni and Zamagni (2007), and also Augimeri (1992) and Milbank (1990). Germany is covered by Tribe (1997).

18 This argument is made by Facarcllo (1999) and Waterman (2008a).

19 The Papal texts may be found on the Vatican website. They are discussed by Waterman (1991c, 1999, 2013, 2016), Barrera (2001) and Yuengert (2014) among others.

20 Bernard Lonergan's work is particularly interesting and discussed by Ormerod *et al.* (2012).

21 The key text is Kuyper (1898) and his relevant essays are collected with an introduction in Kuyper (1998). Oslington (2010) discusses the mutation of Kuyper's thought into an unhelpful sectarian Christian economics.

22 Early American economics is discussed by Dorfman (1947–59) and Emmett (2015). The 19th-century clerical economists such as Francis Wayland, Alonzo Potter and John McVickar have been analysed by Heyne (1986), Noll (2002) and Davenport (2008). The use of the term "clerical laissez-faire" for these and other writers is due to Henry May and has been picked up by subsequent historians as a dismissive description of these writers. The sense seems to be that both religion and laissez-faire are things we have now grown out of.

23 A recent work on Malthus (Bashford and Chaplin 2016) discusses the global reception and impact of Malthus' work, including in America. It also emphasises the role of Benjamin Franklin's *Observations Concerning the Increase of Mankind* 1751 on Malthus' thinking about population. There is little attention to the theological dimensions of Malthus' work or its reception. Even if early American political economists as I argue above were unconcerned about starvation and other Malthusian checks to population operating, it may still be true that Malthusian anxieties encouraged expansion of colonies and dispossession of native peoples' lands in the New World.

24 WG Sumner is discussed by Samuels (1987) and Bannister (1973) who has also edited a collection on Sumner's work *On Liberty, Society, and Politics: The Essential Essays of William Graham Sumner*, Indianapolis, Liberty Fund 1992.

25 The foundation of the American Economic Association is discussed by Ely (1936), Coats (1985) and Bateman and Kapstein (1999). Coats (1987) and Everett (1946) discuss Ely with some attention to his religious background. Bateman (2008, 2011) reflects further on this and subsequent developments, along with Emmett (2014).

26 Tim Leonard (2016) building on earlier work highlights the unwholesome role of eugenics in the Progressive movement and American economics of this period. It may be that this pseudo-religious framework played something of the role that natural theology did in earlier periods in Britain and to a lesser extent America.

27 The most comprehensive discussion of JB Clark's work with attention to its religious background is Henry (1995). Leonard (2003) is also valuable.

8 Reflections on the contemporary relationship between economics and theology

Introduction

This short final chapter is not part of the main argument of the book, but addresses a question asked by some readers along the way about what the historical and theological arguments of the previous chapters might mean for the contemporary relationship between economics and theology.

What can we learn from this episode about what promotes fruitful and unfruitful exchange between economists and theologians?

During the 18th and early 19th centuries in Britain I have argued that political economy was embedded in and nourished by a larger natural theological framework. Economics and theology have now parted ways, and the cultural situation in the 21st century is now quite different. Theology no longer has the cultural power it once enjoyed. What lessons might nevertheless be learnt from this history for contemporary attempts to relate economics to theology? Here are a few suggestions, with no attempt to tie them back rigorously to the historical and theological arguments of the previous chapters.

- **Integration is potentially powerful**. Natural theology as an integrating framework contributed to the birth of economics as a discipline, and then to its demise and the separation of economics from theology.
- **Engage with the mainstream, or a potential replacement mainstream**. Natural theology sustained religious interaction with mainstream economic discussion in Britain in this period, not just a sectarian backwater of economic discussion. Mainstream economics today is perhaps more receptive than it has been for decades to engagement with other disciplines, and some within the profession are seeking to connect economics to larger questions and frameworks as it struggles for legitimacy in the early 21st century.
- **Approaches that attempt to reduce economics to theology, or the reverse, are unhelpful**. During the fruitful period of interaction between economics and theology, such attempts on both sides were held at bay by the natural theological framework.

- **Relating economics and theology is not just an intellectual question; the political and pastoral dimensions are very important**. This is part of the reason it is hard, and the experience in 18th and 19th-century Britain showed how a way of relating the two could be intellectually, pastorally and politically serviceable.
- **Theology has nothing to fear from economics, neither has economics anything to fear from theology**. If interaction has been fruitful for both disciplines in the past, is there any reason to expect it will not be in the present, if well done?

Frameworks for contemporary engagement[1]

If there is to be a renewal on engagement between economics and theology, what intellectual frameworks might support this engagement?

Revival of scientific natural theology

The British tradition of scientific natural theology nourished and shaped the development of political economy in 18th and 19th-century Britain, but this tradition is now well and truly dead. While some of the intellectual issues remain, the 21st-century pastoral and political context is quite different.

There is a contemporary revival of interest in natural theology in some scientific circles, or perhaps more accurately some science and theology circles. Alister McGrath, successor to John Hedley Brooke and Peter Harrison as Professor of Science and Religion at the University of Oxford, is one prominent advocate of a renewal of natural theology (McGrath 2003, 2008). The American Lutheran theologian Philip Hefner's (1993) suggestion of understanding ourselves as created co-creator, though not without its critics, is a variation of this theme which may have potential for sustaining fruitful interaction between economics and theology. A post-Darwinian evolutionally natural theology is another variation that may be fruitful in relation to economics. Perhaps picking up some elements of Charles Babbage's approach discussed in the previous chapter. Or picking up Neil Ormerod's (2010, 2015) work. Or Sarah Coakley's (2012) engagement with evolutionary theory.

Natural law

Natural law can be a bridge between theology and other disciplines, such as ethics. It is usually associated with Roman Catholicism, and the most powerful versions build on the work of Thomas Aquinas (Kerr 2002). Natural law theory need not be Catholic or Thomist, as Stephen Grabill's (2006) discussion of Protestant natural law thinking shows. This Protestant natural law tradition was important to Adam Smith. Among Catholics, natural law has been used as an integrating framework for economics and theology in recent times by Albino Barrera (2004, 2011), Andrew Yuengert (2012), Mary Hirschfeld (2012, 2013), Samuel Gregg (2016) and others.

Common grace

In the Reformed tradition, the doctrine of common grace provides perhaps the most promising integrative framework for economics and theology. This doctrine has been neglected in some recent attempts to construct a Christian economics which claims inspiration from Abraham Kuyper (for instance, Tiemstra 2009; Tiemstra *et al.* 1990); attempts which as well as neglecting common grace turn Kuyper's fundamental antithesis which applies to all people into a sectarian program. A recovery of the original doctrine in Kuyper (1898, 1998, 2015) is needed if common grace is to have a chance of operating as an integrative framework. The issues are further discussed in Mouw (2001), McGowan (2009) and Oslington (2010).

Eastern Orthodox theology

Various Eastern Orthodox writers have used the doctrine of divine wisdom as an integrating framework for economics and theology (for instance, Bulgakov 1937, 2000). More recently, Dotan Lesham (2013, 2016a, 2016b) has proposed the concept of oikonomia in the Eastern Christian Fathers as a point of integration. Each has potential for probing the theological meaning of a market economy.

Pneumatology

The work of the Holy Spirit is another potentially fruitful integrating theological theme for economics and theology (for instance, Volf 1991; Welker 1994, 1999, 2009; Clifton 2014; Yong 2015).

In each case, we must remember that integration is not just an intellectual issue, but integration happens in persons, institutions and wider political contexts. A proposed framework must work in these dimensions as well as dealing with the intellectual issues. As it worked in each of these dimension in 18th and 19th-century Britain.

Above all, there is not one answer to the question of the relationship between economics and theology. Faithful and fruitful answers will be embodied in persons and vary with the context.

Note

1 This section is a substantially revised and updated version of my previous St Marks Day Lecture at St Marks National Theological Centre in Canberra (Oslington 2005).

Appendix

Analysis of key terms in English books

This appendix provides information on the usage of key terms in the main text, using Google N-grams, which indicate the incidence of a phrase in a very large collection of English books from 1750 to the present time which have been dig-itised by Google. The N-grams were obtained using https://books.google.com/ngrams, and full specifications of N-grams are available at https://books.google.com/ngrams/info.

The use of Google N-grams is discussed by Jean-Baptiste Michel, Yuan Kui Shen, Aviva Presser Aiden, Adrian Veres, Matthew K. Gray, Joseph P. Pickett, Dale Hoiberg, Dan Clancy, Peter Norvig, Jon Orwant, Steven Pinker, Martin A. Nowak and Erez Lieberman Aiden (2010) 'Quantitative Analysis of Culture Using Millions of Digitized Books', *Science*. www.sciencemag.org/content/early/2010/12/15/science.1199644.

Google N-grams are one source of information about usage of terms, and I have used them alongside other sources, following the approach of Peter Harrison (2015).

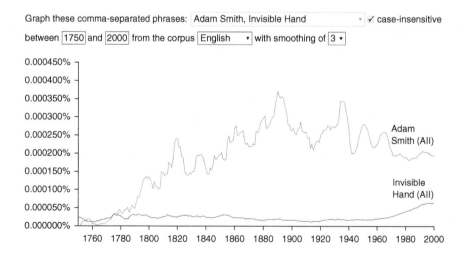

Graph these comma-separated phrases: Malthus, David Ricardo ▾ ✓ case-insensitive

between 1750 and 2000 from the corpus English ▾ with smoothing of 3 ▾

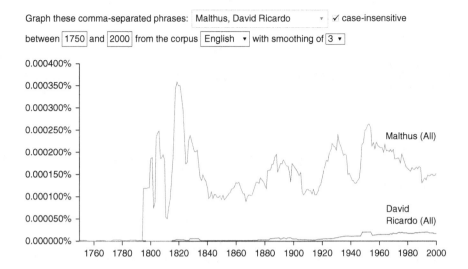

Graph these comma-separated phrases: Thomas Chalmers ▾ ✓ case-insensitive

between 1750 and 2000 from the corpus English ▾ with smoothing of 3 ▾

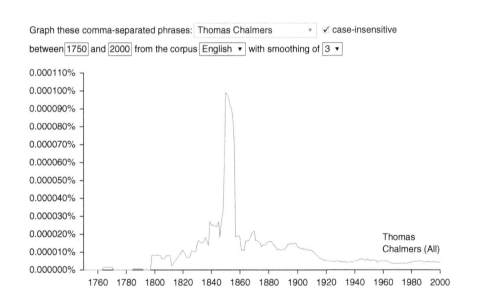

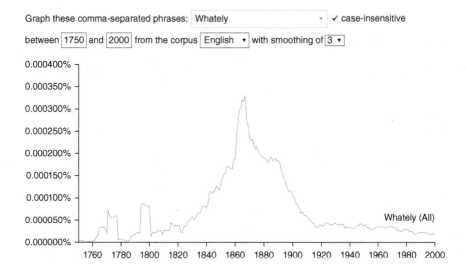

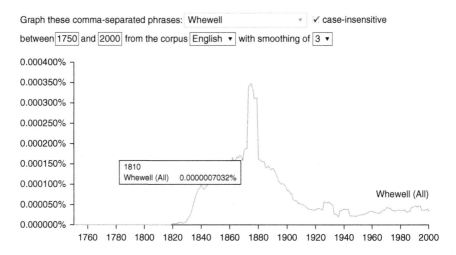

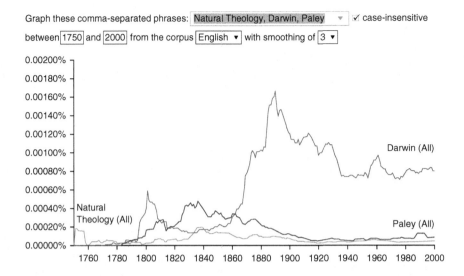

Graph these comma-separated phrases: Natural Theology, Darwin, Paley ▾ ✓ case-insensitive

between 1750 and 2000 from the corpus English ▾ with smoothing of 3 ▾

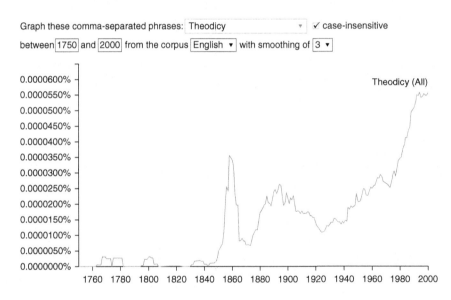

Graph these comma-separated phrases: Theodicy ▾ ✓ case-insensitive

between 1750 and 2000 from the corpus English ▾ with smoothing of 3 ▾

Bibliography

Akenson, D. H. (1981). *A Protestant in Purgatory: Richard Whately, Archbishop of Dublin.* South Bend, IN, Archon Books.

Akerlof, G. (1970). "The Market for Lemons: Quality, Uncertainty and the Market Mechanism". *Quarterly Journal of Economics* 84(3): 488–500.

Anderson, G. A. (2009). *Sin: A History.* New Haven, CT, Yale University Press.

Anderson, G. M. (1988). "Mr Smith and the Preachers: The Economics of Religion in the Wealth of Nations". *Journal of Political Economy* 96: 1066–88.

Aquinas, Thomas (1264). *Summa Contra Gentiles.* Translated in 4 volumes. South Bend, IN, University of Notre Dame Press 1975.

Arbo, Matthew B. (2014). "Theodicy and Commerce". *Studies in Christian Ethics* 27(May): 131–43.

Ashworth, W. J. (1996). "Memory, Efficiency, and Symbolic Analysis: Charles Babbage, John Herschel, and the Industrial Mind". *Isis* 87(4): 629–53.

Aspromourgos, A. (2009). *The Science of Wealth.* London, Routledge.

Augimeri, Paul (1992) *The Economic Ideas of Antonio Genovesi 1713–1769.* PhD thesis, University of Sydney.

Babbage, Charles (1832). *On the Economy of Machinery and Manufactures.* 2nd edition. London, Charles Knight.

Babbage, Charles (1838). *The Ninth Bridgewater Treatise, a Fragment.* 2nd edition. London, John Murray.

Backhouse, R. E. and S. Medema (2009). "The Definition of Economics". *Journal of Economic Perspectives* 23(1): 221–33.

Bacon, Francis (1605). *The Advancement of Learning Divine and Human.* Translated by Wood, edited by Dever. New York, Collier 1901.

Bacon, Francis (1620). *Novum Organum* edited by Urbach and Gibson. Chicago, IL, Open Court 1994.

Baker, Francis (1980). "John Wesley and Bishop Joseph Butler: A Fragment of Wesley's Manuscript Journal August 1739". *Proceedings of the Wesley Historical Society* 42(May): 93–100.

Bannister, R. C. (1973). "William Graham Sumner's Social Darwinism: A Reconsideration". *History of Political Economy* 5(1): 89–109.

Barr, John (1993). *Biblical Faith and Natural Theology.* Oxford, UK, Clarendon Press.

Barrera, Albino (2001). *Modern Catholic Social Documents and Political Economy.* Washington, DC, Georgetown University Press.

Barrera, Albino (2004). *Economic Compulsion and Christian Ethics.* Cambridge, UK, Cambridge University Press.

Barrera, Albino (2005). *God and the Evil of Scarcity*. South Bend, IN, University of Notre Dame Press.

Barrera, Albino (2011). *Market Complicity and Christian Ethics*. Cambridge, UK, Cambridge University Press.

Barrera, Albino (2013). *Biblical Economic Ethics: Sacred Scriptures Teachings on Economic Life*. Lanham, MA, Lexington Books.

Barth, Karl (1932–70). *Church Dogmatics*. Edited and translated by G. W. Bromiley, T. F. Torrance and G. T. Thomson. Edinburgh, UK, T&T Clark, 14 volumes, 1977.

Barth, Karl (1938). *The Knowledge of God and the Service of God According to the Teaching of the Reformation*. Translated by J. L. M. Haire and I. Henderson. London, Hodder & Stoughton.

Barth, Karl and Emil Brunner (1946). *Natural Theology: Comprising "Nature and Grace" and "No!"*. Translated by Peter Fraenkel. London, Geoffrey Bles.

Bashford, A. and J. E. Chaplin (2016). *The New Worlds of Thomas Robert Malthus: Re-Reading the Principle of Population.* Princeton, NJ, Princeton University Press.

Bastiat, Frederic (1850). *Economic Harmonies.* Translated by W. H. Boyers. Princeton, NJ, Van Nostrand 1964.

Bateman, B. W. (2008). "2007 Presidential Address: Reflections on the Secularization of American Economics". *Journal of the History of Economic Thought* 30(1): 1–20.

Bateman, B. W. (2011). "In a Space of Questions: A Reflection on Religion and Economics at the Beginning of the Twenty-First Century". *History of Political Economy* 43(2): 389–411.

Bateman, B. W. and H. S. Banzhaf (eds) (2008). *Keeping Faith, Losing Faith: Religious Belief and Political Economy*. Durham, NC, Duke University Press.

Bateman, B. W. and E. B. Kapstein (1999). "Between God and the Market: The Religious Roots of the American Economic Association". *Journal of Economic Perspectives* 13(4): 249–58.

Becher, H. (1991). "William Whewell's Odyssey: From Mathematics to Moral Philosophy" in *William Whewell, a Composite Portrait* edited by M. Fisch and S. Schaffer. Oxford, UK, Oxford University Press.

Becker, Gary (1976). *The Economic Approach to Human Behaviour*. Chicago, IL, University of Chicago Press.

Bensaude-Vincent, B. and W. R. Newman (eds) (2007). *The Artificial and the Natural: An Evolving Polarity.* Cambridge, MA, MIT Press.

Bentham, J. (1789). *An Introduction to the Principles of Morals and Legislation*. London, Athlone Press 1970.

Bentham, J. (1822). *The Influence of Natural Religion Upon the Temporal Happiness of Mankind* (written with George Grote and published under the pseudonym Philip Beauchamp). London, R. Carlile.

Bentham, J. (1952). *Jeremy Bentham's Economic Writings* edited by W. Stark. 3 volumes. London, Published for the Royal Economic Society by Allen & Unwin.

Berg, Maxine (1980). *The Machinery Question and the Making of Political Economy 1815–1848*. Cambridge, UK, Cambridge University Press.

Berg, Maxine (1987). "Charles Babbage" in *New Palgrave: A Dictionary of Economics* edited by J. Eatwell, M. Milgate and P. Newman. London, Macmillan.

Berger, Peter L. (2005). "Religion and the West". *The National Interest* Summer: 112–9.

Berkeley, George (1737). "The Querist" in *The Works of George Berkeley* edited by A. A. Luce and T. E. Jessop, 9 vols. London, Thomas Nelson and Sons, 1957.

Bishop, J. D. (1995). "Adam Smith's Invisible Hand Argument". *Journal of Business Ethics* 14(3): 165–80.

Bitterman, H. (1940). "Adam Smith's Empiricism and the Law of Nature". *Journal of Political Economy* 48(4): 487–520.

Blaug, Mark (1996). *Economic Theory in Retrospect.* 5th edition. Cambridge, UK, Cambridge University Press.

Blaug, Mark (2008). "Invisible Hand" in *New Palgrave Dictionary of Economics* edited by S. Durlaf and L. Blume. 2nd edition. London, Palgrave Macmillan.

Boer, R. (2003). *Marxist Criticism of the Bible.* London, Sheffield Academic.

Boer, R. and C. Petterson (2015). *Idols of Nations: Biblical Myth at the Origins of Capitalism.* Minneapolis, MN, Fortress Press.

Boisguilbert, Pierre (1697). *Le Detail De La France,* in *Pierre de Boisguilbert ou la Naissance de l'économie politique,* edited by J. Hecht. Paris, Institut National d'Études Démographiques 1966.

Boisguilbert, Pierre (1704). *A Treatise on the Nature of Wealth, Money, and Taxation.* Translated by Peter Groenewegen. Sydney: Centre for the Study of the History of Economic Thought, 2000.

Bonar, James (1885). *Malthus and His Work.* London, Macmillan.

Bouwsma, W. J. (1975). "The Two Faces of Humanism: Stoicism and Augustinianism in Renaissance Thought" in *Itinerarium Italicum: The Profile of the Italian Renaissance in the Mirror of Its European Transformations* edited by P. Kristeller, T. Brady and H. Oberman. Leiden, The Netherlands, Brill.

Bowley, M. (1937). *Nassau Senior and the Classical Economists.* London, Allen and Unwin.

Boyle, Robert (1979). *Selected Philosophical Papers of Robert Boyle* edited by M. A. Stewart. Manchester, UK, Manchester University Press.

Brennan, G. and A. M. C. Waterman (eds) (1994). *Economics and Religion: Are They Distinct?* Boston, MA, Kluwer.

Brennan, G. and A. M. C. Waterman (2008). "Christian Theology and Economics: Convergence and Clashes" in *Christian Theology and Market Economics* edited by I. Harper and S. Gregg. Cheltenham, UK, Edward Elgar: 77–93.

Brennan, G. and C. White (2013). "Action and Motive in Economic and Christian Ethics: A Dialogue of the Deaf?" Seminar at Ridley College, Melbourne.

Brent, Richard (1993). "God's Providence: Liberal Political Economy as Natural Theology at Oxford 1821–1862" in *Public and Private Doctrine: Essays in British History Presented to Maurice Cowling* edited by M. Bentley. Cambridge, UK, Cambridge University Press.

Brent, Richard (2004a). "Edward Copleston" in *Oxford Dictionary of National Biography* edited by L. Goldman. Oxford, UK, Oxford University Press.

Brent, Richard (2004b). "Richard Whately" in *Oxford Dictionary of National Biography* edited by L. Goldman. Oxford, UK, Oxford University Press.

Brett, Mark G. (2008). *Decolonizing God: The Bible in the Tides of Empire.* Sheffield, UK, Sheffield Phoenix Press.

Brewer, Anthony (2009). "On the Other Invisible Hand". *History of Political Economy* 41(3): 519–43.

Brooke, J. H. (1988). "The God of Isaac Newton" in *Let Newton Be!* edited by J. Fauvel. Oxford, UK, Oxford University Press.

Brooke, J. H. (1991a). *Science and Religion: Some Historical Perspectives.* Cambridge, UK, Cambridge University Press.

Brooke, J. H. (1991b). "Indications of a Creator: Whewell as Apologist and Priest" in *William Whewell, a Composite Portrait* edited by M. Fisch and S. Schaffer. Oxford, UK, Clarendon Press.

Brooke, J. H. (2003). "Darwin and Victorian Christianity" in *The Cambridge Companion to Darwin* edited by M. J. S. Hodge and G. Radick. Cambridge, UK, Cambridge University Press.

Brooke, J. H. and G. Cantor (1998). *Reconstructing Nature: The Engagement of Science and Religion.* Edinburgh, UK, T&T Clark.

Brooke, J. H., R. Re-Manning and F. Watts (eds) (2013). *The Oxford Handbook of Natural Theology.* Oxford, UK, Oxford University Press.

Brown, S. J. (1982). *Thomas Chalmers and the Godly Commonwealth in Scotland.* Oxford, UK, Oxford University Press.

Brown, S. J. (2004). "Chalmers, Thomas" in *Oxford Dictionary of National Biography* edited by L. Goldman. Oxford, UK, Oxford University Press.

Brown, S. J. (2008). *Providence and Empire: Religion, Politics and Society in the United Kingdom, 1815–1914.* Harlow, UK, Pearson Longman.

Bruce, Steve (2011). *Secularization: In Defence of an Unfashionable Theory.* Oxford, UK, Oxford University Press.

Bruni, L. S. and S. Zamagni (2007). *Civil Economy: Efficiency, Equity, Public Happiness.* Bern, Switzerland, Peter Lang.

Bruni, L. S. and S. Zamagni (2014). "Economics and Theology in Italy since the 18th Century" in *Oxford Handbook of Christianity and Economics* edited by P. Oslington. Oxford, UK, Oxford University Press.

Bulgakov, S. N. (1937). *Sophia, the Wisdom of God: An Outline of Sophiology.* Translated from Russian by Patrick Thompson. New York, Paisley Press.

Bulgakov, S. N. (2000). *Philosophy of Economy.* New Haven, CT, Yale University Press. Translated, with an introduction by Catherine Evtuhov based on 1912 Russian text.

Burke, Edmund (1769). *Observations on the Present State of the Nation* in *The Portable Edmund Burke* edited by Issac Kramnick. Harmondsworth, UK, Penguin 1999.

Burke, Edmund (1780). *Parliamentary Speech on Economical Reform* in *The Portable Edmund Burke* edited by Issac Kramnick. Harmondsworth, UK, Penguin 1999.

Burke, Edmund (1790). *Reflections on the Revolution in France* in *The Portable Edmund Burke* edited by Issac Kramnick. Harmondsworth, UK, Penguin 1999.

Burke, Edmund (1795). *Thoughts and Details on Scarcity* in *The Portable Edmund Burke* edited by Issac Kramnick. Harmondsworth, UK, Penguin 1999.

Burke, Edmund (1796). *Four Letters on a Regicide Peace* in *The Portable Edmund Burke* edited by Issac Kramnick. Harmondsworth, UK, Penguin 1999.

Butler, Joseph (1726). *Fifteen Sermons Preached at the Rolls Chapel.* London, Bell & Sons 1958.

Butler, Joseph (1736). *The Analogy of Religion: Natural and Revealed to the Constitution and Course of Nature.* London, J. M. Dent 1906.

Calvin, John (1559). *Institutes of the Christian Religion* edited by John McNeill, translated from Latin by Ford Lewis Battles. Philadelphia, PA, Westminster Press 1960.

Campanelli, G. (1987). "William Whewell" in *The New Palgrave: A Dictionary of Economics* edited by J. Eatwell, M. Milgate and P. Newman. London, Macmillan.

Campbell, T. D. (1971). *Adam Smith's Science of Morals.* London, Allen and Unwin.

Cantillon, Richard (1755). *Essay on the Nature of Commerce in General.* Translated by Henry Higgs. Rutgers University, NJ, Transaction Books 2001.

Carmichael, Gershom (1729). "Synopsis of Natural Theology" in *The Writings of Gershom Carmichael* edited by J. Moore and M. Silverthorne. Indianapolis, IN, Liberty Fund 2002.

Chalmers, T. (1808) *Enquiry into the Extent and Stability of National Resources.* Edinburgh, UK, John Moir.

Chalmers, T. (1813). "Christianity" in *David Brewster's Edinburgh Encyclopædia*. Edinburgh, UK, Blackwood. Volume VI, 355–96.

Chalmers, T. (1814). *The Influence of Bible Societies on the Temporal Necessities of the Poor*. Glasgow, UK, John Smith and Son.

Chalmers, T. (1817). *A Series of Discourses on Christian Revelation Viewed in Connection with the Modern Astronomy*. Glasgow, UK, John Smith and Son.

Chalmers, T. (1819–26). *The Christian and Civic Economy of Large Towns* 3 volumes. Glasgow, UK, Collins.

Chalmers, T. (1821). *Discourses on the Application of Christianity to the Commercial and Ordinary Affairs of Life*. Glasgow, UK, John Smith and Son.

Chalmers, T. (1827). *On the Use and Abuse of Literary and Ecclesiastical Endowments*. Glasgow, UK, Collins.

Chalmers, T. (1832). *On Political Economy: In Connection with the Moral State and Moral Prospects of Society*. Glasgow, UK, Collins.

Chalmers, T. (1833). *On the Power Wisdom and Goodness of God Manifested in the Adaption of External Nature to the Moral and Intellectual Constitution of Man*. London, William Pickering. Reprinted by Henry Bohn, London.

Chalmers, T. (1837). *On Natural Theology*. Glasgow, UK, Collins.

Chalmers, T. (1844). "The Political Economy of the Bible". *North British Review* 2: 1–52. Chalmers is reviewing *The Perils of the Nation, an Appeal to the Legislature, the Clergy, and the Higher and Middle Classes* published by Robert Benton Seeley in 1843.

Chalmers, T. (1846). *An Earnest Appeal to the Free Church of Scotland on the Subject of its Economics*. Glasgow, UK, Collins.

Chalmers, T. (1849). *Sermons 1798–1847* edited by William Hanna. Edinburgh, UK, Thomas Constable.

Chalmers, T. (1853). *A Selection from the Correspondence of the Late Thomas Chalmers* edited by William Hanna. Edinburgh, UK, Thomas Constable.

Chalmers, T. (1912). *Problems of Poverty: Selections from the Economic and Social Writings of Thomas Chalmers* edited by Henry Hunter. London, Nelson.

Chambers, Robert (1844). *Vestiges of the Natural History of Creation*. London, John Churchill.

Checkland, S. G. (1951). "The Advent of Academic Economics in England". *Manchester School of Economic and Social Studies* 19: 43–70.

Cheyne, A. C. (1985). "Thomas Chalmers: Then and Now" in his *The Practical and the Pious: Essays on Thomas Chalmers*. Edinburgh, UK, Saint Andrew Press.

Clark, J. B. (1886). *The Philosophy of Wealth: Economic Principles Newly Formulated*. Boston, MA, Ginn & Co.

Clark, J. B. (1899). *The Distribution of Wealth*. New York, Macmillan.

Clark, J. C. D. (2000). *English Society, 1660–1832: Religion, Ideology, and Politics During the Ancien Regime*. Cambridge, UK, Cambridge University Press.

Clark, W. E. (1903). *Josiah Tucker: Economist*. New York, Columbia University Press.

Clifton, Shane (2014). "Pentecostal Approaches to Economics" in *Oxford Handbook of Christianity and Economics* edited by P. Oslington. Oxford, UK, Oxford University Press.

Clifton, Shane (2015). "Theodicy, Disability, and Fragility: An Attempt to Find Meaning in the Aftermath of Quadriplegia". *Theological Studies* 76(4): 765–84.

Clines, D. J. A. (1968). "The Image of God in Man". *Tyndale Bulletin* 19: 53–103.

Coakley, Sarah (2012). *Sacrifice Regained: Evolution, Cooperation and God*. Gifford Lectures at University of Aberdeen. Unpublished.

Coase, R. (1976) "Adam Smith's View of Man". *Journal of Law and Economics* 19(3): 529–46.

Coase, R. (1977). "The Wealth of Nations". *Economic Inquiry* 15(3): 309–25.

Coats, A. W. (1960). "The First Two Decades of the American Economic Association". *American Economic Review* 50(4): 555–74.

Coats, A. W. (1985). "The American Economic Association and the Economics Profession". *Journal of Economic Literature* 23(4): 1697–727.

Coats, A. W. (1987). "Richard Ely" in *New Palgrave: A Dictionary of Economics* edited by J. Eatwell, M. Milgate and P. Newman. London, Macmillan.

Cole, G. A. (1988). "Ethics and Eschatology: Paley's System Reconsidered". *Reformed Theological Review* 47: 33–43.

Cole, G. A. (1991). "Theological Utilitarianism and the Eclipse of the Theistic Sanction". *Tyndale Bulletin* 42(2): 226–44.

Cole, G. A. (2007). "William Paley's Natural Theology: An Anglican Classic?" *Journal of Anglican Studies* 5: 209–25.

Coleman, W. O. (2002). *Economics and Its Enemies: Two Centuries of Anti-Economics* Basingstoke, UK, Palgrave.

Collins, Hugh (1985). "Political Ideology in Australia: The Distinctiveness of a Benthamite Society". *Daedalus* 114(1): 147–69.

Collison Black, R. D. (1960). *Economic Thought and the Irish Question, 1817–1870.* Cambridge, UK, Cambridge University Press.

Collison Black, R. D. (1987). "Richard Whately" in *The New Palgrave: A Dictionary of Economics* edited by J. Eatwell, M. Milgate and P. Newman. London, Macmillan.

Copleston, Edward (1819). *Letter to the Right Hon Robert Peel, On the Pernicious Effects of a Variable Standard of Value.* Oxford, UK, Murray.

Cornish, Rory (2004). "Tucker, Josiah" in *Oxford Dictionary of National Biography* edited by L. Goldman. Oxford, UK, Oxford University Press.

Corsi, P. (1987). "The Heritage of Dugald Stewart: Oxford Philosophy and the Method of Political Economy". *Nuncius* 2: 89–144.

Corsi, P. (1988). *Science and Religion: Baden Powell and the Anglican Debate, 1800–1860.* Cambridge, UK, Cambridge University Press.

Cremaschi, Sergio (2014). *Utilitarianism and Malthus' Virtue Ethics: Respectable, Virtuous and Happy.* London, Routledge.

Crenshaw, J. L. (2005). *Defending God Biblical Responses to the Problem of Evil.* Oxford, UK, Oxford University Press.

Cunliffe, C. (2004). "Butler, Joseph" in *Oxford Dictionary of National Biography* edited by L. Goldman. Oxford, UK, Oxford University Press.

Darwall, Stephen (1999). "Sympathetic Liberalism: Recent Work on Adam Smith". *Philosophy and Public Affairs* 28(2): 139–62.

Darwin, Charles (1859). *Origin of Species by Means of Natural Selection.* Harmondsworth, UK, Penguin 1969.

Davenport, Stewart (2008). *Friends of the Unrighteous Mammon, Northern Christians and Market Capitalism, 1815–1860.* Chicago, IL, Chicago University Press.

De Marchi, N. (1987). "Senior, Nassau William" in *The New Palgrave: A Dictionary of Economics* edited by J. Eatwell, M. Milgate and P. Newman. London, Macmillan.

De Marchi, N. and R. P. Sturges (1973). "Malthus and Ricardo's Inductivist Critics: Four Letters to William Whewell". *Economica* 40(160): 379–93.

Dempsey, B. W. (1958). *The Functional Economy.* Upper Saddle River, NJ, Prentice Hall.

De Vivo, G. (1987). "David Ricardo" in *New Palgrave: A Dictionary of Economics* edited by J. Eatwell, M. Milgate and P. Newman. London, Macmillan.

Dixon, W. and D. Wilson (2010). "Thomas Chalmers: The Market, Moral Conduct, and Social Order". *History of Political Economy* 42(4): 723–46.

Dorfman, Joseph (1947–59). *The Economic Mind in American Civilization*, 5 volumes. New York, Viking Press.

Durkheim, E. (1893). *The Division of Labor in Society*. Translated from French by W. D. Halls. Glencoe, IL, Free Press 1960.

Elashker, A. and R. Wilson (2006). *Islamic Economics: A Short History* Leiden, The Netherlands, Brill.

Elliott, Mark W. (2013). *Providence Perceived: Divine Action from a Human Point of View*. Berlin, De Gruyter.

Ely, Richard T. (1936). "The Founding and Early History of the Organisation of the American Economic Association". *American Economic Review* 26(March): 141–50.

Emmett, Ross B. (2003). "Exegesis, Hermeneutics, and Interpretation" in *A Companion to the History of Economic Thought* edited by W. J. Samuels, J. E. Biddle and J. B. Davis. Malden, MA, Blackwell.

Emmett, Ross B. (2011). "Man and Society in Adam Smith's Natural Morality: The Impartial Spectator, the Man of System, and the Invisible Hand" in *Adam Smith as Theologian* edited by P. Oslington. London, Routledge, pp. 125–32.

Emmett, Ross B. (2014). "Economics and Theology after the Separation" in *Oxford Handbook of Christianity and Economics* edited by P. Oslington. Oxford, UK, Oxford University Press.

Emmett, Ross B. (2015). "The History of American Economics" in *A Companion to the History of American Science* edited by M. A. Largent. New York, John Wiley & Sons.

Evans, Gillian R. (1982). *Augustine on Evil*. Cambridge, UK, Cambridge University Press.

Evensky, J. (2005). *Adam Smith's Moral Philosophy: A Historical and Contemporary Perspective on Markets, Law, Ethics, and Culture*. New York, Cambridge University Press.

Everett, J. R. (1946). *Religion in Economics: A Study of John Bates Clark, Richard T. Ely and Simon N. Patten*. Morningside Heights, NY, Kings Crown Press.

Faccarello, G. (1999). *The Foundations of Laissez-Faire: The Economics of Pierre De Boisguilbert*. London, Routledge.

Faccarello, G. (2005). "A Tale of Two Traditions. On Pierre Force's Self-Interest before Adam Smith". *European Journal of the History of Economic Thought* 12(4): 701–12.

Faccarello, G. (2014). "Theology and Economics in France in the 18th and 19th Centuries" in *Oxford Handbook of Christianity and Economics* edited by P. Oslington. Oxford, UK, Oxford University Press.

Fergusson, David (2006). "Types of Natural Theology" in *The Evolution of Rationality: Interdisciplinary Essays in Honor of J. Wentzel Van Huyssteen* edited by F. L. Shults. Grand Rapids, MI, Eerdmans.

Fergusson, David (ed.) (2007). *Scottish Philosophical Theology 1700–2000*. Exeter, UK, Imprint Academic.

Fergusson, David (2010). "The Theology of Providence". *Theology Today* 67(3): 261–78.

Fergusson, David (2013). "Providence and its Secular Displacements" in *Oxford Handbook of Theology and Modern European Thought* edited by N. Adams, G. Pattison and G. Ward. New York, Oxford University Press

Fergusson, David (2014). *Creation*. Grand Rapids, MI, Eerdmans.

Fisch, M. (1991). *William Whewell, Philosopher of Science*. Oxford, UK, Clarendon Press.

Fisch, M. and S. Schaffer (1991). *William Whewell, a Composite Portrait*. Oxford, UK, Clarendon Press.

Fleischacker, Samuel (2004). *On Adam Smith's Wealth of Nations: A Philosophical Companion*. Princeton, NJ, Princeton University Press.

Foley, Duncan (2006) *Adam's Fallacy: A Guide to Economic Theology*. Cambridge, MA, Harvard University Press.

Force, J. E. (1990). "Newton's God of Dominion: The Unity of Newton's Theological, Scientific and Political Thought" in *Essays on the Context, Nature, and Influence of Isaac Newton's Theology* edited by J. E. Force and R. H. Popkin. Boston, MA, Kluwer

Force, Pierre (2003). *Self-Interest before Adam Smith: A Genealogy of Economic Science*. Cambridge, UK, Cambridge University Press.

Forget, E. (1999). *The Social Economics of Jean-Baptiste Say: Markets and Virtue*. New York, Routledge.

Francis, Keith A. (2012). "Paley to Darwin: Natural Theology Versus Science in Victorian Sermons" in *Oxford Handbook of the British Sermon 1689–1901* edited by K. A. Francis and W. Gibson. Oxford, UK, Oxford University Press.

Frey, R. G. (1992). "Butler on Self-Love and Benevolence" in *Joseph Butler's Moral and Religious Thought Tercentenary Essays* edited by C. Cunliffe. Oxford, UK, Clarendon.

Friedman, B. M. (2010). "The Influence of Religious Thinking on the Smithian Revolution" in *Adam Smith as Theologian* edited by P. Oslington. London, Routledge, pp. 19–23.

Gadamer, Hans Georg. (1960). *Truth and Method*. Translated by Garrett Barden and John Cumming. London, Sheed and Ward 1975.

Gascoigne, John (1988). "From Bentley to the Victorians: The Rise and Fall of British Newtonian Natural Theology". *Science in Context* 2(2): 219–56.

Gascoigne, John (2002). *The Enlightenment and the Origins of European Australia*. Cambridge, UK, Cambridge University Press.

Gascoigne, John (2010) "Darwin and the British Natural Theology Tradition". *St Mark's Review* 211: 35–42.

Gay, Peter, Ed. (1968). *Deism: An Anthology*. Princeton, NJ, Van Nostrand.

Gill, Robin (2012). *Sociological Theology*, 3 volumes. Burlington, VT, Ashgate Publishers.

Goldstrom, J. M. (1966). "Richard Whately and Political Economy in Schoolbooks, 1833–80". *Irish Historical Studies* 15(58): 131–46.

Gonzales, Justo. (1990). *Faith and Wealth: A History of Early Christian Ideas on the Origin, Significance and Use of Money*. San Francisco, CA, Harper and Row.

Goodwin, C. D. (2008). "History of Economic Thought" in *New Palgrave Dictionary of Economics* edited by S. Durlaf and L. Blume. London, Palgrave Macmillan.

Gordon, B. (1975). *Economic Analysis before Adam Smith*. London, Macmillan.

Gordon, B. (1989). *The Economic Problem in Biblical and Patristic Thought*. Leiden, The Netherlands, Brill.

Goudzwaard, B. and R. Jongeneel (2014). "Reformed Christian Economics" in *Oxford Handbook of Christianity and Economics* edited by P. Oslington. Oxford, UK, Oxford University Press.

Grabill, S. J. (2006). *Rediscovering the Natural Law in Reformed Theological Ethics*. Grand Rapids, MI, Eerdmans.

Grampp, W. (2000). "What Did Smith Mean by the Invisible Hand?" *Journal of Political Economy* 108(3): 441–65.

Gray, E. (1983). *The Malthus Library Catalogue*. New York, Pergamon Press.

Gregg, Samuel (2016). *For God and Profit: How Banking and Finance Can Serve the Common Good*. New York, Crossroad Publishing.

Gregory, Brad S. (2012). *The Unintended Reformation: How a Religious Revolution Secularized Society*. Cambridge, MA, Belknap Press.

Gregory, C. A. (1987). "Jones, Richard" in *The New Palgrave: A Dictionary of Economics* edited by J. Eatwell and M. Milgate. London, Macmillan.

Griswold, Charles (1999). *Adam Smith and the Virtues of Enlightenment*. Cambridge, UK, Cambridge University Press.

Groenewegen, P. D. (1977). *The Economics of A. R.J. Turgot*. The Hague, Martinus Nijhoff.

Groenewegen, P. D. (1987). "Boisguilbert, Pierre Le Pesant, Sieur De" in *The New Palgrave: A Dictionary of Economics* edited by J. Eatwell, M. Milgate and P. Newman. London, Macmillan.

Groenewegen, P. D. (1989). "New Light on the Origins of Modern Economics". *Economic Record* 65(189): 136–49.

Groenewegen, P. D. (1999). "From Optimism in Progress to Pessimism: Some Major Implications of Malthus First Essay on Population for Attitudes to Growth and Welfare in the Nineteenth Century" in *Reflections on Economic Development* edited by G. F. Davanzati and V. Giola. Lecce, Italy, Edizioni Milella, pp. 27–37.

Groenewegen, P. D. (2001). "Thomas Carlyle, 'the Dismal Science', and the Contemporary Political Economy of Slavery". *History of Economics Review* 34(1): 74–94.

Groenewegen, P. D. (2002). "Boisguilbert and Eighteenth Century Economics" in P. D. Groenewegen *Eighteenth Century Economics*. London, Routledge.

Groenewegen, P. D. and B. J. McFarlane (1990). *A History of Australian Economic Thought*. London, Routledge.

Haakonssen, Knud (1981). *The Science of a Legislator: The Natural Jurisprudence of David Hume and Adam Smith*. Cambridge, UK, Cambridge University Press.

Haakonssen, Knud (1984). "From Moral Philosophy to Political Economy: The Contribution of Dugald Stewart" in *Philosophers of the Scottish Enlightenment* edited by V. Hope. Edinburgh, UK, Edinburgh University Press.

Haakonssen, Knud (1998). "Divine/ Natural Law Theories in Ethics" in *The Cambridge History of Seventeenth-Century Philosophy* edited by D. Garber and M. Ayers. Cambridge, UK, Cambridge University Press.

Haakonssen, Knud (ed.) (2005). *Cambridge Companion to Adam Smith*. Cambridge, UK, Cambridge University Press.

Haldane, J. (2011). "Adam Smith, Theology and Natural Law Ethics" in *Adam Smith as Theologian* edited by P. Oslington. London, Routledge, pp. 24–32.

Hanley, Ryan (2009). *Adam Smith and the Character of Virtue*. Cambridge, UK, Cambridge University Press.

Hanley, Ryan (2010). "Scepticism and Naturalism in Adam Smith" in *Adam Smith Review*, volume 5. London, Routledge.

Hanna, William (1852). *Memoirs of Dr Chalmers*, 4 volumes. Edinburgh, UK, Sutherland and Knox.

Harper, I. R. and S. Gregg, Eds. (2008) *Christian Theology and Market Economics*. Cheltenham, UK, Edward Elgar

Harrison, P. (1998). *The Bible, Protestantism and the Rise of Modern Science*. Cambridge, UK, Cambridge University Press.

Harrison P. (2007) *The Fall of Man and the Foundations of Science*. Cambridge, UK, Cambridge University Press

Harrison, P. (2011a). "Adam Smith, Natural Theology, and the Natural" in *Adam Smith as Theologian* edited by P. Oslington. London, Routledge, pp. 77–91.

Harrison, P. (2011b) "Adam Smith and the History of the Invisible Hand". *Journal of the History of Ideas* 72(1): 29–49.

Harrison, P. (2015) *The Territories of Science and Religion*. Chicago, IL, Chicago University Press.

Harvey-Phillips, M. B. (1984). "Malthus Theodicy: The Intellectual Background of His Contribution to Political Economy". *History of Political Economy* 16(4): 591–608.

Hauerwas, S. (1983). *The Peaceable Kingdom: A Primer on Christian Ethics.* South Bend, IN, University of Notre Dame Press.

Hauerwas, S. (2001). *With the Grain of the Universe: The Church's Witness and Natural Theology*. Ada, MI, Brazos Press.

Hauerwas, S. (2011) "Economics and Antagonisms". *History of Political Economy* 43(2):413–5.

Hauerwas, S. (2014). "The End of Charity: How Christians Are (Not) to 'Remember the Poor'". *ABC Religion and Ethics* 10 February. www.abc.net.au/religion/articles/2014/02/10/3941760.htm

Hausman, D. M. and M. McPherson (2006). *Economic Analysis, Moral Philosophy, and Public Policy*. 2nd edition. Cambridge, UK, Cambridge University Press.

Hawtrey, Kim (2014). "Anglicanism" in *Oxford Handbook of Christianity and Economics* edited by P. Oslington. Oxford, UK, Oxford University Press.

Hay, Donald A. (1989). *Economics Today: A Christian Critique*. Leicester, UK, Apollos.

Hebert, Robert F. (2008). "Bastiat, Claude Frédéric" in *New Palgrave Dictionary of Economics* edited by S. Durlaf and L. Blume. 2nd edition London, Palgrave Macmillan.

Hefner, Philip (1993). *The Human Factor: Evolution, Culture, Religion.* Minneapolis, MN, Fortress Press.

Helm Paul. (1994) *The Providence of God*. Leicester, UK, IVP.

Helm, Paul (2004). *John Calvin's Ideas*. Oxford, UK, Oxford University Press.

Henderson, J. P. (1996). *Early Mathematical Economics: William Whewell and the British Case*. Lanham, MD, Rowman & Littlefield.

Hengstmengel, J. (2015). *Divine Oeconomy: The Role of Providence in Early Modern Economic Thought before Adam Smith*, Doctoral Thesis. Erasmus Institute for Philosophy and Economics.

Henry, J. F. (1982). "The Transformation of John Bates Clark: An Essay in Interpretation". *History of Political Economy* 14(2): 166–77.

Henry, J. F. (1995). *John Bates Clark: The Making of a Neoclassical Economist.* New York, Macmillan.

Hess, Peter M. J. (2003). "God's Two Books of Revelation: The Life-Cycle of a Theological Metaphor" in *Encyclopedia of Science and Religion.* www.encyclopedia.com/doc/1G2–3404200522.html.

Heyne, Paul. (1986). "Clerical Laissez-Faire: A Study in Theological Economics" in *Religion, Economics and Social Thought* edited by W. Block and I. Hexham. Vancouver, BC, Fraser Institute.

Heyne, Paul (1994) "Passing Judgements". *Bulletin of the Association of Christian Economists USA* 23(Spring): 9–15.

Heyne, Paul (2008) *"Are Economists Basically Immoral?" and Other Essays on Economics, Ethics and Religion* edited and with an Introduction by Geoffrey Brennan and A. M. C Waterman, Indianapolis, IN, Liberty Fund.

Hick, John (1977). *Evil and the God of Love*. 2nd edition. London, Macmillan.

Hill, Lisa (2001). "The Hidden Theology of Adam Smith". *European Journal for the History of Economic Thought* 8(1): 1–29.

Hilton, Boyd (1985). "Chalmers as Political Economist" in *The Practical and the Pious: Essays on Thomas Chalmers* edited by A. C. Cheyne. Edinburgh, UK, St Andrew.

Hilton, Boyd (1988). *The Age of Atonement: The Influence of Evangelicalism on Social and Economic Thought 1795–1865.* Oxford, UK, Clarendon Press.

Hilton, Boyd (2006). *A Mad, Bad, and Dangerous People? England, 1783–1846.* New York, Oxford University Press.

Himmelfarb, Gertrude (2004). *The Roads to Modernity: The British, French, and American Enlightenments.* New York, Knopf

Hirschfeld, Mary L. (2012). "A Humane Economy: Capitalism and St Thomas Aquinas". *The Tablet* (26 March) 16–18.

Hirschfeld, Mary L. (2013). *Virtuous Consumption in a Dynamic Economy: A Thomistic Engagement with Neoclassical Economics.* PhD Thesis. South Bend, IN, University of Notre Dame.

Hirschman, Albert O. (1977). *The Passions and Interests: Political Arguments for Capitalism before Its Triumph.* Princeton, NJ, Princeton University Press.

Holder, R. D. (2012). *The Heavens Declare: Natural Theology and the Legacy of Karl Barth.* Conshohocken, PA, Templeton Press.

Hont, Istvan (1983). "The 'Rich Country-Poor Country' Debate in Scottish Classical Political Economy" in *Wealth and Virtue: The Shaping of Political Economy in the Scottish Enlightenment* edited by I. Hont and M. Ignatieff. Cambridge, UK, Cambridge University Press.

Hont, Istvan (2005). *Jealousy of Trade: International Competition and the Nation State in Historical Perspective.* Cambridge, MA, Harvard University Press.

Hume, David (1739). *Treatise on Human Nature* edited by E. C. Mossner. Harmonsworth, UK, Penguin 1985.

Hume, David (1752). *Essays Moral, Political and Literary.* Indianapolis, IN, Liberty Fund 1985.

Hume, David (1759). "Digression Concerning the Ecclesiastical State" in *History of England* Reprinted from the corrected 1778 edition, London: T Cadell, edited by William B. Todd. Indianapolis, IN, Liberty Fund 1983. Volume 3 chapter XXIX p134 ff.

Hume, David (1993). *Hume's Dialogues and Natural History* edited by J. Gaskin. Oxford, UK, Oxford University Press. The *Dialogues* were first published in 1779.

Hunter, Ian (2015). "Secularization: The Birth of a Modern Combat Concept". *Modern Intellectual History* 12(1): 1–32.

Hutcheson, Francis (1755). "A System of Moral Philosophy" in *Philosophical Writings* edited by R. S. Downie. London, Dent, 1994.

Hutchison, T. W. (1988). *Before Adam Smith: The Emergence of Political Economy 1662–1776.* Oxford, UK, Basil Blackwell.

Iannaccone, L. (1998). "Introduction to the Economics of Religion". *Journal of Economic Literature* 36(3): 1465–95.

Iannaccone, L. (2010). "The Economics of Religion: Invest Now, Repent Later?" *Faith & Economics* 55(Spring): 1–10.

Iyer, Sriya (2016). "The New Economics of Religion". *Journal of Economic Literature* 54(2): 395–441.

James, Patricia (1979). *Population Malthus: His Life and Times.* London, Routledge.

Jeffner, Anders (1966). *Butler and Hume on Religion. A Comparative Analysis.* Stockholm, Sweden, Diakonistyrelsens Bokforlag.

Jones, Richard (1831) *Essay on the Distribution of Wealth and Sources of Taxation: Rent.* London, J. Murray.

Jones, Richard (1859). *Literary Remains, Consisting of Lectures and Tracts on Political Economy* Edited by John Cazenove and William Whewell. London: J. Murray. Reprint New York, A. M. Kelley 1964.

Kames, Henry Home (1751). *Essays on the Principles of Morality and Natural Religion.* New York, Garland Publishing 1976.

Kant, Immanuel (1791). "On the Failure of All Attempted Philosophical Theodicies" in *Kant on History and Religion* edited by Michael Despland. Montreal, QC, McGill-Queen's University Press 1973.

Keynes, John Maynard (1933). *Essays in Biography.* London, Macmillan.

Keynes, John Neville (1917). *Scope and Method of Political Economy.* 4th ed. London, Macmillan.

Kennedy, G. (2008). *Adam Smith: A Moral Philosopher and His Political Economy.* London, Palgrave Macmillan.

Kennedy, G. (2010). "Paul Samuelson and the Invention of the Modern Economics of the Invisible Hand". *Journal of the History of Ideas* 28(3): 105–20.

Kennedy, G. (2011). "The Hidden Adam Smith and His Alleged Theology". *Journal of the History of Economic Thought* 33(3): 385–402.

Ker, I. T. (1988). *John Henry Newman: A Biography.* Oxford, UK, Clarendon Press.

Ker, I. T. and T. Gornall (eds) (1979). *Letters and Diaries of John Henry Newman.* Oxford, UK, Clarendon Press.

Kerr, Fergus (2002). *After Aquinas: Versions of Thomism.* Malden, MA, Blackwell.

King, John E. (2013). *David Ricardo.* London, Palgrave Macmillan.

King, William (1702). *De Origine Mali.* Later translated by Edmund Law and published as *Essay on the Origin of Evil* in 1731. London, Thurlbourn.

Kittel, G., G. Friedrich and G. W. Bromiley (1985). *Theological Dictionary of the New Testament. Abridged in One Volume.* Grand Rapids, MI, Eerdmans.

Kleer, R. A. (1995). "Final Causes in Adam Smith's Theory of Moral Sentiments". *Journal of the History of Philosophy* 32(2): 275–330.

Kleer, R. A. (2000). "The Role of Teleology in Adam Smith's Wealth of Nations". *History of Economics Review* 31: 14–29.

Knight, Frank H. (1933). *The Economic Organization.* Chicago, IL, University of Chicago.

Knight, Frank H. (1999). *Selected Essays by Frank H. Knight* edited by Ross B. Emmett. Chicago, IL, University of Chicago Press.

Knight, Frank H. and T. W. Merriam (1947). *The Economic Order and Religion.* London, Kegan Paul.

Kretzmann, N. (1999). *The Metaphysics of Creation: Aquinas's Natural Theology in Summa Contra Gentiles* 2 volumes. Oxford, UK, Clarendon Press.

Kuran, Timur (2004). *Islam and Mammon: Critical Perspectives on the Economic Agenda of Islamism.* Princeton, NJ, Princeton University Press.

Kuyper, Abraham. (1898). *Lectures on Calvinism.* Grand Rapids, MI, Eerdmans 1931.

Kuyper, Abraham. (1998). *Abraham Kuyper: A Centennial Reader* edited by James D. Bratt. Grand Rapids, MI, Eerdmans.

Kuyper, Abraham (2015). *Common Grace: God's Gifts for a Fallen World* edited by Jordan Ballor and Melvin Flikkema. Grand Rapids, MI, Lexham Press.

Leathers, C. G. and J. P. Raines (1999). "Adam Smith and Thomas Chalmers on Financing Religious Instruction". *History of Political Economy* 31(2): 337–59.

Leibniz, G. W. (1710). *Theodicy.* Translated from German by E. M. Huggard. Chicago, IL, Open Court 1951.

Le Mahieu, D. L. (1976). *The Mind of William Paley.* Lincoln, NE, University of Nebraska Press.

Le Mahieu, D. L. (1979) "Malthus and the Theology of Scarcity". *Journal of the History of Ideas* 40: 467–74.

Leonard, T. C. (2003). "A Certain Rude Honesty: John Bates Clark as a Pioneering Neoclassical Economist". *History of Political Economy* 35(3): 521–58.

Leonard, T. C. (2016). *Illiberal Reformers: Race, Eugenics, and American Economics in the Progressive Era.* Princeton, NJ, Princeton University Press.

Leshem, Dotan (2013). "Oikonomia Redefined". *Journal of the History Economic Thought* 35(1): 43–61.

Leshem, Dotan (2016a). "What Did the Ancient Greeks Mean by Oikonomia?" *Journal of Economic Perspectives* 30(1): 225–31.

Leshem, Dotan (2016b). *The Origins of Neoliberalism: Modeling the Economy from Jesus to Foucault.* New York, Columbia University Press.

Levy, S. Leon (1970). *Nassau W. Senior 1790–1864.* Newton Abbot, UK, David and Charles Publishers.

Livingstone, D. N. (1987). *Darwin's Forgotten Defenders: The Encounter between Evangelical Theology and Evolutionary Thought.* Grand Rapids, MI, Eerdmans.

Lonergan, Bernard (1999). "An Essay on Circulation Analysis" in *Macroeconomic Dynamics: An Essay in Circulation Analysis. Collected Works of Bernard Lonergan Volume 15* edited by F. Lawrence, P. Byrne and C. Hefling. Toronto, ON, University of Toronto Press. Originally written 1944.

Long, Brendan (2002). *Adam Smith and Adam's Sin.* PhD Thesis, Faculty of Theology, University of Cambridge.

Long, Brendan (2009). "Adam Smith's Theism" in *Elgar Companion to Adam Smith* edited by J. Young. Cheltenham, UK, Edward Elgar.

Long, Brendan (2011). "Adam Smith's Theodicy" in *Adam Smith as Theologian* edited by P. Oslington. London, Routledge, pp. 98–105.

Lovejoy, A. O. (1927). "Nature as Aesthetic Norm". *Modern Language Notes* 444–50. Reprinted in *Essays in the History of Ideas* Baltimore, MD, Johns Hopkins University Press, 1948 pp. 69–77.

Maas, Harro (2008). "A Hard Battle to Fight: Natural Theology and the Dismal Science, 1820–50" in *Keeping Faith, Losing Faith: Religious Belief and Political Economy* edited by B. W. Bateman and H. S. Banzhaf. Durham, NC and London, Duke University Press, pp. 143–67.

Macfie, A. L. (1970) "The Invisible Hand in the Theory of Moral Sentiments" in *The Individual and Society.* London: George Allen and Unwin.

Macfie, A. L. (1971). "The Invisible Hand of Jupiter". *Journal of the History of Ideas* 32: 595–99.

MacIntyre, Alasdair (1981). *After Virtue: A Study in Moral Theory.* London, Duckworth.

MacIntyre, Gordon (2003). *Dugald Stewart: Pride and Ornament of Scotland.* Brighton, UK, Sussex Academic.

Maclaurin, Colin (1748). *An Account of Sir Issac Newton's Philosophical Discoveries.* Privately Printed in London. Reprint Johnson Corporation, New York 1968.

Macpherson, C. B. (1962). *The Political Theory of Possessive Individualism.* Oxford, UK, Oxford University Press.

Macpherson, C. B. (1980). *Burke.* Oxford, UK, Oxford University Press.

Macpherson, C. B. (1987). "Edmund Burke" in *The New Palgrave: A Dictionary of Economics* edited by J. Eatwell, M. Milgate and P. Newman. London, Macmillan.

Mallet, C. E. (1927). *A History of the University of Oxford.* London, Methuen.

Malthus, T. R. (1798). *An Essay on the Principle of Population.* 1st edition, edited by A. Flew. Harmondsworth, UK, Penguin 1970. This was originally published anonymously.

Malthus, T. R. (1803). *An Essay on the Principle of Population*. 2nd edition, edited by Donald Winch. Cambridge, UK, Cambridge University Press 1992.

Malthus, T. R. (1815). *An Inquiry into the Nature and Progress of Rent*. London, John Murray.

Malthus, T. R. (1820). *Principles of Political Economy* edited by John Pullen. Cambridge, UK, Cambridge University Press 1989. A posthumous second edition was published in 1836.

Malthus, T. R. (1827). *Definitions in Political Economy*. London, John Murray.

Malthus, T. R. (1830). *Summary View of the Principle of Population* edited by A. Flew. Harmondsworth, UK, Penguin 1970.

Malthus, T. R., (2004). *Unpublished Papers in the Collection of Kanto Gakuen University, Edited by John Pullen and Trevor Hughes Parry*. 2 Volumes. Cambridge, UK, Cambridge University Press.

Mandeville, Bernard (1732). *The Fable of the Bees; or Private Vices and Public Virtues*. Edited F. B. Kaye. Oxford, UK, Clarendon Press 1924, 2 volumes. This edition also includes his 1705 work *The Grumbling Hive*.

Marcet, Jane (1816). *Conversations on Political Economy: Economy: In Which the Elements of That Science Are Familiarly Explained*. Reprint Cambridge, UK, Cambridge University Press 2010.

Marsden, G. M. (1989). "Evangelicals and the Scientific Culture" in *Religion and Twentieth-Century American Intellectual Life* edited by M. J. Lacey. Cambridge, UK, Cambridge University Press.

Marsden, G. M. (1990). *Religion and American Culture*. San Diego, CA, Harcourt Brace Jovanovich.

Marsden, G. M. (1991). "The Evangelical Love Affair with Enlightenment Science" in *Understanding Fundamentalism and Evangelicalism*. Grand Rapids, MI, Eerdmans.

Marshall, Alfred (1890). *Principles of Economics*. London, Macmillan.

Martineau, Harriet (1832–34). *Illustrations of Political Economy*, 9 volumes. London: Charles Fox.

Marty, Martin E. (1969). *The Modern Schism; Three Paths to the Secular*. New York, Harper & Row.

May, Henry F. (1976). *The Enlightenment in America*. New York, Oxford University Press.

McCloskey, Deirdre (2006). *Bourgeois Virtues: Ethics for an Age of Commerce*. Chicago, IL, University of Chicago Press.

McCloskey, Deirdre (2008). "Adam Smith, the Last of the Former Virtue Ethicists". *History of Political Economy* 40(1): 43–71.

McCloskey, Deirdre (2010). *Bourgeois Dignity: Why Economics Can't Explain the Modern World*. Chicago, IL, University of Chicago Press.

McCloskey, Deirdre (2016). *Bourgeois Equality: How Ideas Not Capital or Institutions Enriched the World*. Chicago, IL, University of Chicago Press.

McGowan, Andrew B. (2009). "Providence and Common Grace" in *The Providence of God* edited by F. A. Murphy and P. G. Ziegler. Edinburgh, UK, T&T Clark.

McGrath, Alister (2003). *A Scientific Theology* 3 volumes. Edinburgh, UK, T&T Clark.

McGrath, Alister (2008). *The Open Secret: A New Vision for Natural Theology*. Oxford, UK, Blackwell.

McGrath, Alister (2011). *Darwinism and the Divine: Evolutionary Thought and Natural Theology*. Oxford, UK, Blackwell-Wiley.

McLean, Murdith (2003). "Did Paley Ignore Hume on the Argument from Design?" in *Faith, Reason, and Economics: Essays in Honour of Anthony Waterman* edited by Derek Hum. Winnipeg, St. John's College Press, University of Manitoba.

McVickar, John (1825). *Outlines of Political Economy*. New York, Wilder and Campbell.

Meek, R. L. (1963). *The Economics of Physiocracy; Essays and Translations*. Cambridge, MA, Harvard University Press.

Meeks, Douglas M. (1990). *God the Economist: The Doctrine of God in Political Economy*. Minneapolis, MN, Fortress Press.

Meeks, Douglas M. (2014). "Economics in the Christian Scriptures" in *Oxford Handbook of Christianity and Economics* edited by P. Oslington. Oxford, UK, Oxford University Press.

Michel, Jean-Baptiste, Yuan Kui Shen, Aviva Presser Aiden, Adrian Veres, Matthew K. Gray, Joseph P. Pickett, Dale Hoiberg, Dan Clancy, Peter Norvig, Jon Orwant, Steven Pinker, Martin A. Nowak and Erez Lieberman Aiden (2010) "Quantitative Analysis of Culture Using Millions of Digitized Books", *Science*. Online. www.sciencemag.org/content/early/2010/12/15/science.1199644.

Milbank, John (1990). *Theology and Social Theory: Beyond Secular Reason*. Oxford, UK, Basil Blackwell. Revised edition was published in 2006.

Mill, J. S. (1848). *Principles of Political Economy with Some of Their Applications to Social Philosophy*. Toronto, ON, University of Toronto Press 1965. Based on the 7th edition 1871. Volumes 2 and 3 of the Works edited by John Robson.

Mizuta, H. (2000). *Adam Smith's Library: A Catalogue*. Oxford, UK, Oxford University Press.

Mochrie, Robbie (2008). "Virtue and the Godly Commonwealth". *Association of Christian Economists UK Journal* (April): 12–29.

Moore, Gregory C. (2013). "Teaching Economics with John Henry Cardinal Newman's Ideal University: A Nineteenth Century Vision for the Twenty-First Century Scholar". *Australasian Journal of Economics Education* 10(2): 60–99.

Moore, James (2006). "Natural Rights in the Scottish Enlightenment" in *The Cambridge History of Eighteenth-Century Political Thought* edited by M. Goldie and R. Wokler. New York, Cambridge.

Moore, J. R. (1979) *The Post-Darwinian Controversies: A Study of the Protestant Struggle to Come to Terms with Darwin in Great Britain and America 1870–1900*. Cambridge, UK, Cambridge University Press.

Montes, L. (2003). "Smith and Newton: Some Methodological Issues Concerning General Economic Equilibrium". *Cambridge. Journal of Economics* 27(5): 723–47.

Montes, L. (2008). "Newton's Real Influence on Adam Smith and Its Context". *Cambridge Journal of Economics* 32 4: 555–76.

Mossner, E. C. (1936). *Bishop Butler and the Age of Reason*. 2nd edition. London, Macmillan.

Mossner, E. C. (1980). *The Life of David Hume*. 2nd edition. Oxford, UK, Oxford University Press.

Mouw, R. J. (2001). *He Shines in All That's Fair: Culture and Common Grace*. Grand Rapids, MI, Eerdmans.

Mouw, R. J. (2012). "The Imago Dei and Philosophical Anthropology". *Christian Scholars Review* 41(3): 253–66.

Murray, M. J. (2009). "Theodicy" in *The Oxford Handbook of Philosophical Theology* edited by T. P. Flint and M. C. Rea. Oxford, UK, Oxford University Press.

Myers, Milton L. (1983). *The Soul of Modern Economic Man: Ideas of Self-Interest, Thomas Hobbes to Adam Smith*. Chicago, IL, University of Chicago Press.

Nelson, R. H. (1991). *Reaching for Heaven on Earth- the Theological Meaning of Economics*. London, Rowan and Littlefield.

Nelson, R. H. (2001). *Economics as Religion: From Samuelson to Chicago and Beyond*. University Park, PA, Pennsylvania State University Press.

Nelson, R. H. (2004) "What Is Economic Theology?" *Princeton Seminary Bulletin* 25(1): 58–79.

Nelson, R. H. (2010). *Two Gods: Economic Religion versus Environmental Religion*, University Park, PA, Pennsylvania State University Press.

Newlands, Samuel (2012). "The Problem of Evil" in *Routledge Companion to Seventeenth-Century Philosophy* edited by D. Kaufman. London, Routledge.

Newlands, Samuel (2016). "Hume on Evil" in *Oxford Handbook of Hume* edited by Paul Russell. New York, Oxford University Press.

Newman, J. H. (1864). *Apologia Pro Vita Sua.* London, J. M. Dent and Sons 1912.

Newman, J. H. (1870). *An Essay in Aid of a Grammar of Assent.* London, Longmans Green 1947.

Newman, J. H. (1871). *Fifteen Sermons Preached Before the University of Oxford.* South Bend, IN, University of Notre Dame Press.

Newman, J. H. (1873). *The Idea of a University* edited by I. Ker. Oxford, UK, Clarendon Press 1976.

Newman, J. H. (1989). *The Genius of John Henry Newman: Selections from His Writings* edited by I. T. Ker. Oxford, UK, Clarendon.

Newton, Isaac (1686). *Philosophiae Naturalis Principia Mathematica.* London, Royal Society.

Newton, Isaac (2004). *Newton: Philosophical Writings* edited by Andrew Janiak. Cambridge, UK, Cambridge University Press.

Noll, M. A. (2002). *God and Mammon: Protestants, Money, and the Market, 1790–1860.* Oxford, UK, Oxford University Press.

Noonan, J. T. (1957). *The Scholastic Analysis of Usury.* Cambridge, MA, Harvard University Press.

Norman, E. R. (1976). *Church and Society in England 1770–1970.* Oxford, UK, Clarendon Press.

Norman, E. R. (1987). *The Victorian Christian Socialists.* Cambridge, UK, Cambridge University Press.

Numbers, R. L. (1993). *The Creationists: The Evolution of Scientific Creationism.* New York, Knopf.

O' Brien, D. P. (1987). "Thomas Chalmers" in *The New Palgrave: A Dictionary of Economics* edited by J. Eatwell, M. Milgate and P. Newman. London, Macmillan.

O' Brien, D. P. (2004). *The Classical Economists Revisited.* Princeton, NJ, Princeton University Press.

O' Donovan, O. and J. Lockwood O' Donovan (1999). *From Irenaeus to Grotius: A Sourcebook in Christian Political Thought.* Grand Rapids, MI, Eerdmans.

Ogereau, Julien. (2014). "Paul's Κοινωνα with the Philippians: Societas as a Missionary Funding Strategy". *New Testament Studies* 60(3): 360–78. Based on Macquarie University PhD thesis.

Ogereau, Julien (2015). "A Survey of Κοινωνα and Its Cognates in Documentary Sources". *Novum Testamentum* 57(3): 275–94.

Ormerod, N. (2010) "Creator God, Evolving World. Providence or Process?" *St Mark's Review* 211: 75–82.

Ormerod, N. (2015) *A Public God: Natural Theology Reconsidered.* Minneapolis, MN, Fortress Press.

Ormerod, N., P. Oslington and R. Koning (2012). "The Development of Catholic Social Teaching on Economics: Bernard Lonergan and Benedict XVI". *Theological Studies* 73(June): 391–421.

Oslington, P. (1995). "Economic Thought and Religious Thought: Al Ghazali". *History of Political Economy* 27(4): 775–80.

Oslington, P. (1998) *Unemployment in an Open Economy*, PhD thesis, Faculty of Economics, University of Sydney. Revised version published as *The Theory of International Trade and Unemployment.* Cheltenham, UK, Edward Elgar 2006.

Oslington, P. (1999). "Islamic Economics" in *The Current State of Economic Science* edited by S. B. Dahiya. Amsterdam, The Netherlands, Jan Tinbergen Institute.

Oslington, P. (2001) "Nassau Senior, John Henry Newman and the Separation of Political Economy from Theology in the Nineteenth Century". *History of Political Economy* 33(4): 825–42.

Oslington, P. (ed.) (2003). *Economics and Religion.* International Library of Critical Writings in Economics, 2 volumes. Cheltenham, UK, Edward Elgar.

Oslington, P. (2005). "Natural Theology as an Integrative Framework for Economics and Theology". *St Mark's Review* 199: 20–31. St Marks Day Lecture for 2005.

Oslington, P. (2008a). "Christianity's Post-Enlightenment Contribution to Economic Thought" in *Christian Morality and Market Economics: Theological and Philosophical Perspectives* edited by I. R. Harper and S. Gregg. Cheltenham, UK, Edward Elgar.

Oslington, P. (2008b). "Public Theology: Some Measures and Australian Reflections". *Colloquium: The Australian and New Zealand Theological Review* 40(2): 183–93.

Oslington, P. (2009). "Whither Christian Economics? Further Reflections in the Light of a Conference: 'The Future of Economics and Theology as an Interdisciplinary Research Field'". *Journal of the UK Association of Christian Economists* Discussion Papers 003: 1–9.

Oslington, P. (2010). "The Kuyperian Dream: Reconstructing Economics on Christian Foundations". Paper Presented at American Academy of Religion Annual Meeting, San Diego. Manuscript.

Oslington, P. (ed.) (2011a) *Adam Smith as Theologian.* New York, Routledge.

Oslington, P. (2011b). "The Future Hope Adam Smith's System". *Studies in Christian Ethics* 24(3): 329–49.

Oslington, P. (2011c) "Using Economics in Biblical Studies". Paper Presented at Society for Biblical Literature Annual Meeting, San Francisco. The annotated references from this paper are now published as "Economics and Biblical Studies" in *Oxford Bibliographies* edited by C. Matthews. New York, Oxford University Press. Available at www.oxfordbibliographies.com.

Oslington, P. (2011d). "Caritas in Veritate and the Market Economy: How Do We Reconcile Traditional Christian Ethics with Economic Analysis of Social Systems?" *Journal of Markets and Morality* 14(2): 359–71.

Oslington, P. (2011e). "Symposium: 'What Do Economists and Theologians Have to Say to Each Other'?" *Faith and Economics* Fall: 1–30.

Oslington, P. (2012a). "God and the Market: Adam Smith's Invisible Hand". *Journal of Business Ethics* 108(4): 429–38.

Oslington, P. (2012b). "Jacob Viner on Adam Smith: Development and Reception of a Theological Reading". *European Journal for the History of Economic Thought* 19(2): 287–301.

Oslington, P., Ed. (2014). *Oxford Handbook of Christianity and Economics.* Oxford, UK, Oxford University Press.

Oslington, P. (2015a). "God and Economic Suffering". *Crux* 49(3): 12–20. Shortened version published as "Where Is God When the Economy Collapses? Rethinking Economic Theodicy". *ABC Religion and Ethics* 3 January 2014.

Oslington, P. (2015b). "Sacred and Secular in Australian Social Services". *Pacifica* 28(1): 79–93.

Oslington, P. (2017). "Natural Theology, Theodicy and Political Economy in 19th Century Britain: William Whewell's Struggle". *History of Political Economy*. Forthcoming.

Oslington, P. (2017). "Anglican Social Thought and the Formation of Political Economy in Britain: Joseph Butler, Josiah Tucker, William Paley and Edmund Burke." *History of Economics Review*. Forthcoming.

Otter, William (1836). "Biographical Memoir of TR Malthus". Appended to the posthumous second edition of Malthus' *Principles of Political Economy*. London, John Murray.

Otteson, James R. (2002). *Adam Smith's Marketplace of Life*. Cambridge, UK, Cambridge University Press.

Paley, William (1785). *Principles of Moral and Political Philosophy* edited by D. Le Mahieu. Indianapolis, IN, Liberty Fund 2002.

Paley, William (1790). *Horae Paulinae, or The Truth of the Scripture History of St Paul*. London, Ward, Lock, and Co.

Paley, William (1794). *View of the Evidences of Christianity*. Dublin, J. Pasley.

Paley, William (1802). *Natural Theology* edited by M. Eddy and D. Knight. Oxford, UK, Oxford University Press 2006.

Paley, William (1806). *Sermons*. London, SPCK.

Pelikan, J. J. (1971). *The Christian Tradition: A History of the Development of Doctrine*. Chicago, IL, University of Chicago Press.

Penelhum, Terrence (1985). *Butler*. London, Routledge & Kegan Paul.

Penelhum, Terrence (1988). "Butler and Hume". *Hume Studies* 14: 251–76.

Peterfreund, S. (2012). *Turning Points in Natural Theology from Bacon to Darwin: The Way of the Argument from Design*. London: Palgrave Macmillan.

Phillipson, N. T. (2008). "Dugald Stewart" in *New Palgrave Dictionary of Economics* edited by S. Durlaf and L. Blume. 2nd edition. London, Palgrave Macmillan.

Phillipson, N. T. (2010). *Adam Smith*. London, Allen Lane.

Plantinga, Alvin (1980). "The Reformed Objection to Natural Theology". *Proceedings of the Catholic Philosophical Society* 15: 49–62.

Plantinga, Alvin (2011). *Where the Conflict Really Lies: Science, Religion, and Naturalism*. New York: Oxford University Press.

Pocock, J. G. A. (1985a). "Josiah Tucker on Burke, Locke, and Price" in J. G. A. Pocock *Virtue, Commerce, and History: Essays on Political Thought and History, Chiefly in the Eighteenth Century*. Cambridge, UK, Cambridge University Press, pp. 157–91.

Pocock, J. G. A. (1985b). "The Political Economy of Burke's Analysis of the French Revolution" in J. G. A. Pocock *Virtue, Commerce, and History: Essays on Political Thought and History, Chiefly in the Eighteenth Century*. Cambridge, UK, Cambridge University Press, pp. 193–212.

Pocock, J. G. A. (2008). "History and Enlightenment: A View of Their History". *Modern Intellectual History* 5: 83–96.

Porter, Roy (2000). *Enlightenment: Britain and the Creation of the Modern World*. Harmondsworth, UK, Penguin.

Prendergast, R. (2000). "The Political Economy of Edmund Burke" in *Contributions to the History of Economic Thought: Essays in Honour of R. D.C. Black* edited by A. Murphy and R. Prendergast. London, Routledge, pp. 251–71.

Preston, R. H. (1993). "Christian Socialism" in *The Blackwell Encyclopedia of Modern Christian Thought* edited by A. McGrath. Oxford, UK, Blackwell.

Pryme, George (1816). *A Syllabus of a Course of Lectures on the Principles of Political Economy*. Cambridge, UK, J. Smith.

Pullen, J. M. (1981). "Malthus' Theological Ideas and Their Influence on His Principles of Population". *History of Political Economy* 13(1): 39–54.

Pullen, J. M. (1987a). "Malthus, Jesus and Darwin". *Religious Studies* 23(June): 233–46.

Pullen, J. M. (1987b). "Thomas Robert Malthus" in *The New Palgrave: A Dictionary of Economics* edited by J. Eatwell, M. Milgate and P. Newman. London, Macmillan.

Pullen, J. M. (1998). "The Last Sixty-Five Years of Malthus Scholarship". *History of Political Economy* 30(2): 343–52.

Pullen, J. M. (2004a). "TR Malthus" in *Oxford Dictionary of National Biography* edited by L. Goldman. Oxford, UK, Oxford University Press

Pullen, J. M. (2004b) "Richard Jones" *Oxford Dictionary of National Biography* edited by L. Goldman. Oxford, UK, Oxford University Press.

Pullen, J. M. (2016). "Variables and Constants in the Theology of TR Malthus". *History of Economics Review* 63(1): 21–32.

Ramsey, I. T. (1973). *Models for Divine Activity.* London, SCM Press.

Raphael, D. D., Ed. (1969). *British Moralists 1650–1800.* Oxford, UK, Oxford University Press.

Raphael, D. D. (1985). *Adam Smith.* Oxford, UK, Oxford University Press.

Raphael, D. D. (2007). *The Impartial Spectator.* Oxford, UK, Clarendon.

Rashid, Salim (1977a). "William Whewell and Early Mathematical Economics". *Manchester School of Economic and Social Studies* 45(4): 381–91

Rashid, Salim (1977b). "Richard Whately and Christian Political Economy at Oxford and Dublin". *Journal of the History of Ideas* 38: 147–55.

Rashid, Salim (1982). "Review of Dean Tucker and 18th Century Economic and Political Thought by George Shelton". *History of Political Economy* 14(4): 611–13.

Rashid, Salim (1983). "Christianity and the Growth of Liberal Economics". *Journal of Religious History* 12(3): 221–32.

Rashid, Salim (1984). "Malthus' Theology: An Overlooked Letter and Some Comments". *History of Political Economy* 16(1): 135–38.

Rashid, Salim (1985). "Dugald Stewart, 'Baconian' Methodology and Political Economy". *Journal of the History of Ideas* 46: 245–57.

Rashid, Salim (1987). "Political Economy as Moral Philosophy; Dugald Stewart of Edinburgh". *Australian Economic Papers* 26(48): 145–56.

Rashid, Salim (1998). *The Myth of Adam Smith.* Cheltenham, UK, Edward Elgar.

Ray, J. (1691). *The Wisdom of God Manifested in the Works of Creation.* London, William and John Innes.

Reumann, J. H. P. (1992). *Stewardship and the Economy of God.* Grand Rapids, MI, Eerdmans.

Ricardo, David (1815). *An Essay on the Influence of a Low Price of Corn on the Profits of Stock* in Collected Works edited by Pierro Sraffa Volume IV. Cambridge, UK, Cambridge University Press 1951.

Ricardo, David (1817). *Principles of Political Economy and Taxation* in *Collected Works* edited by Pierro Sraffa. Volume I. Cambridge, UK, Cambridge University Press 1951.

Richardson, J. D. (1988). "Frontiers in Economics and Christian Scholarship". *Christian Scholars Review* 17(4): 381–400. Reprinted in *Bulletin of the Association of Christian Economists USA* 23 1994.

Richardson, J. D. (2014). "Interface and Integration in Christian Economics" in *Oxford Handbook of Christianity and Economics* edited by P. Oslington. Oxford, UK, Oxford University Press.

Robbins, Lionel (1935). *An Essay on the Nature and Significance of Economic Science.* 2nd revised edition. London, Macmillan.

Robbins, Lionel (1998). *A History of Economic Thought* Edited by Steven Medema and Warren J Samuels. Princeton, NJ, Princeton University Press.

Ross, I. S. (1995). *The Life of Adam Smith.* Oxford, UK, Oxford University Press. A revised second edition was published in 2010.

Ross, I. S. (2004a). "Great Works on the Anvil in 1785: Adam Smith's Projected Corpus of Philosophy". *Adam Smith Review* 1: 40–59.

Ross, I. S. (2004b). "Aspects of Hume's Treatment of the Problem of Evil" in *But Vindicate the Ways of God to Man: Literature and Theodicy* edited by R. Freiburg and S. Gruss. Tübingen, Germany, Stauffenburg.

Ross, I. S. (2010). "Adam Smith's Smile: His Years at Balliol College, 1740–6, in Retrospect". *Adam Smith Review* volume 5. London, Routledge.

Rothschild, Emma (1994). "Adam Smith and the Invisible Hand". *American Economic Review* 84(2): 319–22.

Rothschild, Emma (2001). *Economic Sentiments: Adam Smith, Condorcet and the Enlightenment.* Harvard, MA, Harvard University Press.

Rotwein, Eugene (1955). "Introduction" to his *David Hume: Writings on Economics.* Edinburgh, UK, Thomas Nelson and Sons.

Ruse, Michael (2001). *Can a Darwinian Be a Christian? The Relationship between Science and Religion.* Cambridge, UK, Cambridge University Press.

Samuels, Warren J. (1987). "William Graham Sumner" in *New Palgrave: A Dictionary of Economics* edited by J. Eatwell, M. Milgate and P. Newman. London, Macmillan.

Samuels, Warren J. (2009). "The Invisible Hand" in *Elgar Companion to Adam Smith* edited by J. Young. Cheltenham, UK, Edward Elgar.

Samuels, Warren J. (2011). *Erasing the Invisible Hand: Essays on an Elusive and Misguided Concept in Economics.* Cambridge, UK, Cambridge University Press (with the assistance of Marianne F. Johnson and William H. Perry).

Sayre-McCord, G. (2010). "Sentiments and Spectators: Adam Smith's Theory of Moral Judgment". *Adam Smith Review* 5: 122–44.

Schabas, M. (2003). *The Natural Origins of Economics.* Chicago, IL, University of Chicago Press.

Schabas, M. and C. Wennerlind (eds) (2008). *David Hume's Political Economy.* London, Routledge.

Schneewind, Jerome B. (1968). "Whewell's Ethics" in *Studies in Moral Philosophy: American Philosophical Quarterly Monograph Series* 1 edited by N. Rescher. Oxford, UK, Blackwell, pp. 108–41.

Schumacher, E. F. (1966). "Buddhist Economics" in *Asia: A Handbook* edited by G. Wint. London, Anthony Blond Ltd.

Schumpeter, Joseph A. (1954). *A History of Economic Analysis.* Oxford, UK, Oxford University Press.

Schweiker, W. and C. Mathewes (eds) (2004). *Having: Property and Possession in Religious and Social Life.* Grand Rapids, MI, Eerdmans.

Scotland, N. (1995). *John Bird Sumner: Evangelical Archbishop.* London, Gracewing.

Scotland, N. (2004). "John Bird Sumner" in *Oxford Dictionary of National Biography* edited by L. Goldman. Oxford, UK, Oxford University Press.

Screpanti, E. and S. Zamagni (2005). *An Outline of the History of Economic Thought* 2nd edition. Oxford, UK, Oxford University Press.

Scrope, George Poulett. (1833). *Principles of Political Economy.* Cambridge, UK, Cambridge University Press.

Sedgwick, Adam (1833). *Discourse on the Studies of the University.* Leicester, UK, Leicester University Press 1969.

Sedlacek, T. (2011). *Economics of Good and Evil: The Quest for Economic Meaning from Gilgamesh to Wall Street.* Oxford, UK, Oxford University Press.

Semmel, B. (1965). "The Hume-Tucker Debate and Pitt's Trade Proposals". *Economic Journal* 75 759–70.

Sen, Amartya and Emma Rothschild (2005). "Adam Smith's Economics" in *Cambridge Companion to Adam Smith* edited by K. Haakonssen. Cambridge, UK, Cambridge University Press.

Senior, Nassau W. (1827). "An Introductory Lecture on Political Economy" in *Selected Writings on Economics.* New York, Augustus Kelley 1966.

Senior, Nassau W. (1836). *An Outline of the Science of Political Economy.* London, Clowes and Son. Reprint by Augustus Kelley Publishers.

Shaftesbury, Third Earl of, Anthony Ashley Cooper (1699). *An Inquiry Concerning Virtue, or Merit.* Manchester, UK, Manchester University Press 1977

Shelton, G. W. (1981). *Dean Tucker and Eighteenth Century Economic and Political Thought.* New York, St. Martin's Press.

Shelton, G. W. (1987). "Josiah Tucker" in *The New Palgrave: A Dictionary of Economics* edited by J. Eatwell, M. Milgate and P. Newman. London, Macmillan.

Sher, Richard B. (1985). *Church and University in the Scottish Enlightenment: The Moderate Literati of Edinburgh.* Princeton, NJ, Princeton University Press.

Skinner, Andrew S. (1987). "Adam Smith" in *The New Palgrave: A Dictionary of Economics* edited by J. Eatwell, M. Milgate and P. Newman. London, Macmillan.

Skinner, Andrew S. (1996) *A System of Social Science: Papers Relating to Adam Smith.* Oxford, UK, Clarendon Press

Smith, Adam (1759/1790). *The Theory of Moral Sentiments* edited by D. D. Raphael and A. Macfie. Oxford, UK, Oxford University Press 1975. Abbreviated *TMS.*

Smith, Adam (1776). *An Inquiry into the Nature and Causes of the Wealth of Nations* edited by T. Campbell, A. Skinner and W. Todd. Oxford, UK, Oxford University Press 1976. Abbreviated *WN.*

Smith, Adam (1978). *Lectures on Jurisprudence* edited by R. L. Meek, D. D. Raphael and P. G. Stein. Oxford, UK, Oxford University Press.

Smith, Adam (1980). *Essays on Philosophical Subjects* edited by W. P. D. Wrightman, J. C. Bryce and Ian Simpson Ross. Oxford, UK, Oxford University Press.

Smith, Adam. (1983). *Lectures on Rhetoric and Belles Lettres* edited by J. C. Bryce. Oxford, UK, Oxford University Press.

Smith, Adam (1986). *The Correspondence of Adam Smith* 2nd edition, edited by E. C. Mossner and Ian Simpson Ross. Oxford, UK, Oxford University Press.

Smith, Christian (2014). *The Sacred Project of American Sociology.* New York, OUP.

Snyder, Laura J. (2006). *Reforming Philosophy: A Victorian Debate on Science and Society.* Chicago, IL, University of Chicago Press.

Snyder, Laura J. (2011). *The Philosophical Breakfast Club: Four Remarkable Friends Who Transformed Science and Changed the World.* New York, Broadway Books.

Stark, R. (1999). "Secularization R.I.P". *Sociology of Religion* 60(3): 249–73.

Steedman, Ian (1987). "Wicksteed, Philip Henry" in *The New Palgrave: A Dictionary of Economics* edited by J. Eatwell, M. Milgate and P. Newman. London, Macmillan.

Steedman, Ian (1994). "Wicksteed: Economist and Prophet" in *Economics and Religion: Are They Distinct?* edited by Geoffrey Brennan and A. M. C. Waterman. Boston, MA, Kluwer Academic, pp. 77–101.

Stephen, L. (1876). *History of English Thought in the Eighteenth Century.* London, Smith & Co.

Stephen, L. (1899a). "Butler, Joseph" in *Dictionary of National Biography.* Oxford, UK, Oxford University Press.

Stephen, L. (1899b). "Tucker, Josiah" in *Dictionary of National Biography.* Oxford, UK, Oxford University Press.

Stephen, L. (1899c). "Paley, William" in *Dictionary of National Biography.* Oxford, UK, Oxford University Press.

Stephen, L. (1899d). "Smith, Adam" in *Dictionary of National Biography.* Oxford, UK, Oxford University Press.

Stephen, L (1899e). "William Whewell" in *Dictionary of National Biography.* Oxford, UK, Oxford University Press.

Stewart, Dugald (1792–1827). *Elements of the Philosophy of the Human Mind*, 3 volumes I in Stewart *Collected Works*, volumes II–IV edited by W. Hamilton. Edinburgh, UK, Thomas Constable.

Stewart, Dugald (1795). "Account of the Life and Writings of Adam Smith" in Adam Smith *Essays on Philosophical Subjects.* Now edited by W. P. D. Wrightman, J. C. Bryce and Ian Simpson Ross. Oxford, UK, Oxford University Press 1980. Also in Stewart *Collected Works* volume X edited by W. Hamilton. Edinburgh, UK, Thomas Constable.

Stewart, Dugald. (1810). *Philosophical Essays*, in *Collected Works* volumes V edited by W. Hamilton. Edinburgh, UK, Thomas Constable.

Stewart, Dugald (1855). "Lectures on Political Economy" in *Collected Works* volumes VIII and IX edited by W. Hamilton. Edinburgh, UK, Thomas Constable. Lectures first delivered 1800–1801.

Stewart, M. A. (1991). "The Stoic Legacy in the Early Scottish Enlightenment" in *Atoms, Pneuma, and Tranquillity: Epicurean and Stoic Themes in European Thought* edited by M. J. Osler. Cambridge, UK, Cambridge University Press.

Stewart, M. A. (2003). "Religion and Rational Theology" in *Cambridge Companion to the Scottish Enlightenment* edited by A. Broadie. Cambridge, UK, Cambridge University Press.

Stigler, George (1976). "The Successes and Failures of Professor Smith". *Journal of Political Economy* 84(6): 1199–213.

Stiglitz, Joseph E. (2002). "There Is No Invisible Hand". *The Guardian.* Friday 20 December.

Storkey, Alan (1993). *Foundational Epistemologies in Consumption Theory.* Amsterdam, VU University Press. Based on earlier PhD thesis at Free University of Amsterdam.

Sumner, J. B. (1814). "On Improving the Condition of the Poor". *Quarterly Review*: 146–59.

Sumner, J. B. (1816). *A Treatise on the Records of the Creation; with Particular Reference to the Jewish History, and the Consistency of the Principle of Population with the Wisdom and Goodness of the Deity.* London, Hatchard.

Sumner, J. B. (1817). "The Poor Laws". *British Review* 20: 333–550.

Surin, Kenneth (1986). *Theology and the Problem of Evil.* Oxford, UK, Blackwell.

Swinburne, R. (1991). *The Existence of God.* Revised edition. Oxford, UK, Clarendon Press.

Swinburne, R. (1998). *Providence and the Problem of Evil.* Oxford, UK, Clarendon Press.

Swinburne, R. (2011). "Why Hume and Kant Were Mistaken in Rejecting Natural Theology". *European Journal for Philosophy of Religion* 2(1): 1–24.

Swinburne, R. (2015). "My Natural Theology". Catholic University of Lublin Graduation Address. Available at www.kul.pl/cms/files/57/aktualnosci/DHC_swinburne_richard.pdf.

Tanner, Kathryn (2004). "Economies of Grace" in *Having: Property and Possession in Religious and Social Life* edited by W. Schweiker and C. Matthewes. Grand Rapids, MI, Eerdmans.

Tanner, Kathryn (2005). *Economy of Grace*. Minneapolis, MN, Fortress Press.

Tanner, Kathryn (2016). *Christianity and the New Spirit of Capitalism*. Gifford Lectures at Edinburgh. Unpublished.

Taylor, Charles (1989) *Sources of the Self: The Making of the Modern Identity*. Cambridge, MA, Harvard University Press.

Taylor, Charles (2007). *A Secular Age*. Cambridge, MA, Harvard University Press.

Teixeira, P. and A. Almodovar (2008). "Catholic Economic Thought" in *New Palgrave Dictionary of Economics* edited by S. Durlaf and L. Blume. 2nd edition. London, Palgrave Macmillan.

Teixeira, P. and A. Almodovar (2014). "Economics and Theology in Europe from the 19th Century" in *Oxford Handbook of Christianity and Economics* edited by P. Oslington. Oxford, UK, Oxford University Press.

Tiemstra, J. P. (2009). "Notes from the Revolution: Principles of a New Economics". *Faith & Economics* 54 (Fall): 19–29.

Tiemstra, J. P., W. F. Graham, G. N. Monsma, C. Sinke and A. Storkey (1990). *Reforming Economics: A Christian Perspective on Economic Theory and Practice*. New York, Edward Mellen.

Todhunter, I. (1876). *William Whewell, D. D. Master of Trinity College Cambridge: An Account of His Writings with Selections from His Literary and Scientific Correspondence*. London, Macmillan.

Topham, J. R. (1992). "Science and Popular Education in the 1830s: The Role of the Bridgewater Treatises". *British Journal for the History of Science* 25: 397–430.

Topham, J. R. (1998). "Beyond the Common Context: The Production and Reading of the Bridgewater Treatises". *Isis* 89(2): 233–62.

Topham, J. R. (1999). "Science, Natural Theology, and Evangelicalism in Early Nineteenth-Century Scotland: Thomas Chalmers and the Evidence Controversy" in *Evangelicals and Science in Historical Perspective* edited by D. N. Livingstone, D. G. Hart and M. A. Noll. New York, Oxford University Press.

Torrance, T. F. (1970). "The Problem of Natural Theology in the Thought of Karl Barth". *Religious Studies* 6: 121–35.

Tribe, Keith (1995). "Professors Malthus and Jones: Political Economy at the East India College 1806–1858". *European Journal for the History of Economic Thought* 2: 327–54.

Tribe, Keith (1997). *Strategies of Economic Order: German Economic Discourse, 1750–1950*, revised edition. Cambridge, UK, Cambridge University Press.

Tucker, Abraham (1768). *Light of Nature Pursued*. 6th edition. London, Bohn.

Tucker, Josiah (1749). *A Brief Essay on the Advantages and Disadvantages Which Respectively Attend France and Great Britain, with Regard to Trade*. London, T. Trye. The work was anonymous until the third edition 1753.

Tucker, Josiah (1755). *The Elements of Commerce and the Theory of Taxes*. Privately printed. Published in Tucker (1931).

Tucker, Josiah (1757). *Instructions for Travellers*. London. Reprinted in Tucker (1931).

Tucker, Josiah (1758). "The Great Question Resolved, Whether a Rich Country Can Stand a Competition with a Poor Country (of Equal Natural Advantages) in

Raising of Provisions, and Cheapness of Manufactures". Tract I in Tucker *Four Tracts, on Political and Commercial Subjects*. Gloucester, UK, R. Raikes and J. Rivington 1774.

Tucker, Josiah (1774). *The True Interest of Britain, Set Forth in Regard to the Colonies*. London, T. Cadell. Reprinted in Tucker (1931).

Tucker, Josiah (1775). *A Letter to Edmund Burke*. London, T. Cadell. Reprinted in Tucker (1931).

Tucker, Josiah (1781). *A Treatise Concerning Civil Government*. London, T. Cadell. Reprinted in Tucker (1931).

Tucker, Josiah (1931). *Josiah Tucker: A Selection from His Economic and Political Writings* edited by Robert L Schulyer. New York, Columbia University Press.

Turner, F. M. (1974). "Rainfall, Plagues and the Prince of Wales: A Chapter in the Conflict of Religion and Science". *Journal of British Studies* 8: 46–65.

Turner, F. M. (1978). "The Victorian Conflict between Science and Religion: A Professional Dimension". *Isis* 20(248): 356–76.

Turner, F. M. (1993). "The Secularization of the Social Vision of British Natural Theology" in *Contesting Cultural Authority: Essays in Victorian Intellectual Life*. Cambridge, UK, Cambridge University Press.

Twiss, Travers (1847). *View of the Progress of Political Economy in Europe since the Sixteenth Century*. London, Longman, Brown, Green.

Venturi, Franco (1970). *Utopia and Reform in the Enlightenment*. Cambridge, UK, Cambridge University Press.

Viner, J. (1927) "Adam Smith and Laissez Faire". *Journal of Political Economy* 35: 198–232.

Viner, J. (1932). "Review of R. Schuyler, ed. Josiah Tucker: Selections". *Journal of Political Economy* 40(3): 416–8.

Viner, J. (1950). *A Modest Proposal for Some Stress on Scholarship in Graduate Training* Convocation Address, Brown University, June 1950. Subsequently published by Princeton University Press 1953.

Viner, J. (1960). "The Intellectual History of Laissez Faire". *Journal of Law and Economics* 3(October): 45–69.

Viner, J. (1963). "Possessive Individualism as Original Sin: Review of the Political Theory of Possessive Individualism by CB Macpherson". *Canadian Journal of Economics and Political Science* 29: 548–59.

Viner, J. (1965). *Guide to John Rae's Life of Adam Smith*. New York, Augustus M. Kelley.

Viner, J. (1968). "Adam Smith" in *International Encyclopedia of the Social Sciences* edited by D. Sills. New York, Macmillan, 14, pp. 322–29.

Viner, J. (1972). *The Role of Providence in the Social Order*. Philadelphia, PA, American Philosophical Society.

Viner, J. (1978). *Religious Thought and Economic Society* edited by J. Melitz and D. Winch. Durham, NC, Duke University Press.

Vivenza, Gloria (2001). *Adam Smith and the Classics: The Classical Heritage in Adam Smith's Thought,* Oxford, UK, Oxford University Press.

Vivenza, Gloria (2005). "The Agent, the Actor, and the Spectator". *History of Economic Ideas* 13: 37–56.

Vivenza, Gloria (2008). "A Note on Adam Smith's First Invisible Hand". *Adam Smith Review* 4: 26–9.

Vivenza, Gloria (2009). "Adam Smith and Aristotle" in *Elgar Companion to Adam Smith* edited by J. Young. Cheltenham, UK, Edward Elgar.

Volf, Miroslav (1991). *Work in the Spirit: Toward a Theology of Work.* New York, Oxford University Press.

Volf, Miroslav (2011) *Public Faith: How Followers of Christ Should Serve the Common Good.* Ada, MI, Brazos Press

Voltaire (1759). *Candide.* Translated from the French by J. Butt. Harmondsworth, UK, Penguin 1966.

Walsh, Vivian (1961). *Scarcity and Evil.* Saddle River, NJ, Prentice Hall.

Walsham, Alexandra (1999). *Providence in Early Modern England.* Oxford, UK, Oxford University Press.

Waszek, N. (1984). "Two Concepts of Morality: A Distinction of Adam Smith's Ethics and Its Stoic Origin". *Journal of the History of Ideas* 45(4): 591–606.

Waterman, A. M. C. (1987). "Economists on the Relation between Political Economy and Christian Theology: A Preliminary Survey". *International Journal of Social Economics* 14(6): 46–68.

Waterman, A. M. C. (1991a). *Revolution, Economics and Religion: Christian Political Economy 1798–1833.* Cambridge, UK, Cambridge University Press.

Waterman, A. M. C. (1991b) "The Canonical Classical Model of Political Economy in 1808 as viewed from 1825: Thomas Chalmers on the National Resources". *History of Political Economy* 23(2): 221–41.

Waterman, A. M. C. (1991c). "The Intellectual Context of Rerum Novarum". *Review of Social Economy* 49(4): 465–82. Reprinted in Waterman 2004.

Waterman, A. M. C. (1994). "Whately, Senior and the Methodology of Classical Economics" in *Economics and Religion: Are They Distinct?* edited by G. Brennan and A. M. C. Waterman. Boston, MA, Kluwer. Reprinted in Waterman 2004.

Waterman, A. M. C. (1996). "Why William Paley Was 'the First of the Cambridge Economists'". *Cambridge Journal of Economics* 20(6): 673–86.

Waterman, A. M. C. (1998). "Malthus, Mathematics, and the Mythology of Coherence". *History of Political Economy* 30(4): 571–99.

Waterman, A. M. C. (1999). "Market Social Order and Christian Organicism in Centesimus Annus". *Journal of Markets and Morality* 2(2): 220–33. Reprinted in Waterman 2004.

Waterman, A. M. C. (2001). "The Beginning of Boundaries: The Sudden Separation of Economics from Christian Theology" in *Economics and Interdisciplinary Research* edited by G. Erreygers. Reprinted in Waterman 2004.

Waterman, A. M. C. (2002). "Economics as Theology: Adam Smith's Wealth of Nations". *Southern Economic Journal* 68(4): 907–21. Reprinted in Waterman 2004.

Waterman, A. M. C. (2003). "Should We Listen to the Churches When They Speak on Economic Issues?" *Agenda* 10(3): 277–88. Reprinted in Waterman 2004.

Waterman A. M.C. (2004) *Political Economy and Christian Theology since the Enlightenment: Essays in Intellectual History.* London: Palgrave Macmillan.

Waterman, A. M. C. (2008a). "Is 'Political Economy' Really a Christian Heresy?" *Faith and Economics* 51(Spring): 31–55.

Waterman, A. M. C. (2008b). "English School of Political Economy, 1798–1909" in *New Palgrave Dictionary of Economics* 2nd edition, edited by S. Durlaf and L. Blume. London, Palgrave Macmillan.

Waterman, A. M. C. (2008c). "Paley, William" in *New Palgrave Dictionary of Economics* 2nd edition, edited by S. Durlaf and L. Blume. London, Palgrave Macmillan.

Waterman, A. M. C. (2008d). "The Changing Theological Context of Economic Analysis Since the Eighteenth Century" in *Keeping Faith, Losing Faith: Religious Belief and Political Economy* edited by B. W. Bateman and H. S. Banzhaf. Durham, NC, Duke University Press, pp. 121–42.

Waterman, A. M. C. (2013). "The Relation between Economics and Theology in Caritas in Veritate". *Erasmus Journal for Philosophy and Economics* 6(2). Electronic journal.

Waterman, A. M. C. (2014). "Theology and the Rise of Political Economy in Britain in the 18th and 19th Centuries" in *Oxford Handbook of Christianity and Economics* edited by P. Oslington. Oxford, UK, Oxford University Press.

Waterman, A. M. C. (2016). "Rerum Novarum and Economic Thought". *Faith and Economics* 67: 29–56.

Watts, Fraser (2002). *Theology and Psychology*. London, Ashgate.

Wayland, F. (1835). *Elements of Moral Science*. Boston, MA, Gould, Kendall and Lincoln

Wayland, F. (1837). *Elements of Political Economy*. Boston, MA, Gould, Kendall and Lincoln.

Webb, Charles (1915). *Studies in the History of Natural Theology*. Oxford, UK, Clarendon Press.

Weber, Max (1905). *The Protestant Ethic and the Spirit of Capitalism*. Translated by Talcott Parsons. London, Allen and Unwin 1976.

Werhane, Patricia H. (1991). *Adam Smith and His Legacy for Modern Capitalism*. New York, Oxford University Press.

Werhane, Patricia H. (2000). "Business Ethics and the Origins of Contemporary Capitalism: Economics and Ethics in the Work of Adam Smith and Herbert Spencer". *Journal of Business Ethics* 24(3): 185–98.

Wesley, John (1760) "The Use of Money" in *On Moral Business: Classical and Contemporary Resources for Ethics in Economic Life* edited by M. Stackhouse, D. McCann and S. Roels. Grand Rapids, MI, Eerdmans 1995, pp. 194–7.

Welker, M. (1994). *God the Spirit*. Minneapolis, MN, Fortress Press.

Welker, M. (1999). *Creation and Reality*. Minneapolis, MN, Fortress.

Welker, M. (2009). "The Holy Spirit" in *Oxford Handbook of Systematic Theology* edited by K. Tanner, J. Webster and I. R. Torrance. Oxford, UK, Oxford University Press.

Whately, E. J. (1886). *Life and Correspondence of Archbishop Whately*. London, Longmans Green.

Whately, R. (1826). *Elements of Logic*. London, J. W. Parker. Includes additions to appendix by Nassau Senior on definitions in political economy.

Whately, R. (1828) "Review of Oxford Lectures on Political Economy". *Edinburgh Review* Sept 170–84.

Whately, R. (1832). *Introductory Lectures on Political Economy*. 2nd edition. London, J. W. Parker.

Whately, R. (1833). *Easy Lessons on Money Matters*. London, J. W. Parker.

Whately, R. (1859). *Dr Paley's Works*. London, J. W. Parker.

Whewell, W. (1827). *Sermons Preached at St Marys Church, Cambridge*. Unpublished Manuscript, Trinity College Cambridge. Whewell papers R.6.17

Whewell, W. (1829–50). *Mathematical Exposition of Certain Doctrines of Political Economy*. New York, A. M. Kelley Reprint 1971. Contains 1 "Mathematical Exposition of Some Doctrines of Political Economy", *Transactions Cambridge Philosophical*

Society 1829. 2 "Mathematical Exposition of Some Leading Doctrines in Mr Ricardo's Principles of Political Economy", *Transactions Cambridge Philosophical Society* 1831. 3 "Mathematical Exposition of Some Doctrines of Political Economy: Second Memoir", *Transactions of the Cambridge Philosophical Society* 1850.

Whewell, W. (1831a). "Review of Herschel's *Preliminary Discourse on the Study of Natural Philosophy*". *Quarterly Review* 90: 374–407.

Whewell, W. (1831b) "Review of Richard Jones *Essay on the Distribution of Wealth: Rent*". *British Critic* 10: 41–61.

Whewell, W.(1832) "On the Uses of Definitions". *Philological Museum*. Whewell papers 164.c.83.5.

Whewell, W. (1833). *Astronomy and General Physics Considered with Reference to Natural Theology. The Bridgewater Treatises on the Power, Wisdom and Goodness of God as Manifested in Creation.* London, William Pickering.

Whewell, W. (1837a). *On the Foundations of Morals: Four Sermons.* London, J. W. Parker.

Whewell, W. (1837b). *The History of the Inductive Sciences: From the Earliest to the Present Times.* 3 Volumes. London, J. W. Parker.

Whewell, W. (1840). *The Philosophy of the Inductive Sciences, Founded Upon Their History.* 2 Volumes. London, J. W. Parker.

Whewell, W. (1845a). *Elements of Morality, Including Polity.* 2 Volumes. London, J. W. Parker.

Whewell, W. (1845b). *Indications of the Creator.* London, J. W. Parker.

Whewell, W. (1849). *Of Induction, with Especial Reference to Mr. J. Stuart Mill's System of Logic.* London, J. W. Parker.

Whewell, W. (1852). *Lectures on the History of Moral Philosophy in England.* London, J. W. Parker.

Whewell, W. (1853). *Of the Plurality of Worlds.* London, J. W. Parker.

Whewell, W. (1860). *On the Philosophy of Discovery.* London, J. W. Parker.

Whewell, W. (1862). *Six Lectures on Political Economy.* Cambridge, UK, Cambridge University Press.

Wicksteed, Philip H. (1910). *The Common Sense of Political Economy.* London, Macmillan.

Williams, Rowan (2010). "Theology and Economics: Two Different Worlds?" *Anglican Theological Review* 92(4): 607–16.

Wilson, R. (1997). *Economics, Ethics and Religion; Jewish, Christian and Islamic Economic Thought.* London, Macmillan.

Winch, D. (1971). "The Emergence of Economics as a Science" in *The Fontana Economic History of Europe* volume 3 edited by C. Cipolla. London, Fontana.

Winch, D. (1978). *Adam Smith's Politics: An Essay in Historiographic Revision.* Cambridge, UK, Cambridge University Press.

Winch, D. (1983). "The System of the North: Dugald Stewart and His Students" in *That Noble Science of Politics* edited by J. Burrow, S. Collini and D. Winch. Cambridge, UK, Cambridge University Press.

Winch, D. (1987) *Malthus.* Oxford, UK, Oxford University Press.

Winch, D. (1993). "Robert Malthus: Christian Moral Scientist, Arch-Demoralizer, or Implicit Secular Utilitarian?" *Utilitas: A Journal of Utilitarian Studies* 5(2): 239–54.

Winch, D. (1996). *Riches and Poverty: An Intellectual History of Political Economy in Britain, 1750–1834.* Cambridge, UK, Cambridge University Press.

Winch, D. (1997) "Adam Smith's Problem and Ours" *Scottish Journal of Political Economy* 44(4): 384–402.

Winch, D. (2004). "Adam Smith" in *Oxford Dictionary of National Biography* edited by L. Goldman. Oxford, UK, Oxford University Press.

Winch, D. (2009). *Wealth and Life: Essays on the Intellectual History of Political Economy in Britain, 1848–1914.* Cambridge, UK, Cambridge University Press.

Winch, D. (2014). "A Short Comment on the Long History of Smith Biography". *Adam Smith Review* 7: 181–85.

Witham, Larry (2005). *The Measure of God: Our Century-Long Struggle to Reconcile Science and Religion.* San Francisco, CA, Harper.

Witzum, Amos and J. T. Young (2012). "Utilitarianism and the Role of Utility in Adam Smith". *European Journal for the History of Economic Thought* 20(4): 572–602.

Yeo, Richard (1979). "William Whewell, Natural Theology and the Philosophy of Science in Mid-Nineteenth Century Britain". *Annals of Science* 36: 493–512.

Yeo, Richard (1993). *Defining Science: William Whewell, Natural Knowledge and Public Debate in Early Victorian Britain.* Cambridge, UK, Cambridge University Press.

Yeo, Richard (2004). "Whewell, William". *Oxford Dictionary of National Biography.* Oxford, UK, Oxford University Press

Yong, Amos (2015). "Global Pentecostalisms Navigating the Public Square: Revitalizing Political Theology?" in *Oxford Handbook of Political Theology* edited by S. Casey and M. Kessler. Oxford, UK, Oxford University Press.

Young, Frances M. and David F. Ford (1987). *Meaning and Truth in 2 Corinthians.* London, SPCK.

Young, J. T. (1997). *Economics as a Moral Science: The Political Economy of Adam Smith.* Cheltenham, UK, Edward Elgar.

Young, J. T. (2008). "Law and Economics in the Protestant Natural Law Tradition: Samuel Pufendorf, Francis Hutcheson, and Adam Smith". *Journal of the History of Economic Thought* 30(3): 1–14.

Young, J. T. (ed.) (2009). *Elgar Companion to Adam Smith.* Cheltenham, UK, Edward Elgar.

Young, Robert M. (1985). *Darwin's Metaphor: Nature's Place in Victorian Culture.* Cambridge, UK, Cambridge University Press.

Yuengert, A. M. (2012). *Approximating Prudence: Aristotelian Practical Wisdom and Economics Models of Choice.* New York, Palgrave Macmillan.

Yuengert, A. M. (2014). "Roman Catholic Economics" in *Oxford Handbook of Christianity and Economics* edited by P. Oslington. Oxford, UK, Oxford University Press.

Index

 **Taylor & Francis eBooks**

Helping you to choose the right eBooks for your Library

Add Routledge titles to your library's digital collection today. Taylor and Francis ebooks contains over 50,000 titles in the Humanities, Social Sciences, Behavioural Sciences, Built Environment and Law.

Choose from a range of subject packages or create your own!

Benefits for you

- » Free MARC records
- » COUNTER-compliant usage statistics
- » Flexible purchase and pricing options
- » All titles DRM-free.

Benefits for your user

- » Off-site, anytime access via Athens or referring URL
- » Print or copy pages or chapters
- » Full content search
- » Bookmark, highlight and annotate text
- » Access to thousands of pages of quality research at the click of a button.

 REQUEST YOUR **FREE** INSTITUTIONAL TRIAL TODAY **Free Trials Available**
We offer free trials to qualifying academic, corporate and government customers.

eCollections – Choose from over 30 subject eCollections, including:

Archaeology	Language Learning
Architecture	Law
Asian Studies	Literature
Business & Management	Media & Communication
Classical Studies	Middle East Studies
Construction	Music
Creative & Media Arts	Philosophy
Criminology & Criminal Justice	Planning
Economics	Politics
Education	Psychology & Mental Health
Energy	Religion
Engineering	Security
English Language & Linguistics	Social Work
Environment & Sustainability	Sociology
Geography	Sport
Health Studies	Theatre & Performance
History	Tourism, Hospitality & Events

For more information, pricing enquiries or to order a free trial, please contact your local sales team:
www.tandfebooks.com/page/sales

 Routledge
Taylor & Francis Group

The home of
Routledge books

www.tandfebooks.com

Printed in the United States
by Baker & Taylor Publisher Services